The Art of Today

The Art of Today

Brandon Taylor

The Everyman Art Library

Acknowledgments

I must thank numerous individuals and organisations for their timely assistance, including Marion Busch of the Museum Boymans-Van Beuningen, Rotterdam; Richard Francis of the Museum of Contemporary Art, Chicago; Victoria Henry of the Canadian Museum of Civilization, Ottawa; Wolfram Kiepe of the Berlinische Galerie, Berlin; Portland McCormick of the Museum of Contemporary Art, Los Angeles; Matthew Slotover of Frieze Magazine, London; the Ronald Feldman Gallery, New York; the Andrea Rosen Gallery, New York; the Sidney Janis Gallery, New York; the Galerie Gerald Piltzer, Paris; the Gallery Sties, Kronberg; the Neue Galerie am Landesmuseum, Graz; the Martin-Gropius-Bau, Berlin; and the library staff of the Tate Gallery, London. The book was read in manuscript by Tim Barringer, Adam Clark-Williams, Thomas Crow, Stephen Johnstone and Tim Renshaw, all of whom made suggestions which have greatly improved the text. My assistant, Liz Atkinson, helped with a mass of elusive detail. Josephine Dobbin-Felici translated from the Italian. My wife, Lucia, gave valuable advice on an early draft. I must particularly thank the many artists who supplied me with information.

First published in Great Britain in 1995 by
George Weidenfeld and Nicolson Ltd
The Orion Publishing Group, Orion House
5 Upper St Martin's Lane
London WC2H 9EA

A catalogue-in-publication record for this book is available from the British Library

ISBN 0297 83515 7 (h/b)
ISBN 0297 83366 9 (p/b)

Series Consultant Tim Barringer (Birkbeck College, London)
Designer Karen Stafford, DQP, London
Picture Editor Susan Bolsom-Morris
Printed and bound by Toppan, Singapore

Frontispiece SHERRY LEVINE *Large Gold Knot: 2*, page 99 (detail)

Contents

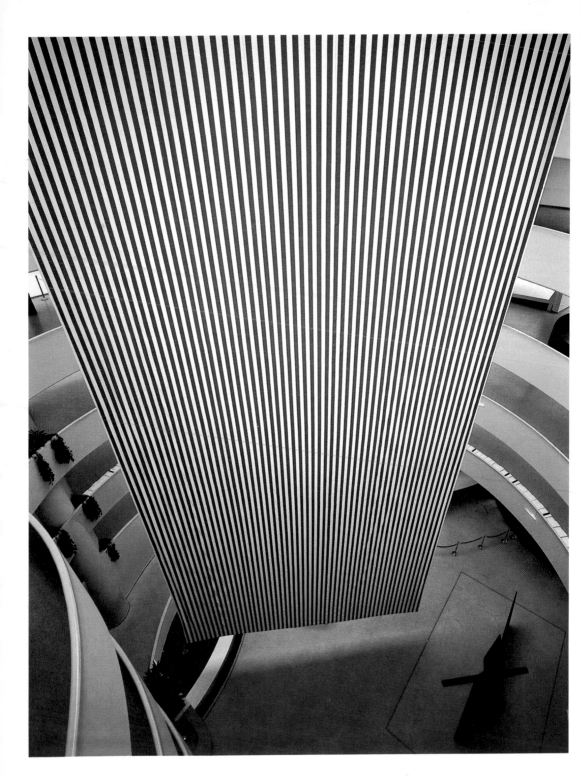

Tradition and Avant-Garde

A s the twentieth century has unfolded, the tension between tradition and avant-garde art has taken many forms. The particular rebellion which sets the scene for this book began in the later 1950s and continued through the 1960s, culminating with an explosion of dissent among younger artists around 1968. Throughout this period, a minority of artists in Europe and North America began to sense that the visual culture of the modern world, as presented by the major art museums and a significant number of professional critics, was beginning to appear as so many forms of individual (usually male) "expression." Successive movements in modern art were becoming routinely seen as mere formal novelties, each one more audaciously liberating than the ones before, while evolving out of, hence replacing, those forerunners. According to this orthodoxy – identified in the pages that follow as Modernism – modern art since Impressionism was an outpouring of the (male) artist's creative personality, while tending progressively but inexorably towards abstraction. It then looked for a sympathetic response to that outpouring in the cultivated and art-loving observer.

Modernism in this sense, then, was not merely a set of art objects, but an historical and critical framework within which most modern art could be conventionally "understood." In the years after World War II, it was chiefly identified in America with Abstract Expressionism, most famously exemplified by the paintings of Jackson Pollock and his school, and by the art criticism of Clement Greenberg and those who followed him.

In the late 1950s and early 1960s, however, artists who could be called avant-garde in Europe and America had already begun to challenge both Abstract Expressionist painting and the ortho-

1. DANIEL BUREN
Inside (Centre of Guggenheim), 1971. Acrylic on cloth, 65′ 7½″ x 29′ 9¾″ (20 x 9.1 m). Installed at the Solomon R. Guggenheim International Exhibition, 1971, for one day before the opening. Collection of the artist.

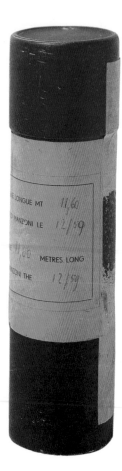

2. PIERO MANZONI
Linea Lunga Metri 11.60,
1959. Ink on paper in
cylindrical cardboard
container, 7³/₄ x 2¹/₃″
(20 x 6 cm).

dox Modernist lens through which it was seen. Among those who pioneered this challenge were the American artists Robert Rauschenberg, Jasper Johns, and Larry Rivers, alongside British counterparts such as Peter Blake and Richard Hamilton, who developed informal, collage-like discontinuities in works that were generally receptive to mass-media imagery. At the same time, the move into performance, "happenings," and installation on the part of American artists Allan Kaprow, Jim Dine, and Claes Oldenburg helped generate the European-centred Fluxus group, whose most prominent member, the German artist Joseph Beuys, pronounced a virtual moratorium on painting, while making a speciality of installations and lecture-events in which the social and psychological dimensions of art were incorporated into the very work.

Pioneer dissenters such as the Italians Lucio Fontana and Piero Manzoni had already contested the dominance of painting as the central mainstay of modern visual culture: the latter had resorted by the early 1960s to producing mechanically drawn lines, rolled up in a tube in order not to be seen, but only known (FIG. 2). A later formation, *arte povera,* or poor art, arose in Italy in the later 1960s around Jannis Kounellis, Mario Merz, Michelangelo Pistoletto, and others, in which animal, vegetable, and mineral material was used to evoke a sense of the "dull absurdity" of contemporary reality. Further north, the Danish painter Asger Jorn, affiliated to a group known as the Situationist International, repainted low-quality genre paintings in a spirit of irony, or rebellion, or both. All these examples, from the decade leading to 1968, embodied a potent mixture of jokes, refusals, and the open juxtaposition of dissonant styles, arranged in nonorthodox arrangements and deploying a motley of low cultural resources such as media imagery, found objects, and urban detritus, treated with the rank bad manners and extravagant nihilism of a disaffected minority culture.

What followed directly upon the heels of these provocative early avant-gardes were two tendencies that were to prove important in the decades that followed. American Minimal artists of the mid-1960s enacted another form of escape from orthodox Modernism by constructing simple, blank, geometrical objects that were characterised by formal symmetry, absence of traditional composition, and little colour. These "simple objects" were understood at the time to challenge the dominance of Modernist painting from another angle: existing between painting and sculpture, they purported to make the viewer self-conscious of his or her perceptual assumptions, cultural expectations and artistic values. At the same time they elevated industrially made forms, often used repetitively, into the culture of art (FIG. 3). In the later 1960s, a generation of so-called Conceptual artists across an international spectrum began to resume the earlier tendency to experiment with found materials, photography, and ordinary ephemera. By shifting attention systematically away from the ineffable visual experience of art objects and towards the attitudes and processes of conceiving them or making them, Conceptualists sought to occupy a space outside the dominant cultural conventions governing the production and consumption of art.

One result of all these forms of avant-garde activity was that by the early 1970s it was no longer necessary for paintings to be primarily coloured, or flat, nor for sculptures to be upright or have volume. Following in the footsteps of the French artist-iconoclast, Marcel Duchamp, artists proclaimed that anything in or out of the gallery – lines drawn on the ground, a set of photocopied documents, a filing cabinet, a sheet of instructions, a gallery performance – could under certain conditions of production and display qualify as "art." The intended result was to frustrate the market mechanism by making art objects which were resistant to being sold, collected, and evaluated by conventional means.

When, therefore, the meaning of "avant-garde" came under renewed scrutiny in the mid-1970s, it did so against a background of skirmishes already fought and some victories won. By this time, however, the political setting had changed, especially in the United States. The radical social agenda of the later 1960s that provided a supportive context for earlier avant-garde art – the anti-Vietnam War protests, the students' and workers' strikes, the growth of feminism – was widely perceived to be past history. By 1975 or so, Conceptual art itself was becoming popular, even stale. By the later 1970s and early 1980s it was widely considered

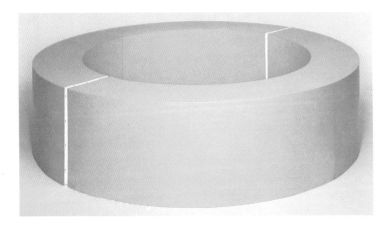

3. ROBERT MORRIS
Untitled, 1965-66.
Fibreglass and fluorescent lights, 2' x 8' (0.6 x 2.8 m).
Dallas Museum of Fine Arts.

to have been, at best, a ground-clearing exercise coincident with a wider mood of disaffection or, at worst, an embarrassment whose time had passed. By the early 1980s the almost abandoned practices of painting and sculpture were being ushered back onto centre stage in an effort to reassure an expanding public for new art that social revolution was no longer on the agenda, and that older traditions, particularly from the European past, were fit to be resumed. In such a climate the continued existence of an avant-garde could by no means be taken for granted.

The conjunction which resulted, of a hugely expanded public interest in contemporary arts at a time of relative political and social reaction, is a theme with many variations. It is over-simple to see the Western political retrenchment after 1979-80 – Reaganism in America and Thatcherism in Great Britain – as being entirely coincident with capitulation to the capitalist market. Indeed, relations between avant-garde ambition and the market in the 1980s proved to be infinitely worrisome and complex. For example, the conservative "return" to painting ran parallel to and partially concealed a set of more challenging artistic projects that effectively form a major part of this book: art now turned back to the possibilities of the Duchampian ready-made (the "found" or "encountered" object); it proposed a dialogue about the concept and purposes of the photograph; and it declared a return to an openly narrative or story-telling method. Such concerns, which seemed suddenly beleagured in the days of the painting "revival," have come in the last fifteen or twenty years to constitute the best new art of our time.

A parallel development since the early 1970s has been the growth of a new public and a new market for contemporary art. This expanded constituency has posed altogether different questions about the relationship between public culture and dissent. The twentieth-century avant-garde from Cubism and Surrealism onward has, on the whole, fitted easily into a public and commercial culture. Yet hand-in-hand with the expansion of the art network has gone a rapid growth in the training of art historians, critics, and curators whose understanding of contemporary art has resulted in a professionalisation and institutionalisation of the avant-garde attitude itself. By this logic, the embalming of what purports to be avant-garde art in museum collections, survey exhibitions, and popular books has had the effect of depriving it of the very resistant and critical qualities by which it often came into being. The twist within this paradox is that the museum apparatus is, ostensibly at least, necessary to making challenging new art visible to a substantial interested public.

An early instance of this tension may be found in controversies that erupted in 1971 at New York's prestigious Guggenheim Museum. Early in that year, a show of new art was selected for the Guggenheim International (an annual survey of recent art), featuring twelve American artists and eight from the rest of the world. Yet a furore was raised when a work by the French artist, Daniel Buren (see FIG. 1) – a striped painting in two parts, the larger part hung in the centre of the Guggenheim atrium and the smaller part outside, across 88th Street – had its larger part withdrawn by the museum. Buren's response was that the work, "placed in the centre of the museum, irreversibly laid bare the building's secret function of subordinating everything to its narcissistic architecture." The museum, said Buren – he might have been speaking about any museum – "unfolds an absolute power which irremediably subjugates anything that gets caught/shown in it." Several weeks later, a planned exhibition by the German-born artist Hans Haacke at the same museum was also withdrawn. The project that Haacke offered for this show was a photographic documentation of Manhattan real-estate holdings, with information on ownership and value culled from public records (FIG. 4), together with an opinion poll on visitors' political views. Museum officials stated that the work was a "muckraking venture" which compromised their charter obligation of "pursuing aesthetic and educational motives that are self-sufficient and without ulterior motives." The issue was once more that of the artist's right to radical expression in the face of the museum's wish to make reference to the social environment only in symbolic and generalised terms.

Other radical agendas since the 1970s have extended an avant-garde mentality to groups defined in terms of gender. The rise of feminist consciousness and the quest for gay and lesbian identity have produced perhaps the most thoroughgoing general shifts of emphasis in the visual arts in the past twenty years. At repeated intervals throughout these two decades, feminism has raised crucial questions about the role of women in the visual media. Why had women been for so long under-represented in museum collections, exhibitions, and books? Now that they were being trained as artists in equal numbers to men, the question became how a specifically feminist art could be made and understood. Could the art of gays be recognised and discussed? Such questions threatened the coherence of a system of cultural production and reproduction that had traditionally served up predominantly heterosexual male culture for a heterosexual male public. But there are paradoxes here, too. The pioneer Pop,

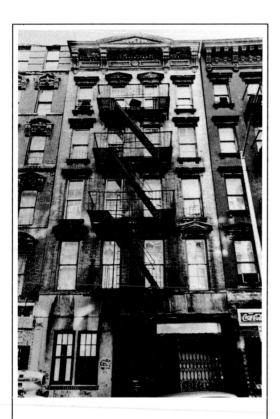

228 E 3 St.
Block 385 Lot 19
24 x 105' 5 story walk-up old law tenement

Owned by Harpmel Realty Inc.   608 E 11 St.   NYC
Contracts signed by Harry J. Shapolsky, President('63)
              Martin Shapolsky, President('64)

Acquired from John The Baptist Foundation
c/o The Bank of New York, 48 Wall St. NYC
for $237 000.- (also 5 other properties) , 8-21-1963

$150 000.- mortgage (also on 5 other properties) at 6%
interest as of 8-19-1963 due 8-19-1968
held by The Ministers and Missionaries Benefit Board of
The American Baptist Convention, 475 Riverside Dr. NYC

Assessed land value $8 000.- total $28 000.-(1971)

4. HANS HAACKE
Shapolsky et al. Manhattan Real Estate Holdings, a Real-Time Social System, as of May 1, 1971 (detail), 1971. One photograph and typewritten sheet.

The Guggenheim Museum's rejection of this work demonstrated the challenge of the radical assumption that information could be art, as well as the capacity of Haacke's tableaux, deployed in different contexts thereafter, powerfully to unmask the links between culture and power.

Minimalist, and Conceptual artists of the 1960s had almost all been men; how could women, as a group or as individuals, overturn the values of male culture if that culture were already a field of contestation among men? The dilemma has proved powerful; and in the 1990s it is still being insisted – rightly – that too few of the early feminist challenges reached the economic level. The recent activist work of the American group, the Guerrilla Girls, protests against the imbalance between male and female access to status in the arts – here in the form of a commercially printed poster that juxtaposes the prices paid for a white male avant-garde hero, Jasper Johns, with those paid for the art of women artists, both white and of colour (FIG. 5). Such activism suggests that a powerful patriarchy and the economics of a rampant capitalist market are still inextricably entwined. It remains controversial how far the most challenging new work by women and sexual minorities has managed to soften or unsettle that partnership.

The feminist challenge implicit in this particular Guerrilla Girls' poster is made paradoxical at another level by the fact that in the larger task of de-masculinising culture, Jasper Johns may

5. GUERRILLA GIRLS
Untitled poster, 1989. 16³/₄ x 21¹/₂″ (42.5 x 54.5 cm).

WHEN RACISM & SEXISM ARE NO LONGER FASHIONABLE, WHAT WILL YOUR ART COLLECTION BE WORTH?

The art market won't bestow mega-buck prices on the work of a few white males forever. For the 17.7 million you just spent on a single Jasper Johns painting, you could have bought at least one work by all of these women and artists of color:

Bernice Abbott	Elaine de Kooning	Dorothea Lange	Sarah Peale
Anni Albers	Lavinia Fontana	Marie Laurencin	Ljubova Popova
Sofonisba Anguisolla	Meta Warwick Fuller	Edmonia Lewis	Olga Rosanova
Diane Arbus	Artemisia Gentileschi	Judith Leyster	Nellie Mae Rowe
Vanessa Bell	Marguérite Gérard	Barbara Longhi	Rachel Ruysch
Isabel Bishop	Natalia Goncharova	Dora Maar	Kay Sage
Rosa Bonheur	Kate Greenaway	Lee Miller	Augusta Savage
Elizabeth Bougereau	Barbara Hepworth	Lisette Model	Vavara Stepanova
Margaret Bourke-White	Eva Hesse	Paula Modersohn-Becker	Florine Stettheimer
Romaine Brooks	Hannah Hoch	Tina Modotti	Sophie Taeuber-Arp
Julia Margaret Cameron	Anna Huntingdon	Berthe Morisot	Alma Thomas
Emily Carr	May Howard Jackson	Grandma Moses	Marietta Robusti Tintoretto
Rosalba Carriera	Frida Kahlo	Gabriele Münter	Suzanne Valadon
Mary Cassatt	Angelica Kauffmann	Alice Neel	Remedios Varo
Constance Marie Charpentier	Hilma af Klimt	Louise Nevelson	Elizabeth Vigée Le Brun
Imogen Cunningham	Kathe Kollwitz	Georgia O'Keeffe	Laura Wheeling Waring
Sonia Delaunay	Lee Krasner	Meret Oppenheim	

Information courtesy of Christie's, Sotheby's, Mayer's International Auction Records and Leonard's Annual Price Index of Auctions.

Please send $ and comments to: Box 1056 Cooper Sta. NY, NY 10276 **GUERRILLA GIRLS** CONSCIENCE OF THE ART WORLD not be a target, but an ally. Artists of both sexes sympathetic or attuned to the gay sensibility of Johns, Rauschenberg, and Warhol have extended the revolution in media – notably photography and the fascination exerted by mass culture – to questions of attitude and style. In much recent work, elements of decoration, stylistic inconsistency and visual contradiction have gained an important place. A certain studied lack of seriousness, a deliberate cultivation of degrees of incompetence and falling-short, impudent illusionism, and indifference to established formal frameworks have become vital qualities in the best art of the period. And this development has also had consequences for our notions of avant-garde. The question for some has been whether the pluralism and diversity implicit in the "rebellion of gender" is really compatible with an *historical* concept of avant-garde. Throughout the period covered by this book, it has been said, no single artistic movement, but rather a free-floating and unpredictable diversity, has been in a position to make claims upon the high ground of opposition to existing culture.

The image of an inalienable gulf between contestatory minority cultures and a stable centre is, at any rate, too simple. Throughout the history of Modernism – however understood – relations between the margins and the centre have been dialectical and constantly shifting. What has arguably changed since the 1970s is not the existence of the avant-garde, but its obvious and unproblematic visibility. The retreat of political radicalism in the 1970s and 1980s, the pluralism of visual culture in the wake of Conceptualism, and the rise of the well-intentioned curator who was also sympathetic to dissenting forms of culture, have made it less and less possible to identify the avant-garde with a single set of combative individuals or groups. It has also become less and less possible to see dissenting culture as *political*, and more customary to applaud it for its reflective and even theoretical qualities.

This latter shift has encouraged the growth of a visual culture that has proved economically efficient as well as philosophically highly challenging. "How can it be otherwise," Thomas Crow has argued, "when disembodied information about the smallest event in a studio in a Brooklyn backstreet or a Venice Beach alleyway can mobilize human energies, financial transfers, and intellectual attention on a global scale? That sort of cultural leverage, the extent of which – in material terms – would have to be measured in multiple orders of magnitude, is new in the world ...With their low costs of entry and potential for exponential returns, the fine arts seem closer in this respect to computer software, the most potent form of intellectual property of our era."

Yet within that fast-expanding culture, a development that has begun to puzzle commentators has been a resurgence of iconographical energy. A striking contrast can be observed between Minimalist work of the mid-1960s and such projects of the 1990s as those of the Polish artist Miroslaw Balka (FIG. 6). Minimalist objects could be said in themselves to express little, refer to little, suggest little; as a category of made object they may be said to have been mute and undeclarative. At least according to its early readings, Minimalism required the presence of the viewer in an abstract, ungendered personification to function (for good or ill) in the completion of the work. To be in the presence of Balka's *190x60x11, 190x60x11*, on the other hand, is to be drawn into an encounter with an object which is overflowing with significations. Its bed-like format and scale, the traces of ordinary activity on its marble slabs, and the electric wires that heat them, all refer inescapably to human functions such as lying, sleeping, surviving, establishing a base or home. While Minimalists attempted to unsettle and reposition the spectator, Balka's work suggests readings and anecdotes relating to the body and the world.

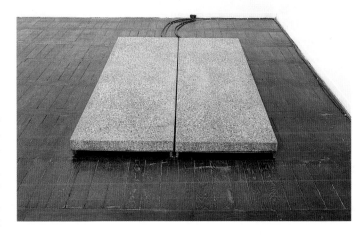

6. MIROSLAW BALKA *190x60x11, 190x60x11*, 1992-93. Terrazzo, steel, heating cables, and felt, 6'3" x 23½" x 4⅓" (190 x 60 x 11 cm). Lannan Foundation, Los Angeles.

The significance of this difference must not be underestimated. The type of open contradiction between forms and expectations engineered widely in the late 1960s and early 1970s will be taken by some to provide a kind of standard for the evaluation of more recent art. Yet the insurrection mounted by Minimal and early Conceptual art could not be repeated without change today. What follows from that realisation? If anything, it is that the dissenting spirit of the 1960s has become transformed, at best, into a highly plural as well as energetic field of activity which turns out to possess startling philosophical and theoretical depths, but a more conformist relation to both its specialist and general public. Of course, that assessment cuts both ways. It is one that occupies the pages of this book.

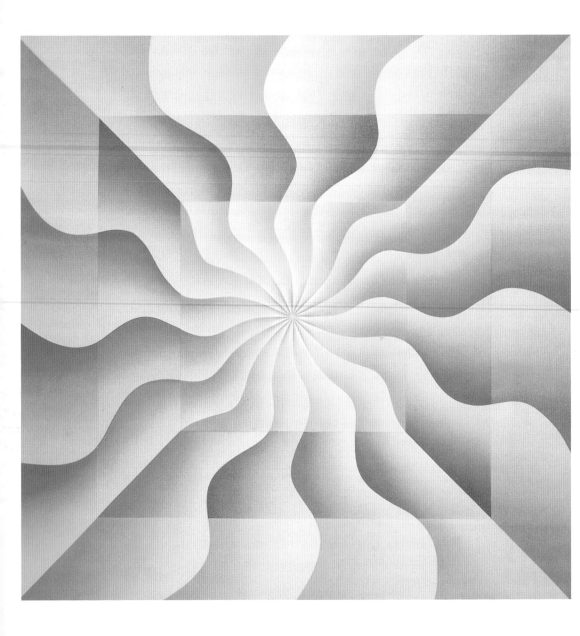

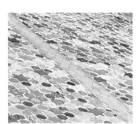

ONE

Alternatives to Modernism: the 1970s

7. JUDY CHICAGO
Christina of Sweden, 1972.
Sprayed acrylic on canvas,
3′4″ x 3′4″ (1.1 x 1.1 m).
Collection Janet Bajan,
Santa Fe, New Mexico.

Adopting the name of her
birthplace as her own to
establish a new identity as
an independent woman
artist, Judy Chicago tried in
her *Great Ladies* series, in
her words, "to make my
form-language and colour
reveal something really
specific about a particular
woman in history...the
whole quality of a
personality." Others in the
series – all queens – were
Marie Antoinette, Catherine
the Great, and Victoria.

The early 1970s was a time when the prospects for avant-garde art looked rich indeed throughout the Western world. Particularly for younger artists who had been caught up in the mood of opposition to established culture in the late 1960s, it seemed that the formal victories won against traditional forms of modern painting and sculpture in those years held the key to a host of new philosophical and aesthetic possibilities. And yet by the end of the decade the mood was very different. Not only had the social radicalism of the late 1960s and early 1970s subsided, but a new set of priorities had come to occupy centre stage such as to make that radicalism seem misplaced, or at best utopian.

The formal end of American involvement in the Vietnam War in 1973 and the Watergate scandal which ended Nixon's presidency (FIG. 8) were quickly followed by a series of shocks to the international economy caused by oil-price rises and a sequence of deepening social crises in housing, women's rights, the enfranchisement of ethnic and sexual minorities, as well as in relations between the developed and the developing world. Widespread disenchantment with traditional patriarchal culture was accompanied by a perception that the social and artistic alternatives of the 1960s had not been, and could not be, sustained. The mood of the Western art community toward the end of the 1970s can be described as one of confusion. A New York critic, attempting to summarise the condition of art at the end of the decade, ended her recitation of the key buzzwords of

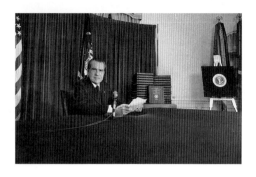

8. President Nixon in his White House office in April 1974, surrounded by evidence offered in support of his claim that he was not involved in covering up an illegal break-in at the Democratic Party's Watergate campaign headquarters in 1972. He subsequently resigned as a result of public pressure.

the period – Minimalism, Formalism, Post-Minimalism, Process art, Scatter Works, Earthworks, Conceptualism, Body art, Photo-Realism – with the despairing cry that "after the early 1970s words fail us; the glossary dissolves...there are no more terms that really work." Speaking of "schizophrenia," "dissociation," and "a double bind," she sensed that artists were viewing all the tried alternatives to orthodox Modernism as empty, over-used, exhausted, at the same time feeling uncertain where else to go.

Between the perception of hope and the experience of exhaustion lay an expanse of artistic experiment. Attempts were made throughout the decade to propagate and extend an earlier radicalism at a time when the pull of the wider culture was often in a contrary direction.

A New Women's Art

Of all the major realignments in visual culture of the last twenty or so years, perhaps the most significant has resulted from a sustained reflection on questions of gender. In the early 1970s the crisis of confidence in traditional male culture was deepest among women artists allied to feminism in any of its then current variations. Prefigured by West Coast artists of the 1960s such as Miriam Schapiro and Judy Chicago, women's groups had also been active in New York, where a group known as Women Artists in Revolution (WAR) had in 1969 grown out of the wider Art Workers' Coalition (AWC). It was followed by The Women's Art Committee (WAC), founded in 1970. The critic Lucy Lippard and the black artist Faith Ringgold protested that the Whitney Annual exhibitions discriminated against women; they and others took steps to organise their own shows and run their own galleries.

Against this background, a number of key critical ideas about women's art emerged in public in 1971 with the publication of Linda Nochlin's essay, "Why Have There Been No Great Women Artists?" in *Art News*, and Lucy Lippard's catalogue for the show, *26 Contemporary Women Artists*, of which she was the curator for the Aldrich Museum in Connecticut. Nochlin addressed the much-debated question of whether there was a distinctive *feminine* sensibility or essence in women's art. She argued forcibly that there was not, nor was there likely to be. She agreed that there were no "great" women artists in the mould of Michelangelo or Manet, but suggested that the reasons lay in male-dominated educational and institutional structures that suppressed women's talents. Indeed, since concepts of "genius," "mastery," and "talent" had been devised by men to apply to men, it was remarkable that women had achieved as much as they had.

Lippard's approach to the question was almost the exact opposite. "I have no clear picture of what, if anything, constitutes 'women's art'" she wrote, "although I am convinced that there is a latent difference in sensibility...I have heard suggestions that the common factor is a vague 'earthiness,' 'organic images,' 'curved lines' and, most convincingly, a centralised focus."

"Centralised focus" was a term devised by the West Coast artist Judy Chicago, who in her works of the early 1970s explored the symbolic meanings available within (as well as taboos against) the forms of the vagina (see FIG. 7). Referring to Georgia O'Keeffe's early efforts to illuminate the darknesses of female identity, Lippard wrote that "there is now evidence that many women artists have defined a central orifice whose formal organisation is often a metaphor for a woman's body." By 1973 Lippard had identified a more generalised range of female imagery, comprising "a unifying density, an overall texture, often sensuously tactile and often repetitive to the point of obsession; the preponderance of circular forms and central focus (sometimes contradicting the first aspect); a ubiquitous linear 'bag' or parabolic form that turns in on itself; layers, or strata; an indefinable looseness or flexibility of handling; a new fondness for the pinks and pastels and the ephemeral cloud-colours that used to be taboo."

The critic Lawrence Alloway, strongly refuting the idea that women's art could be defined in relation to ancient symbolism or ritual, offered the mildly patronising suggestion that "a plethora of soft sculpture, fetishes and simulated shelters is generationally rather than sexually attributable. Such work is largely produced by young artists motivated by an optimistic belief in a non-specialised technology and a primitivist ideal that we can live on our personal resources." The objection was surely addressed in part to the work of the California-based artist Lynda Benglis, whose pigmented and moulded foam pieces seemed designed to contest the appearance of male-dominated Minimalism, with its multiple technological and mathematical references. Benglis herself, however, continued to feel underrepresented in an art system run predominantly by men; in a

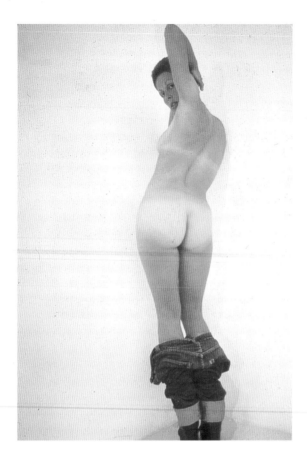

9. LYNDA BENGLIS
Invitation to an exhibition at
the Paula Cooper Gallery,
New York, 4-19 May 1974.
Photograph by Annie
Liebowitz.

notorious gesture of 1974 she confronted this "male" ethos by taking
out advertisements for her own work,
in which she parodied men's view of
women, posing as a pin-up (FIG. 9) or,
in the final advert, wearing nothing
but sunglasses and a giant latex dildo.

Simultaneously with these researches into a women's aesthetic –
researches which continued to be
developed and debated through the
1970s – a diversity of other women's
art activity reflected on the body, and
on differences between male and
female. Photo-pieces exploring gender and identity by artists such as
Martha Wilson, Rita Myers, and
Ketty La Rocca, for instance, con-
trasted formally and materially with
the hard technological Minimalism of
Donald Judd and Carl Andre. A kind
of homage to the pioneering tradition
of fragile floor- or wall-pieces
launched by Eva Hesse (who died
prematurely from cancer in 1970) is
illustrated by Rosemary Castoro's
epoxy, fibreglass and steel installation-sculpture, *Symphony*, of
1974 (FIG. 10). It is also suggestive of physical movement and the
organic body. Several of Castoro's pieces refer to the imagery of
dance: she studied choreography and worked on occasion with
the experimental dancer and film-maker, Yvonne Rainer. Such
works showed not merely the latent vitality to be found in heterodox materials and combinations, but that the tendency in
American male aesthetics to deny the body and its references
was by no means universalisable.

Such new art by American women of the early 1970s was
significant for many reasons. It constituted the first phase of
committed philosophical engagement by female artists with
questions of how feminism could be embodied in art, and it
took up the issue of how women could use the body or body-
image to explore female identity without inviting the accusation
that they were playing upon the very kinds of voyeuristic
responses that for other reasons they wanted to preclude. Col-
laborations and discussions among women artists were at the

same time beginning to permeate the institutional frameworks of education, exhibition, and the understanding and criticism of art. Projects such as Womanhouse at the California Institute of the Arts in 1971 and 1972 (a vast environmental sculpture made by and for women) or the 1973 New York Cultural Center exhibition, *Women Choose Women*, or the founding of *Heresies* magazine in New York (planned from 1975 and first published early in 1977) could be taken as suggesting that art could get along nicely without men. Art-historical revisions such as Carol Duncan's essay, "Virility and Domination in Early 20th-Century Vanguard Painting," published in *Artforum* late in 1973, directed a note of much-needed scepticism at a still-resistant male avantgarde establishment. A suggestion underlying these developments was that advanced, critical work in culture needed to concern itself with questions of gender and with the ideological relations of gender to politics and art-world power.

A similar suggestion was raised by forms of art produced by American women which introduced variations on the tendency of male Minimalist art to involve the viewer in a set of reflective relationships to the art-work. Diverting attention away from the art-work as an invitation to philosophical speculation to one of physical and human empathy, the early work of the Belgian artist Marie-Jo Lafontaine, who subsequently worked in video, painting, and installation, took the cotton of canvas before it was woven and dyed it black. Once woven back into material and hung as a series of monochrome canvases, the works stood as an eloquent testimony to women's craft, to repetitive and exhausting labour (the artist's own), yet to an ongoing refusal to

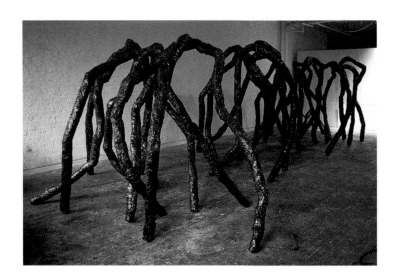

10. ROSEMARY CASTORO *Symphony*, 1974. Pigmented epoxy and fibreglass over styrofoam and steel rods, 6'4" x 9' x 24' (1.9 x 3.2 x 8.4 m).

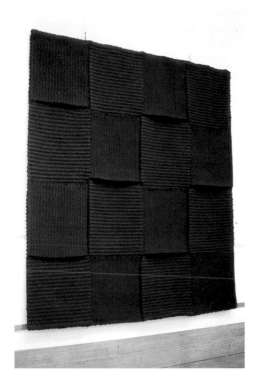

11. MARIE-JO LAFONTAINE
Monochrome Noir, 1977.
Woven cotton, 6'6" x 6'6"
(2 x 2 m).

adorn a pre-existing surface with composed forms (FIG. 11). In America, Jackie Winsor incorporated labour-intensive repetitions of binding, tying, or nailing, and using twine, rope, and cut trees, reflecting her childhood on the bleak Newfoundland coast. Winsor's elaborately made boxes of the mid-1970s, which display a fondness for detail *within* or *upon* the cube, provide an elegant instance of a feminine variation on, and challenge to, a dominant male aesthetic (FIG. 12).

Other women artists went directly to the land. Alice Aycock took the forms of Minimalism into or under the ground surface, building caves and subterranean structures which could be interpreted as metaphors for seeking, interiority, or for an atavistic, self-burying impulse. Mary Miss's *Untitled* necessitated a laborious journey to view it on a vacant landfill along the Hudson River in New York City, but to Lippard it gave rise to a blank and "vaguely disappointing" experience until its ever more deeply buried circles were aligned (FIG. 13). The spaces between the planks of *Untitled* were sealed by black tar, whose lines echoed the structure of the empty landscape. But otherwise the planks are only a false façade. "If certain pieces take on a geometrical aspect," the artist said, eager to rebut any association with Minimalism, "it is not from any interest in this particular form. Though there is a very physical basis to my sculpture, the desired result is not to make an object."

However, although American women's art of the early to mid-1970s cut across the tensions between Modernist formalism and the anti-formalism of Minimalist art − art forms produced and critically fought over by men − for many women the issue was never one of contesting the rules of practice on the same theoretical territory as men.

Further, only a minority of radical women artists was much exercised by Marxism − that political affiliate of the avant-garde − whose traditional emphasis on the relationship between the means of production and the formation of social class seemed largely to overlook or disdain feminist concerns. In the words of the British critic Griselda Pollock "the nature of societies in which art has been produced has been not only...feudal or capitalist,

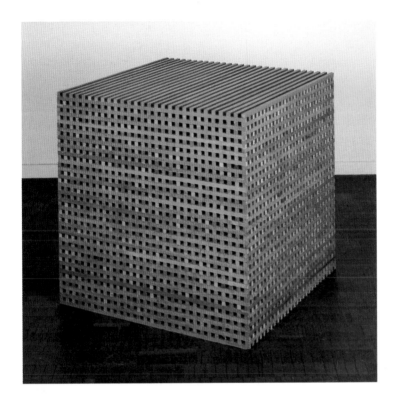

but patriarchal and sexist." What was required was a binding
together of feminism with reformulated Marxist concerns.

A second difficulty for feminists concerned the very concept
of "avant-garde," whose tradition of utopian or revolutionary
thought seemed to imply the adoption of an "outsider" position
from which to mount an assault on traditional bases of power
and class. Not only had this posi-
tion been occupied since its origins
in Romanticism largely by men,
but some feminists pointed to the
fact that women had always been
outsiders anyway. If anything, they
needed to establish a powerful position within the mainstream.

The resources of Conceptual
art, especially photography, helped
them to establish that position.
Among Martha Rosler's earliest
works using photography was a
series of collages which mixed
images of the Vietnam War with

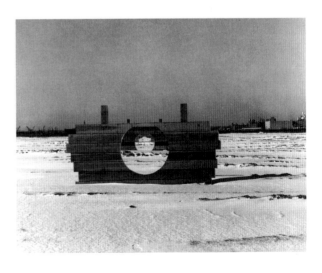

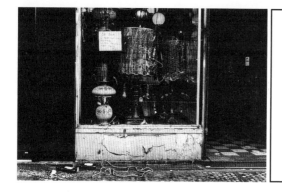

```
comatose     unconscious

passed out      knocked out

        laid out

out of the picture

out like a light
```

14. MARTHA ROSLER
The Bowery: in two inadequate descriptive systems, (detail showing two photographs), 1974-75. Forty-five black-and-white photographs.

The artist has said that "the photos here are radical metonymy, with a setting implying the condition [of inebriation] itself...If impoverishment is a subject here, it is more centrally the impoverishment of representational strategies tottering about alone than that of a mode of surviving."

American domestic scenes of the same time. Called *Bringing the War Home: House Beautiful* (1967-72), they appeared in the alternative art press in the early 1970s, and were Rosler's response to the distance established by news reporting in *Life* and other mainstream publications from the personal responsibility (and conditions of response) of viewers at home.

In a series entitled *The Bowery: in two inadequate descriptive systems* (1974-75), Rosler took different representations aimed at capturing the reality of drunks living on the streets of lower Manhattan and placed them next to, and made them critical of, each other. *The Bowery* can be seen as a work which followed the structuralist thinking of the French anthropologist Claude Lévi-Strauss. Like structuralist analysis in other fields, it sought to shift the viewer's attention from the thing represented to the representational systems themselves. Each panel pair showed a photographic record of a derelict Bowery storefront next to a lexicon of terms used to describe inebriation (FIG. 14). Pitting her work against what she saw as the "victim photography" of documentary journalism, which "insists on the tangible reality of generalised poverty and despair," but in which the "victims of the camera – that is, of the photographer – are often docile," Rosler located the problem of social deprivation within the politics of representation itself. In her own account:

> The words begin outside the world of skid row and slide into it, as people are thought to slide into alcoholism and skid to the bottom of the row. ...[The project is] a work of refusal. It is not defiant antihumanism. It is meant as an act of criticism: the text you are reading now runs on the parallel track of another descriptive system. There are no stolen images [of drunks]...what could you learn from them that you didn't already know?

Comparable intellectual motives can be seen at work in the multi-part *Post-Partum Document* (1973-78) by the British artist Mary Kelly. Kelly's *Document* (FIG. 15) depicts the rearing of a male child by periodically reproducing his bodily imprint on various types of matter, from diapers to writing paper; it also contains a record of the mother's anxieties about her son, and a section of her diary that records her activities as an artist in relation to her role as mother. Several kinds of discourse around the growing child's activities are represented in particular typefaces, carefully arranged both to be read and for their visual effect; what Kelly called the "scripto-visual" manner. Not only was the immediate topic of *Document* ground-breaking, but its form and theoretical basis arguably outstripped anything previously achieved by a European feminist artist. The larger philosophical significance of the *Document* lies in its attempt to fuse two perceptions of female subjectivity, one derived from the writings of

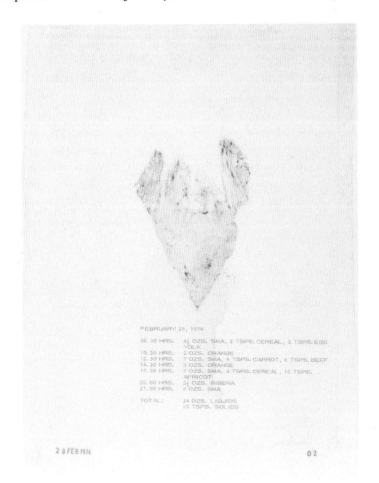

15. MARY KELLY
*Post-Partum Document,
Documentation I,* 1974.
Mixed media, 28 units, each
14 x 11" (35.6 x 28 cm). Art
Gallery of Ontario, Canada.

Freud (on narcissism), the other from Lacan (on Freud). It was also intended as a commentary on the steps through which, as Kelly put it, "maternal 'femininity' is constructed within the mother-child relationship" and the process by which the identity of a child is gradually formed through engagement with, and eventual entry into, the symbolic order which is language.

The two latter projects suggest that American women's art in the Conceptualist vein tended in the 1970s to the empirical, the positivist, and the descriptive, while European work tended to the psychoanalytically based, the private, and the subjective. However, both Rosler and Kelly represent positions of powerful theoretical engagement within a field of alternative practice that was widely perceived as "avant-garde." In offering topics or modes of representation that contested the concerns of the patriarchy, both can be seen as having forged a kind of union between sexual politics and visual culture at a time when their possible connections had not yet been understood.

Performance Art

Performance art by its nature – both by women and men – provided further examples during the 1970s of how feminist or other "radical" content could be embodied in alternative forms and media. Deriving at some distance from Dada, alternative theatre and the "happenings" movement of the 1960s, performance art resisted being treated as a commodity (it could be neither bought nor sold), while replacing the normal materials of art with nothing more, nor less, than the artist's own body. Performance art throughout the later 1960s and 1970s attracted small but influential art-world audiences and continues to resonate vividly both in recollection, in photo-documentation, and in the eye-witness account. In hindsight certain projects – significant too for purposes of comparison between American and European forms – stand out as exemplary.

It was immediately clear to Lucy Lippard, for example, that European body and performance art had different characteristics from that of the Americans. More abrasive, more physically challenging, more dangerously sited in relation to issues of pain, wounding, rape, and disease than the relatively celebratory North American work, European body art seemed to contain pointers to the different social and philosophical traditions – and their contemporary crises – on the two continents.

In the United States, Carolee Schneemann continued the vein of performances she had begun as early as 1963, involving

16. CAROLEE SCHNEEMANN *Interior Scroll*, 1975. Performance.

Interior Scroll was first performed in 1975 before an audience of women artists on Long Island. "The reading was done on top of the table, taking a series of life model 'action poses,' the book balanced in one hand," said Schneemann. "At the conclusion I dropped the book and stood upright on the table. The scroll was slowly extracted as I read from it, inch by inch."

the body as a symbol and a resource. In her *Interior Scroll* of 1975 (FIG. 16) she used her body as a "stripped-down, undecorated, human object." As Schneemann put it, "I approached the table dressed and carrying two sheets. I undressed, wrapped myself in one sheet, spread the other over the table and told the audience I would read from *Cézanne, She Was a Great Painter* [a feminist text written by the artist in 1974]. I dropped the covering sheet and standing there painted large strokes defining the contours of my body and face." The performance culminated in her reading a selection of texts secreted in her vagina. The idea of interior knowledge seemed to Schneemann "to have to do with the power and possession of naming – the movement from interior thought to external signification, and the reference to an uncoiling serpent, to actual information (like a ticker tape, torah in the ark, chalice, choir loft, plumb line, bell tower, the umbilicus and tongue)." The body becomes the source of self-knowledge and truth. "I assumed," says Schneemann, "that the carved figurines and incised female shapes of Paleolithic, Mesolithic artefacts were carved by women...that the experience and complexity of her personal body was the source of conceptualising or interacting with materials, of imagining the world and composing its images."

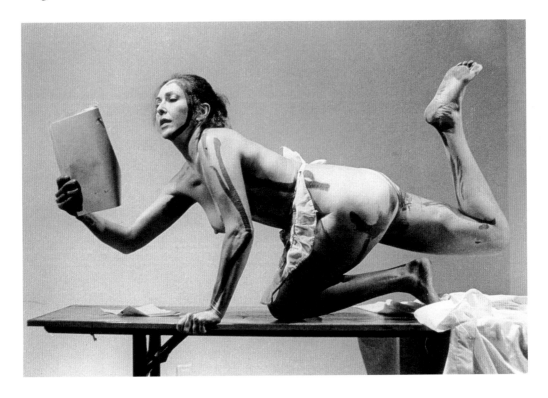

In Europe, by contrast, a gendered Conceptualism in which the artist "performed" postures and attitudes in front of the camera had produced photo-pieces on sexuality by artists like Urs Lüthi (Vienna) and Katherina Sieverding (Düsseldorf), Annette Messager (Paris) and Renate Weh (Germany). Film and video work by Ulricke Rosenbach (Germany) and Marina Abramovic (Yugoslavia) had extended the genre to moving images, the latter inviting physical danger in a piece that involved the artist recording her and her audience's reactions as she swallowed pills designed to cure schizophrenia. Rebecca Horn's films of the mid-1970s, such as *Dreaming Under Water* (1975), featured torture-like contraptions attached to the body – elongated fingers, head-dresses, cages and harnesses – which were menacingly sadistic and tender at the same time.

In America, Chris Burden in California stands out among male artists attending to the vulnerable or mortal body (including Vito Acconci, Dennis Oppenheim, or Barry Le Va), by incorporating something of the dare-devil or frontiersman into his work. Following a performance in 1971 in which an intended grazing by shooting resulted, accidentally, in a real wound, Burden continued in the mid-1970s to place himself in situations of

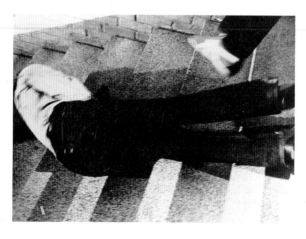

17. CHRIS BURDEN
Kunst Kick, 19 June 1974.
Performance at the Basle Art Fair, Switzerland.

real danger, though of an increasingly less harrowing sort. The documentation of Burden's performance *Kunst Kick* at the 1974 Basle Art Fair (FIG. 17) reads: "At the public opening [of the Art Fair]...at twelve noon, I laid down at the top of two flights of stairs in the Mustermesse. Charles Hill repeatedly kicked my body down the stairs, two or three steps at a time." The description itself suggests how the artist reduced himself to a body to be violated by stress or mistreatment, inducing a tension between guilt and disengagement in his small yet voyeuristic audiences. Burden's dead-pan tone also indicates a level of irony or pseudo-science in the project, and might be said to parody the reification of persons in advanced technological society.

Burden's principal male counterpart in Europe since the time of the Vienna "Actionists" – a group interested in body-ritual including Hermann Nitsch, Günter Brus, Arnulf Rainer, and Valie Export – has been the Englishman, Stuart Brisley. In the

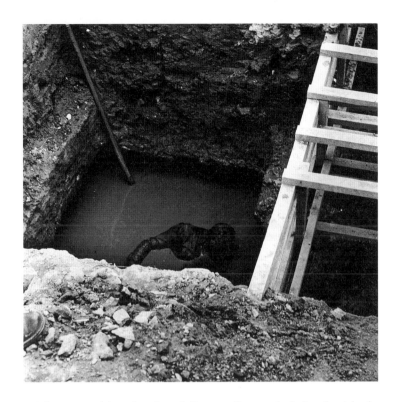

18. STUART BRISLEY
Survival in Alien Circumstances, with Christopher Gericke, 1977. Performance at *Documenta 6*, Kassel, Germany.

Ever sensitive to displays of conspicuous waste, Brisley moved his performance from the centre of Kassel on hearing of the project of the American Conceptual artist, Walter de Maria, to drill a hole 1 kilometre deep in the Friedrichsplatz at the alleged cost to an American sponsor of £200,000 ($300,000). Brisley is seen here at work with his young German collaborator, Christopher Gericke.

mid-1970s Brisley developed forms of extended ritual with the body that engaged issues of power *versus* autonomy, control *versus* freedom, consumption *versus* denial. In *Ten Days,* first performed in Berlin in 1972 and then in London in 1978, the artist refused food for ten days over the Christmas period while watching the meals ritually served to him slowly rot. In *Survival in Alien Circumstances* (FIG. 18), performed at the art fair, *Documenta 6*, in Kassel in 1977, he dug a hole 6 feet (2 m) deep in a location where he encountered rubble, bones from human war victims, and dank water. At the bottom of the hole Brisley built a wooden structure in which he lived alone for a fortnight.

The most controversial case of a female body artist performing *in extremis* was that of Gina Pane in Paris. From 1968 for the best part of a decade Pane used her body as the site of her art; cutting and otherwise torturing body parts in front of an audience and the camera (FIG. 19). As she wrote at the time, "to live one's body signifies discovering one's weakness, the tragic and pitiless servitude of its limitations, of its wear and tear and its precariousness; signifies becoming aware of its phantasms, which are none other than the reflection of myths created by society: a society that cannot accept the language of the body without reacting, because it doesn't fit into the automatism necessary to

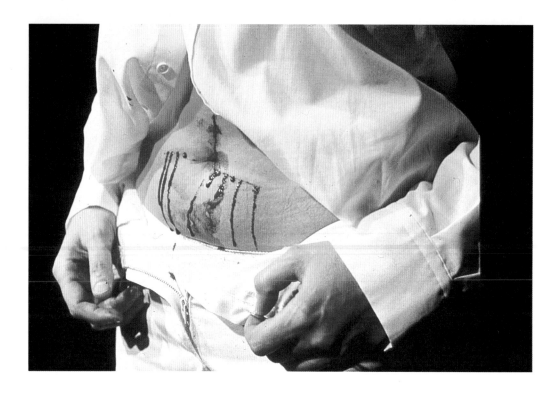

19. GINA PANE
Psyche, 24 January 1974.
Performance at the Galerie
Stadler, Paris.

the functioning of its system." "The wound is the memory of the body," she later wrote; "it was impossible for me to reconstruct an image of the body without the flesh being present, without it being placed frontally, without veils and mediations." Pane used the photograph as a witness and as a "logical support" for the body in its self-inflicted travails. "It can grasp the heart of that dialectic through which a behaviour becomes significant by becoming communicable for a community."

By the mid-1970s the absence of a shared agenda of radical protest within the Western art community had caused the links between European and American art to grow thin. Symptomatic of a desire to address this estrangement was the re-entry into the New York art world in May 1974 of the German artist, Joseph Beuys. Beuys was already known for his involvement in the iconoclastic Fluxus movement, and had a reputation in the United States for his charismatic teaching and his shamanic performances. He had given a speaking performance in a New York gallery in January of that year, developing his message of the need for conscious creativity in all human beings, and the necessity to transcend social conditioning. On his second visit, he gave a three-day performance at the René Block Gallery in SoHo entitled *I Like America and America Likes Me* (FIG. 20). Beuys assembled a pile of hay, two lengths of felt, a flashlight, a pair of gloves, a musical triangle, 50 copies of the *Wall Street Journal* (fresh daily), and a hooked walking-stick which he used to cajole and signal to a coyote, on hire from an animal farm in New Jersey. Beuys was transported to the gallery directly from the plane, wrapped up all the while in a type of felt similar to that which had saved him after crash-landing as a war-time pilot. Each day, for three days, he struck the triangle as a signal for a tape-recording of loud engine noise to begin, then excited the coyote by throwing his gloves at it. He wrapped himself again in the felt, which "covered everything but the top of his hat, to become a muffled piece of human sculpture. His walking-stick, hooked like a shepherd's staff, periscoped from the top of the felt like a dousing rod to tune in on the coyote's spirit. Beuys bent and turned according to the actions of the coyote, which...nipped and tugged at the edges of the felt. Beuys passed through a series of chosen positions as if in slow-motion salaam to the animal; when he reached floor level, he lay down, still totally covered." This eyewitness report adequately conveys how a European artist could convey the notion of a wild and original "nature" that technological and capitalist America was accused of threatening to destroy.

Conceptually, too, such works were built upon radical premises. Like other performance artists on both continents, Beuys aimed to transform the artistic product from a marketable object of exchange to a set of actions consisting entirely of the

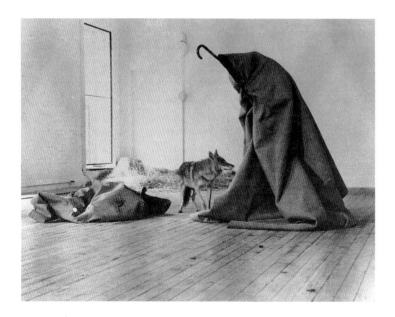

20. JOSEPH BEUYS
I Like America and America Likes Me, 1974.
Performance at the René Block Gallery, New York.

To Beuys the presence of the coyote pointed to Native Americans' history of persecution, as well as to "the whole relationship between the United States and Europe." "I wanted to concentrate only on the coyote. I wanted to isolate myself, insulate myself, see nothing of America other than the coyote...and exchange roles with it."

labour of the artist. Neither theatre nor sculpture nor real ritual, such events dramatised a new and important paradox in art: that of the artist attacking the dominant institutions of cultural power in the space of, and with the qualified compliance of, those institutions themselves. The paradox of mutual dependency of the subversive artist and the established art system continued throughout the 1970s to be a source of heated debate among those who saw themselves as carriers of a politically avant-garde tradition.

The Trials of Conceptualism

In the face of a new willingness in the museums and galleries to accommodate radical art – feminist, performance, and Conceptual art of many kinds – the dilemma, particularly for the younger artists who were interested in the avant-garde tradition, was to discover how and in what form such dissenting gestures could be developed.

We have mentioned the mounting pressure from feminists on both sides of the Atlantic to abandon a politics of class and power for one of gender and power, even a politics of place and identity. Masculine radicalism based on aspects of Conceptualism soon became endangered by the fact that museums and the commercial art world themselves became converted enthusiastically to its cause. The short-lived but important small-circulation journal *The Fox*, published in New York by an offshoot of the English Conceptual art group Art and Language, promoted the rhetorical style of a self-doubting Conceptualism taken towards the limits of an increasingly frustrated Marxist analysis of art. *The Fox* trenchantly analysed the dilemma whereby even the most radical activity tended eventually to be made subject to capitalist appropriation and the concomitant workings of social power. Some members of this grouping soon left the field of art altogether to work in education or grass-roots politics; others were soon to reassemble in Great Britain to pursue the critical practice of, surprisingly, painting.

Other radical male artists who had come of age in the late 1960s also had to face the unwelcome reality that revolutionary commitment in Western society was fading fast, and that without that essential backdrop they faced real dilemmas of how to continue. Such an artist was Gordon Matta-Clark, who in 1969 -72 had discreetly violated actual buildings, destabilising them by cutting out panels or whole walls, hence making vivid his awareness of inner-city deprivation. Until his early death in 1978

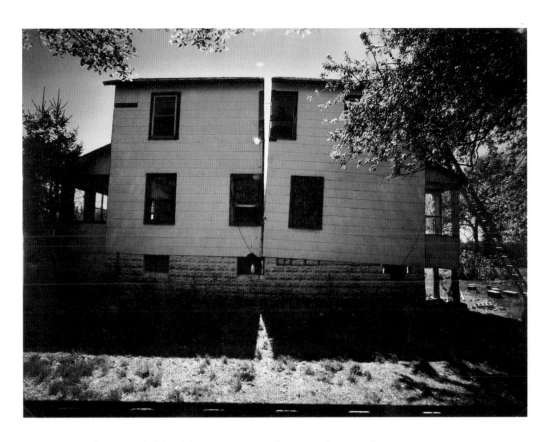

he continued to "undo" buildings in a way that owed as much to the Surrealism of his father, Robert Matta, as to the anti-form art movements of the 1960s. In his punningly titled *Splitting* of 1974 (FIG. 21), Matta-Clark cut in half a New Jersey house from which the tenants had been abruptly evicted to make room for a planned (but never finished) urban renewal project. Housing had become a familiar theme for some artists on both continents in the mid-1970s, following crises in property prices, urban planning, and mounting unemployment. Yet the danger was that works like *Splitting* would become routine exercises and begin to tire critics and dealers alike. The uneasy alliance between artistic radicalism and a market economy was already showing signs of wearing thin.

For the California artist Michael Asher, the question was one of elaborating a unique set of projects in "situational aesthetics" which took a museum or gallery as a physical resource and intervened in its palpable, material character in order to suggest a re-reading of the normal processes whereby art was produced, displayed, and commodified. In a project at the Otis Art Institute in Los Angeles in 1975, Asher negotiated for the gallery to be

21. GORDON MATTA-CLARK *Splitting* (*in Englewood*), 1974. Cibachrome, 3′6¹/₄″ x 2′8¹/₄″ (1.1 x 0.8 m). Private collection.

After visiting the house, the artist Alice Aycock recalled "starting at the bottom of the stairs where the crack was small. You'd go up...it kept widening as you made your way to the top, where the crack was one or two feet wide...you sensed the abyss in a kinaesthetic and psychological way."

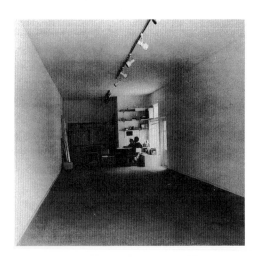

22. MICHAEL ASHER
Project at the Claire Copley
Gallery, Los Angeles, 1974.

This photograph shows the
area created with the
partition between office and
gallery spaces removed. "In
the unified office/exhibition
space," said Asher, "the
gallery personnel seemed to
become aware of their
activities, and viewers
became more aware of
themselves as viewers."

closed for the duration of the "show": in the entrance lobby he positioned a notice saying "In the present exhibition I am the art" – functioning to confound the identity of producer and viewer, as well as to frustrate expectations of solace and refinement in the viewing space. A year earlier, also in Los Angeles, Asher had taken a private gallery, removed the partition between gallery and office space, and by cleaning up resulting discontinuities in carpet and paint decor made the whole space, empty of paintings save for those stacked conventionally at the office end, mysteriously one (FIG. 22). The result was to deconstruct the distinction between aesthetic experience and commerce. "Viewers were confronted with the way in which they had become traditionally lulled into viewing art and, simultaneously, the unfolding of the gallery structure and its operational procedure...Without that questioning, a work of art could remain enclosed in its abstracted aesthetic context, creating a situation where a viewer could mystify its actual and historical meaning." Simultaneously, Asher's deconstruction began to shift the authorship of the work from individual to team. Henceforward, the radical curator would be part and parcel of the work.

Asher's projects cannot be bought or sold and survive only precariously in documentation and critical writing. However, it was becoming clear that most galleries and museums were finding it convenient to acknowledge the more conventional types of Conceptual art – texts, notices, diagrams, instructions, photographs – and to make their less demanding formats the pretext for even speedier commercial transactions than before. Simple to transport, display, document, and insure, Conceptual art in several of its forms risked becoming a ready answer to the dealer's prayer for formal novelty combined with radical pretension.

Such an assessment could not be made of Conceptualism in a wider international field. Not only was the pre-history of the best work produced in Poland and Russia in the 1970s and 1980s – to take two significant examples – at variance with their counterparts in Western Europe and America, but the support systems and audiences of the socialist bloc countries were scarcely to be compared.

In such countries, the market, which proved so central and so problematic for Western artists, simply did not exist. In the

USSR, state-approved versions of Socialist Realism in the form of images of the glorious march of Communism, the individual's happy subservience to the state, and so on, were in the late 1960s still normal fare. The maintenance of the production machinery which regulated this work had since at least 1945 lain like a suffocating blanket over the arts of all of Eastern Europe. Abstract art was both officially banned and unknown in any detail.

The atmosphere in avant-garde circles in Moscow in the early 1970s can be judged partly in terms of the extent to which oppositional art provoked the state authorities. The infamous bulldozing by the KGB of an avant-garde exhibition in Beljaevo Park in 1974 is the prime example, and yet the publicity generated paradoxically served to release as much as to constrain the younger generation: the exhibition was re-staged two weeks later to much popular interest. By this time Moscow artists had coined the term "*Sots* Art" (from the Russian for "socialist") to denote a cruel Pop-art pastiche of official Soviet realism. The *Sots* work of Vitaly Komar and Alexandr Melamid, two artists who still work together, makes use of a mixture of Duchampian, Minimalist, and Pop-art ideas learned from Western art magazines, combined with a home-grown cynicism that harks back to the absurdist literary group of the 1920s, Oberiu. One painting, dating from 1972 and representing a kind of Eastern Conceptualism (FIG. 23), took an official Communist slogan and reduced each letter to a monochrome rectangle, making the literal content of the slogan unintelligible. At another level the repetitiveness and blankness of Minimal painting function to characterise the missing message itself, whatever it was. "Official" reality became subject to parody within the codes of art, which was coincidentally a condition of the artists' freedom from the attentions of the censor.

For most Soviet artists, unable to travel to the West yet privy to the occasional tit-bit of art-world information from New York and elsewhere, the work of certain Western Conceptualists, land artists, and musicians came to assume almost mythic importance. The group in Moscow around Andrei Monastyrsky, known as Collective Actions, began in the mid-1970s to develop the ideas of the composer John Cage concerning the role of chance and randomness in musical composition. Invited participants would travel to a destination outside Moscow, and there Collective Actions would perform ritualistic actions of an enigmatic nature not announced in advance. In *Appearance* (1976), for example, two performers appeared from a forest and handed a note to the viewer signifying his or her participation in the

23. VITALY KOMAR and ALEXANDR MELAMID *Quotation*, 1972. Oil on canvas, 2'7" x 3'10½" (0.8 x 1.2 m). Private collection.

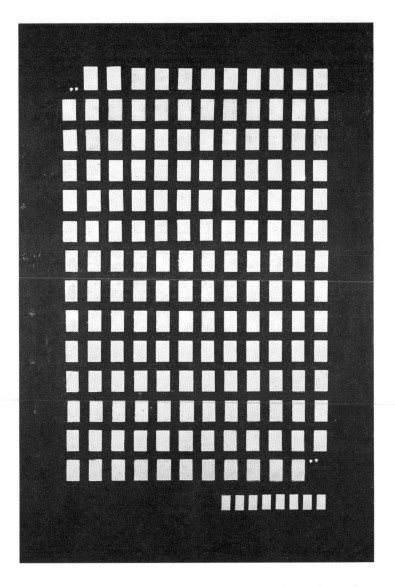

event (an example of the Russian tendency to dovetail visual art with language). *Lieblich*, of the same year, involved an electric bell which sounded under the snow when the viewer approached: the group's concept of "sounding silence" was directly inspired by John Cage. In *Third Variant* (FIG. 24) characters performed empty actions and cleansing gestures like lying in a ditch (a gesture found in the novelist Carlos Castaneda's *Journey to Ixtlan* and in Samuel Beckett's novel *Molloy*) until the audience disappeared of its own accord. Such forms of art lay beyond the confines of both official art and its opposition, and merely travelling to the event and taking part took on a kind of ritual significance.

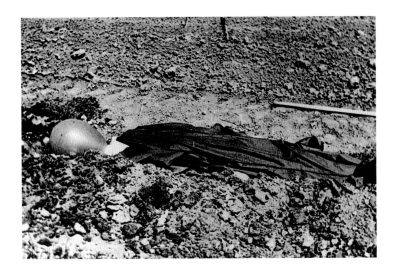

24. ANDREI MONASTYRSKY
and COLLECTIVE ACTIONS
Third Variant, 1978.
Performance.

In this performance a
character dressed in violet
emerged from a forest,
walked across a space and
lay in a ditch. A second
character's head (in the
form of a balloon) blew up
before he, too, lay in the
ditch. The characters
continued to lie there until
the audience wandered
away.

Russian irony in the face of fabled Western art also found
expression in the work of a group of Moscow Performance
artists: Mikhail Roshal, Viktor Skersis, and Gennady Donskoy,
who made a document in which they purported to have purchased the soul of Andy Warhol for 100 roubles. Another action
by this trio, wittily entitled *Underground Art* (1979), took place in
the same park as the bulldozed show of five years before. The
artists, partly buried in the ground, spoke into a microphone
about their lives as artists in the USSR and drew with mud on a
canvas above their heads. A video recording of the event – a
novel form of documentation in Russia in 1979 – shows the artists
emerging from the hole and asking "Where is Chris Burden
when we need him?" Such self-mocking art-world gestures, many
of them barely publicised and sometimes not even recorded, suggest that the pervasive irony of Western Conceptualism could be
usefully adapted to all manner of situations, however distant or
dissimilar.

The Spectre of Affirmative Painting

The last example shows that painting under the influence of
Conceptualism could be oblique and transgressive: *Underground
Art* was in part a nihilistic painting about painting itself. By
comparison, directly affirmative painting, such as the sensuous
colour abstraction of Jules Olitski in America or John Hoyland
in Great Britain, looked thin and unconvincing. At the very
least, it now seemed to lack the kind of critical purchase that
Conceptualism had made a possibility.

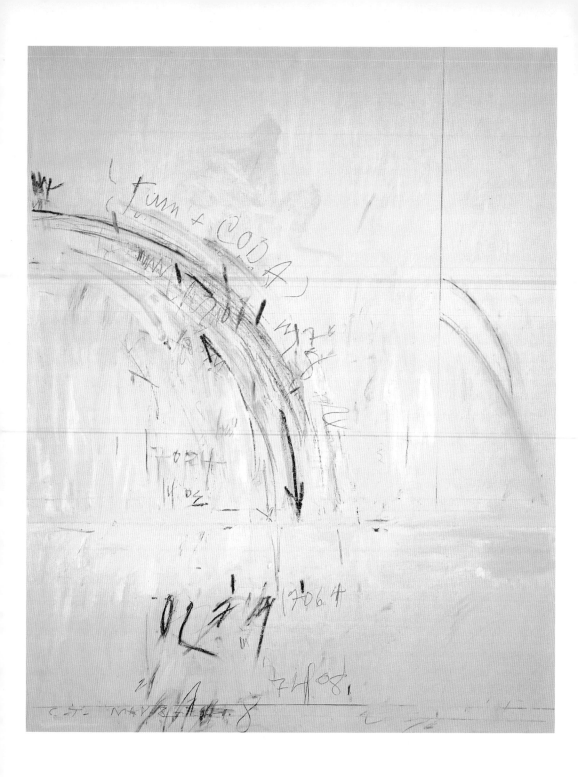

Alternatives to Modernism: the 1970s

In the mid-1970s, only certain artists could be described as pushing the medium of painting to the limits of thought and practice: Sigmar Polke and Gerhard Richter in Germany, or the American artists Brice Marden, Robert Ryman, and Cy Twombly, by now living in Rome, whose faint, scribbled abstractions bore all the marks of irresolution necessary to painting's contemporary re-definition (FIG. 25). "It is as if the painting were conducting a fight against culture," the French theorist Roland Barthes said of Twombly's work, "jettisoning its magniloquent discourse and retaining only its beauty." Assimilating Twombly's manner to the anti-individualistic style of Eastern art, Barthes said that "it does not grasp at anything: it is situated, it floats and drifts between the desire which, in subtle fashion, guides the hand, and politeness, which is the discreet refusal of any captivating ambition." Twombly's ethic was to be located, Barthes said, "outside painting, outside the West, outside history, at the very limit of meaning."

A different way out of the reductive pull of Minimalist painting towards the blank, uninflected monochrome, was the tendency of the American Frank Stella in the mid-1970s, who now complicated the pictorial surface in a progressively flamboyant way. Following his own Minimalist black and aluminum stripe paintings of 1958-60, and his development of a type of Cubist wall-relief painting in the early 1970s, Stella turned in his *Exotic Bird* series (FIG. 26) to irregular curves, wild brushstrokes, and violent colour on a vast and assertive scale. Stella's reputation as one of the most intelligent and prescient painters of his

Opposite
25. CY TWOMBLY
Turn and Coda, 1974. Oil-based house paint, oil paint, wax crayon, and lead pencil on canvas, 8'2¼" x 6'6¾" (2.5 x 2 m). Private collection.

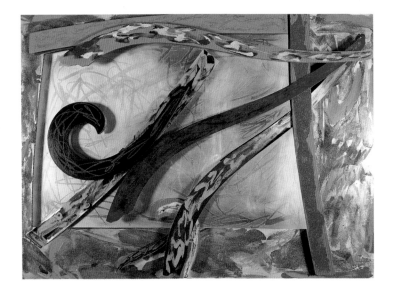

26. FRANK STELLA
Bermuda Petrel, 1976. Lacquer and oil on metal, 5'1½" x 6'11½" x 14" (1.5 m x 2.1 m x 35.5 cm).

The works in the largest of the *Exotic Bird* paintings required factory-made aluminum surfaces treated with ground glass and lacquer that the artist merely directed to be made. "I could make the structural schemes for such paintings just by sliding templates around the surface [of a drawing]," Stella recalled. To die-hard Conceptualists, Stella's art after his Minimalist phase looked increasingly baroque and cumbersome.

generation ensured that his new work was registered in many studios as being a direction to watch.

Yet one's sense at the time was of a certain redundancy in much abstract painting that was maximalising merely for the sake of change. A similar judgement afflicted a type of women's painting that surfaced internationally towards the end of the 1970s, known as "pattern painting." This deployed colourful, repeated detail across generally large formats (FIG. 27). Critics who supported this work made much of the way back that it offered from the supposedly barren exercises of the Conceptualist turn. "We need an art that will acknowledge Third World and/or those forms traditionally thought of as women's work: an art that will enliven a sterile environment...Naked surfaces are being filled in," wrote the *Artforum* critic John Perrault. "The grids of Minimal-type painting are being transformed into nets or lattices that are sensuous and have content that goes beyond self-reference."

Celebrated in shows such as the twenty-artist *Pattern Painting* at New York's P.S.1 Gallery in November-December 1977, pattern painting can nevertheless be said to have answered to a mood (the desire for sensuousness and colour at the end of a confining decade) rather than to a thought. Its appeal was to types of ethnic decorativeness (Celtic, Native American, Islamic), celebrated in ways that did little more than attach style to a format. Even installations such as those of Cynthia Carlson, in which entire gallery environments were submitted to the urge to eclecticism and profusion, functioned more as a model-kit for architecture that wanted to renovate its form-language than as a contribution to art. The achievement of pattern painting, neverthe-less, was to demonstrate the willingness of women painters to work outside the confining protocols of Modernist critical formulae.

And yet the relatively poor staying-power of pattern painting in the late 1970s reflected a deeper transformation within the art world in the wake of Conceptualism's popularisation. For it would soon become obvious that more than mere sensuousness was required to overcome the despondency that enervated much of the art world at the time. The most direct challenge to the protocols of formalist Modernism art lay not in maximal abstraction as a way of trumping Minimalist abstraction, but through a complete escape from abstraction as such, in a return to various forms of attention to the figure.

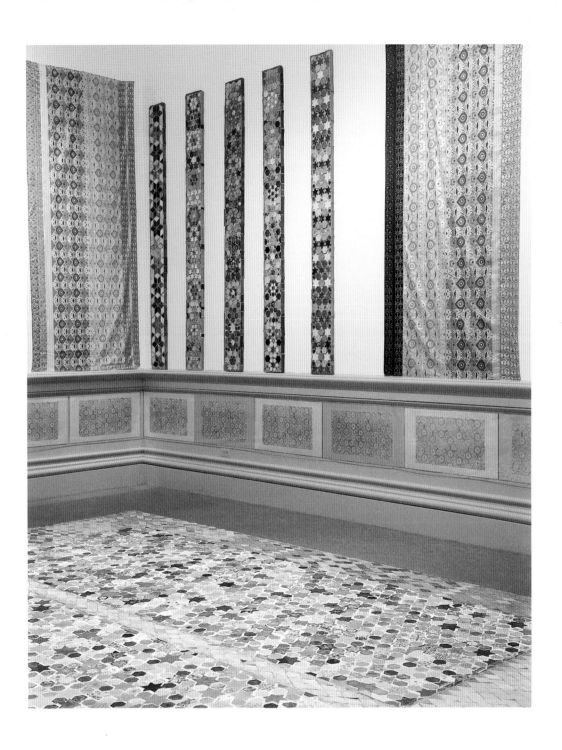

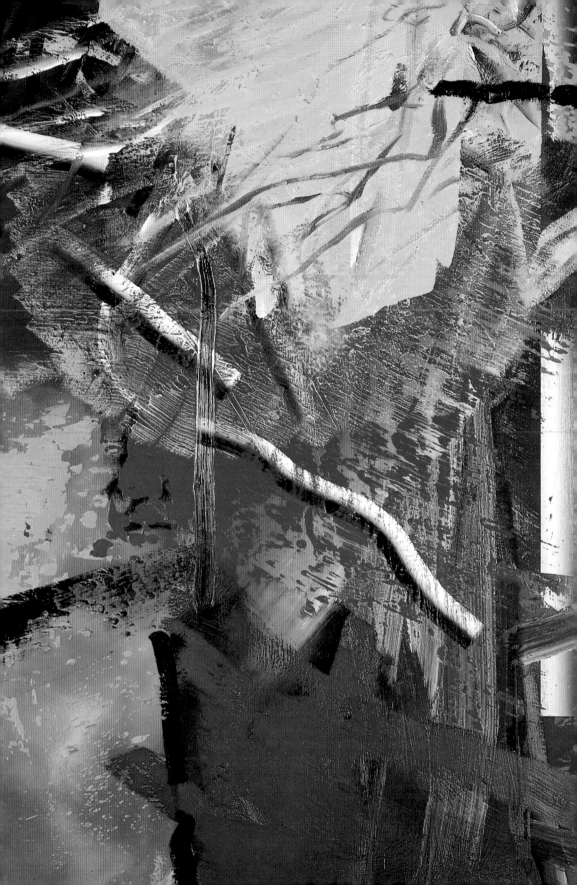

TWO

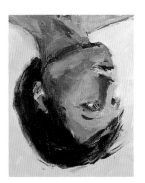

Painting and Politics: 1976-90

B y about 1975 painting was widely viewed as a renewable resource. Yet the dilemmas of the medium were by this stage legion. On the one hand, those alive to the hard-won achievements of Conceptualism remained cheerful about the collapse of Modernist protocols in the later 1960s and scepti-cal of claims that an intuitive "quality" was to be found in some painting projects. For others, a way out of the growing lethargy in the Conceptualist camp was becoming desirable.

A thinly concealed case for the restoration of a figurative richness in the visual arts can be found in Lucy Lippard's cata-logue for the 9th Paris Biennale in 1975. Lippard remarked that women's art might "indicate ways to move back towards a more basic contact between artists and real life...By confronting other levels of seeing again, we may be able to come to terms more quickly with that volcanic layer of suppressed imagery so rarely acknowledged today." Though issued on behalf of feminism, that remark proved prescient in different ways. Painting had not, of course, ceased in the later 1960s and early 1970s, but had unconvincingly tried to extend a formalist Modernist aesthetic. Its various critical and practical reinterpretations in the mid-1970s were still united by the use of oil or acrylic on canvas, much of it at a scale approaching that of Abstract Expressionism. Yet it emerged that much of the new painting included the image of the human figure, some of it with an allegorical or nar-rative content. A further complication was that most of the new figurative art was executed by men.

The Return of the Figure and of "Expression"

A kind of exemplary reinvestment of confidence and energy in painting could be seen in the work of the American Leon Golub, for whom the probity (or even the possibility) of a *political* figurative art was the important question. The critique of traditional styles and media in the 1960s had made the very notion of figurative art seem outmoded, at best nostalgic. Moreover, the cultural and diplomatic stand-off between the Soviet Union and the United States had contributed to making a serious engagement with figurative realism in the West look unlikely. A committed political "realism" could, perhaps, have emerged only from an older artist. Born in 1922, Golub had been a student in figuratively-inclined WPA art classes in the mid-1930s and had exhibited internationally throughout the 1940s and 1950s. He became engaged in artists' protests against the Vietnam War in the later 1960s (in 1968 he lobbied to have Picasso withdraw *Guernica* from the Museum of Modern Art in New York as a protest against the Unites States' bombing policy in Vietnam). Golub's paintings of the following decade eschewed abstraction while addressing the theme of political power struggles: his *Assassins*, from 1972, and the *Mercenaries* series, from 1976, may be taken as referring to social and political violence in

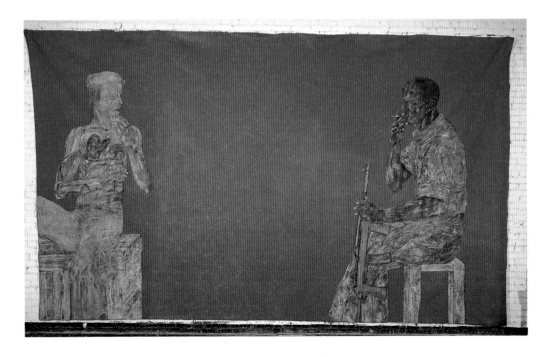

general as much as to CIA-sponsored terrorism in General Pinochet's Argentina or genocide in Pakistan (FIG. 29).

Working against Golub, however, was the uneasy suspicion that, after the minutely detailed recording of the war in Vietnam by television and photography, explicitly narrative and political painting had become a hopeless, though brave, endeavour. That suspicion, of course, sprang from the notion that paintings such as Golub's functioned primarily as illustrations, rather than as aesthetic constructions working critically upon the audience's understanding of what an illustration is.

What could be said of most figurative paintings made in the wake of Conceptualism was that the question of their style in relation to previous figurative styles became crucial. Conceptualism had made vivid a sense that paintings were physically redundant objects. A related realisation was that perhaps all figurative styles had already taken place; hence that "revived" figuration could only offer the experience of deep inauthenticity. Had not pioneer Modernists such as Picasso and Duchamp had to explore how the very languages of representation could be renovated? Had not the very act of painting figures become irredeemably associated with (male) historical institutions, the wielding of political and personal power, the submission of minorities and women, and with the operations of the capitalist market itself?

Many of these questions surfaced in London in 1976, when the former Pop artist, R. B. Kitaj, organised a painting and drawing show entitled *The Human Clay* (the phrase is from the poet W H. Auden: "To me Art's subject is the human clay"). Kitaj included his own work in the show, along with that of Leon Kossoff, Lucian Freud, Francis Bacon, and others, who were now claimed to constitute a "School of London." Setting his face against what he termed "provincial and orthodox vanguardism," that is, post-Duchampian art, the culture of New York and much else, Kitaj's defense of figuration was conducted with some frankly traditionalist claims. "The seam never really gave out," he said, referring to an alleged tradition of pictures of the single human form. "It's not as if an instinct which lies in the race of men from way before Sassetta and Giotto has run its course..." The return to figuration was also for Kitaj a way of "making common cause with working people...It seems to me at least as advanced or radical to attempt a more social art as not to." For all that, however, *The Human Clay* remained a traditionalist exercise of men drawing or painting women (or, less frequently, each other). Lucian Freud, for example, who had

29. LEON GOLUB *Mercenaries III*, 1980. Acrylic on canvas, 10' x 15' (3 x 4.5 m). Eli Broad Family Foundation, Los Angeles.

Golub has said that the mercenaries "are inserted into our space and we're inserted into their space. It's like trying to break down the barriers between depicted and actual space... There is a certain *ressentiment*, an aggressive shoving of these images right back at a society which tolerates these practices."

begun exhibiting in the early 1940s but was still regarded as a contemporary painter of great power – a reputation that survives into the 1990s – was hailed by his supporters in the 1970s as one who had kept alive a tradition of humanising figure painting in which the subject was revealed as candid, classless, and sexually animalistic, in which such revelations were conveyed in and through an encounter involving paint. Freud's detractors saw him as a fabricator of oddly postured, submissive female images, painted in unpleasant oranges and browns and dominated by the presence of the painter, leering down at their prostrate and frequently somnolent bodies from above (FIG. 30).

But the School of London was (and remains) an historical backwater. In a different register, attention throughout Europe and North America was curatorially captured around 1977 and 1978 by what was presented as an exciting "return" of previously lost possibilities. In Germany and Italy, but also across a wider international spectrum, paintings began to be shown which took up a seemingly knowing, parodic posture in relation to previous historical styles. Georg Baselitz, from Berlin, had for well over a decade been exploring the tension between abstract and figurative art, dispersing fragments over the canvas or, after 1969, turning his roughly drawn figures upside down. Another Berlin painter, Markus Lüpertz, author of the *Dithyrambic Manifesto* of 1966, introduced German motifs, including helmets, cannon, and incidents from World War II, into an essentially abstract art. The Dresden-born A.R. Penck (real name Ralf Winkler) had been frozen out of the Western art system during the 1960s, but had been drawn back in through contacts with Baselitz and the Michael Werner Gallery in Cologne. At the same time the work of a number of Italian painters, shortly to be known in Italy as the "transavantgarde" – Enzo Cucchi, Francesco Clemente, Mimmo Paladino, and Sandro Chia, along with Nicola de Maria, Luigi Ontani, and Ernesto Tatafiori – was shown first at home, then in Switzerland and Germany. The work of this group was increasingly eclectic, nostalgic, and ironic, though remaining within the large-canvas format of 1950s abstraction.

The new mood may be captured by a comparison of Harold Szeeman's choice of painters for *Documenta 5* in Kassel in 1972, which in retrospect reads like a compendium of Conceptualism, and Manfred Schneckenburger's selection for *Documenta 6* of 1977. Schneckenburger brought back several painters whom Szeeman had proscribed: Bacon, Baselitz, Lüpertz, and Penck were now placed alongside new work by Nancy Graves, Andy Warhol, Jasper Johns, Frank Stella, Roy Lichtenstein, and

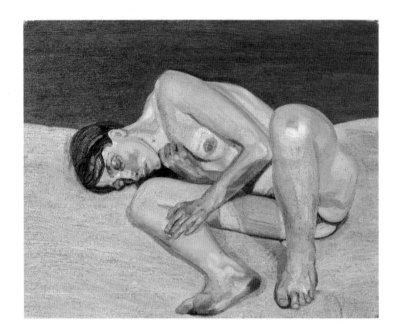

Willem de Kooning. The Italians were not yet in evidence, but Francesco Clemente and Sandro Chia showed at the Sperone Westwater Fischer Gallery in New York in 1979, and with Enzo Cucchi in a threesome at Sperone in 1980. Both shows were greeted with rapture and relief by dealers and critics who had grown weary of the austerities of Conceptualism. By the time of the Venice Biennale of 1980, it was clear that the curatorial community was wholeheartedly committed to the new, highly charged "neo-expressionist" painting, which was yet treated with scepticism by those for whom a return to "narrative" and "painterly expression" could only mean a retreat from serious critical engagement with art.

The critical divide is well exemplified by the reactions to large, high-profile group shows organised in London in 1981 and in Berlin in 1982 by Norman Rosenthal, exhibitions secretary of the Royal Academy in London, and Christos Joachimedes, the Berlin art critic. The Berlin event was titled *Zeitgeist* ("Spirit of the Times") – a weighty expression suggestive of world-historical forces in a Germanic key. The London show, portentously called *A New Spirit in Painting*, showcased artists as diverse as Baselitz, Karl Hödicke, Rainer Fetting, Lüpertz, Sigmar Polke, and Gerhard Richter from Germany; Calzolari, Mimmo Paladino, and Chia (FIG. 31) from Italy; Brice Marden, Julian Schnabel, and Stella from the United States; and Bacon, Alan Charlton, Hockney, Howard Hodgkin, and Kitaj from Great Britain.

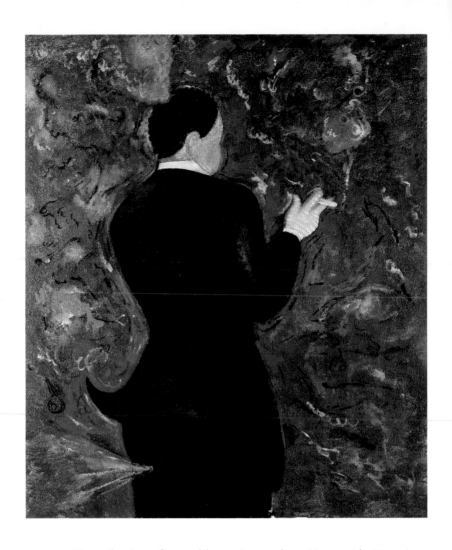

31. SANDRO CHIA
Smoker with Yellow Glove,
1980. Oil on canvas, 4'11" x
4'4" (1.5 x 1.3 m). Bruno
Bischofberger, Zurich.

Referring to his studio in Italy
as like "the stomach of a
whale," Chia described his
paintings and sculptures as
"like the indigested residues
of a former past...I am like a
lion-tamer amongst his beasts
and I feel close to the heroes
of my childhood, close to
Michelangelo, Titian and
Tintoretto."

Contributions from older artists such as Picasso, de Kooning, and Matta served to lend legitimacy to the work of a younger generation. The London exhibition embraced paintings by Baselitz (FIG. 32), furious sexual impastos from Fetting, eclectic performances from Stella, Picasso in his luminous dotage, Lolita-like figuration from Balthus, and monochrome panels from Charlton, Gotthard Graubner, and Robert Ryman. Confidently paraded as including "some of the liveliest and best-known painters in the world today," the "new spirit" exhibition promoted three main ideas: first, that painting in the 1950s had been dominated by New York, resulting in a marginalisation of the European contribution. Second, that the cultural and political mores of the 1960s needed rapid revision: as Joachimedes put it, "the overemphasis on the idea of autonomy in art which brought

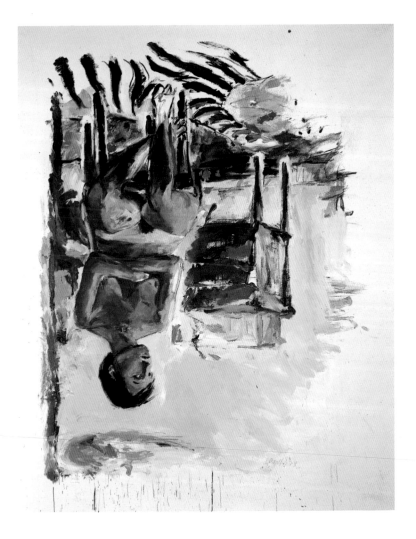

about Minimalism and its extreme appendix, Conceptual art, was bound to be self-defeating: soon the avant-garde of the 1970s, with its narrow, puritan approach, devoid of all joy in the senses, lost its creative impetus and began to stagnate." Third, that despite the continuing importance of abstraction, it was necessary to re-assert a figurative tradition. "It is surely unthinkable," wrote the selectors of the London exhibition "that the representation of human experiences, in other words people and their emotions, landscapes and still lives could forever be excluded from painting." Through a resurrection of what the selectors called "the Northern Expressionist tradition" – referring in part to the early twentieth-century German Expressionism of Ernst Kirchner, Karl Schmidt-Rottluff, and Emil Nolde – artists were now poised to ensure that such themes "must in the long

32. GEORG BASELITZ *Nude Elke*, 1974. Oil on canvas, 8'3" x 8'3" (2.5 x 2.5 m). Private collection.

Trained in the figurative tradition of East Germany, Baselitz began to invert his motifs in 1969 in order to be "delivered of all ballast, delivered from tradition." He now saw himself as German in a wider sense, linked to an expressive tradition stemming from the Gothic and from Romanticism.

run return to the centre of the argument of painting." An underlying ambition of Joachimedes was to "present a position in art which consciously asserts traditional values, such as individual creativity, accountability, quality." He went so far as to call the show – which was a box-office success – an "act of resistance" which was "in the true sense progressive."

And yet *A New Spirit in Painting* re-established painting at the beginning of the 1980s as a male activity (all 38 artists shown were men), structured around qualities of energy, ambition, sensual celebration, and an awareness of national "tradition." The Germans were angst-ridden and obsessed in the manner of earlier German Expressionism, the Americans were confident and pluralist, the British were northern Romantics concerned with the figure, the Italians had survived *arte povera* to return to even earlier roots. National stereotyping within a framework of tradition: here were male artists of the NATO alliance bound into the cultural project of "returning" to European art via the trope of the expressionist surface. Meanwhile, Reaganomics in the United States and Thatcherist monetarism in Great Britain was at this point combining to kick-start the international art market after a fallow period following the oil crises of the mid-1970s (FIG. 33). In the new political dispensation, the possession of large, energetic-seeming paintings was to become as fashionable and worthy as those "people and their emotions, landscapes and still lives" which they purported to celebrate.

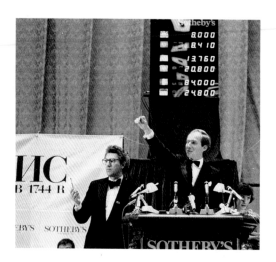

33. A successful bid at Sotheby's sale of Russian avant-garde and Soviet contemporary art in Moscow, 7 July 1988, an event which marked the opening of art and artists from beyond the Iron Curtain to the pressures and expectations of the Western art market.

Immediately following the London show the new *transavantgarde* – to use Achile Benito Oliva's term – became successful with influential dealers across the Atlantic. In the summer and autumn of 1981 the Germans followed the Italians to New York: one-man shows occurred of Georg Baselitz, Anselm Kiefer, Markus Lüpertz, Rainer Fetting, Bernd Zimmer, and the scabrous Salomé, who was also involved in performance and music with the band Randy Animals. They were soon followed by Jörg Immendorff, A.R. Penck, Franz Hitzler, Troels Wörsel, and others. Influential galleries in Europe, such as Michael Werner in Cologne, the Museum Folkwang in Essen, the Kunsthalle in Hamburg, Gian Enzo Sperone in Rome and Konrad Fischer in Düsseldorf, showed representatives of the "new spirit" to a substantial tide of critical endorsement.

Expressionism Contested

The debate which raged on both sides of the Atlantic about the values and priorities of the new painting was furious and partisan. For its supporters, German painting in particular provided a way out of what seemed an artistic and aesthetic *impasse*. It presented a seeming willingness to engage in artistic "pleasure," while responding to supposed anxieties of the mid-European mind about its own past. Bazon Brock in Germany and Donald Kuspit in America argued for placing the new painting within an avant-garde framework which "compelled us to see the seemingly familiar within our tradition in a totally new way" (Brock) or which showed a complex, forced, childishness that was a "political gesture, signalling the helplessness of the individual in the face of social forces beyond his control" (Kuspit). The work of Penck and Jörg Immendorf contained for Kuspit the seeds of a "world-historical art, a seemingly comprehensive, dominating style, sweeping all before it...beheading and relegating to the dustbin of history the art of the 1960s and 1970s that has up to now seemed royal."

Such outbursts were effectively countered by a series of attacks on the new painting launched by *October*, a Marxist-inclined theoretical journal published in New York from 1976. Opposition to painting had been implicit in the early *October* writings of Douglas Crimp and Craig Owens on photography. In the spring of 1981 it was the vigorous and articulate criticism of Crimp and Benjamin Buchloh that hit home. "Only a miracle can prevent [painting] from coming to an end" Crimp wrote *à propos* the Duchampian position of Daniel Buren and the contrary claims made for the colourful new paintings of Frank Stella.

Buchloh elucidated what had been implicit in Buren and Conceptual art generally, namely that "expressive" painting was reactionary in intention and complicit in its support of elite and undemocratic power bases within both art and wider politics. "If the perceptual conventions of mimetic representation...were re-established, if the credibility of iconic referentiality was reaffirmed, and if the hierarchy of figure-ground relationships on the picture plane was again presented as an 'ontological' condition," Buchloh said of the return to "classicism" of the 1920s, after the period of pioneer Cubism, "then what other ordering systems outside of aesthetic discourse had to have already been put in place in order to imbue the new visual configurations with historical authenticity?" Buchloh's implication was that the return to figuration in the early 1980s indeed signalled an attack upon an earlier avant-garde moment which had had "great potential for the critical dismantling of the dominant ideology." For a committed "left" critic wishing to support a painting practice committed to revolutionary re-coding, the new German painting was at best apolitical and undialectical; at worst, it underpinned and tacitly endorsed the wider contemporary political and cultural reaction. "In the pathetic force of their repetition-compulsion," Buchloh complained, "the mock avant-garde of contemporary European painters now benefits from the ignorance and arrogance of a racket of cultural *parvenus* who perceive it as their mission to reaffirm the politics of a rigid conservatism through cultural legitimation." *October* was at times implacable. In any event, it maintained a highly selective perception of which painters were worth supporting or even mentioning. The suspicion generated was that painting *per se* could not be avant-garde.

Yet a few exceptions were permitted to prove the rule. One was Gerhard Richter. Richter had grown up in Dresden, in the former German Democratic Republic and had trained as a painter within an ethos dominated by Socialist Realism, before moving to Düsseldorf in 1961, two months before the Berlin Wall divided his country. He had already seen the work of Jackson Pollock and Lucio Fontana at *Documenta 2* in 1959, and after settling in the West he worked with Sigmar Polke and Konrad Fischer-Leug on an early version of Pop art mockingly known as "Capitalist Realism," which manipulated ready-made signs from advertising and urban imagery.

Over the next fifteen years Richter's work existed at the edges or limits of representation, between painting and the photograph, often with a strong implication of wanting to be neither. A group of paintings of the early 1970s were constituted of grey squiggles; works of 1981 consisted of large wall-mirrors ordered by phone for an exhibition. From about 1978 or 1979 Richter forced this part-despairing, part-exploratory practice to new limits, continuing to dispute the culture of "*peinture*" on the grounds of its associations with traditional aesthetics – "*peinture*," Richter said, "stands in the way of all expression that is appropriate to our times" – while at the same time producing abstract paintings, now in colour, alongside paintings based on mass-produced imagery such as the snapshot and photo-journalism.

Richter's abstract paintings are composed of unorthodox devices: veils of relatively simple colours are spread and dragged over the surface with large spatulas or squeegees, and seem in their multiplicity to make fun of the very idea of colour juxtapositions, while in their random and mechanical mode of production they appear to refute the very idea of composition (see FIG. 28, page 43). In his photo-inspired paintings Richter adopted a similarly perverse authorial position: making it clear that he was knowingly producing the appearance of photographs by the wrong means. Such paintings replicate colour or black-and-white photographs right down to their indistinct focus and lack of convincing depth. A notable series from the later 1980s, 15 grey paintings entitled *18 Oktober 1977*, responded to journalistic photographs of the incarceration and death in the Stammheim prison of Red Army Faction members Andreas Baader, Gudrun Ensslin, and Jan-Carl Raspe. Richter said that

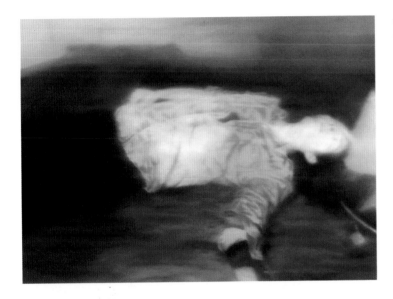

34. GERHARD RICHTER
Shot Down No. 2, 1988. From the series *18 Oktober 1977*. Oil on canvas, 3'3" x 4'6½" (1 x 1.4 m).

he was struck by "the public ambitions of these people, their non-private, impersonal, ideological motivation...the tremendous force, the frightening power of one idea to the point of dying for it." They were "victims, not of a specific ideology on the left or right, but of ideological behaviour *per se*." While feeling that most photographs "generate horror," Richter viewed the resulting paintings, life-size, as sympathetic meditations on the death, probably by suicide, of the captive terrorists. The series as a whole forms a hybrid, metaphorical tableau (FIG. 34).

Yet what is striking in the early reception accorded to Richter was its legislative, sometimes dogmatic, quality. Buchloh, writing in *October*, saw Richter's strategies as an ironic attempt to deal with political history in the best avant-garde manner. Richter, for his part, maintained that he was unattracted to the

35. ART AND LANGUAGE
Portrait of V.I.Lenin with a Cap, in the Style of Jackson Pollock, I, 1979. Oil and enamel on board mounted on canvas, 5'10" x 4'2" (1.7 x 1.2 m). Private collection, Paris.

Using stencils for the gestural moments and an official Communist-party icon for the emergent image of Lenin, such paintings play with the collision and possible annihilation of both Action Painting and "partiinost," upon ground occupied by neither.

Red Army Faction as a political group. "I'm interested in the *raison d'être* of an ideology that sets so much in motion," he said. "Politics just isn't for me," Richter insisted in an interview with Buchloh, "because art has an entirely different function...The reason I don't argue in 'sociological terms' is that I want to produce a picture and not an ideology. It's always its factuality that makes a picture good...call it conservative if you want." Yet Richter recognised that his painting practice was radical vis-à-vis the governing conventions of documentation and artifice. His chief interest has been the idea of representation itself in an age dominated by news photography, and how such photography can could be brought within the confines of a painting tradition now increasingly subject to reflection on its own resources.

A comparable outlook can be identified in the British group, Art and Language, whose members throughout the late 1960s and early 1970s had participated in theoretical discussions and had produced Minimal and Conceptual-type art-works. They also wrote texts, a practice ironically described by two art-historian members of the circle as "a type of post-Frankfurt and post-logical atomism...developed into a culture-critical sloganisation with logical detail." By 1978-79 the group had dwindled to three members: the artists Michael Baldwin and Mel Ramsden, and the art historian Charles Harrison, who had begun to discuss questions of how meaning came to reside in pictures at all – an inquiry which led to the further question of how a picture (any picture) established its various relationships to what it was *of*. The answer, derived from contemporary philosophical analyses of *naming*, was couched in terms of cause. "No answer to the question of what a picture is *of* can be seen as adequate... so long as it requires a suppression of information about, or inquiry into, that picture's genesis," they wrote. It seemed to follow that relations of genesis (via practical resources, painterly and theoretical competencies on the part of the artist and the viewer) stood against and often collided with the sheer iconicity of an image when that iconicity was open and declared.

The opportunity to test the stresses and results of such collisions was presented by an invitation to exhibit work in the Netherlands in 1980. For this, Art and Language began a series of paintings (in itself both an accommodation to fashionable concerns and an extension of the group's previous researches into art's foundations) generically entitled *Portrait of V.I. Lenin with a Cap, in the Style of Jackson Pollock* (FIG. 35), thus combining a Socialist Realist icon with the abstract cavortings of Jackson Pollock's drip paintings of the late 1940s. Described in an auto-

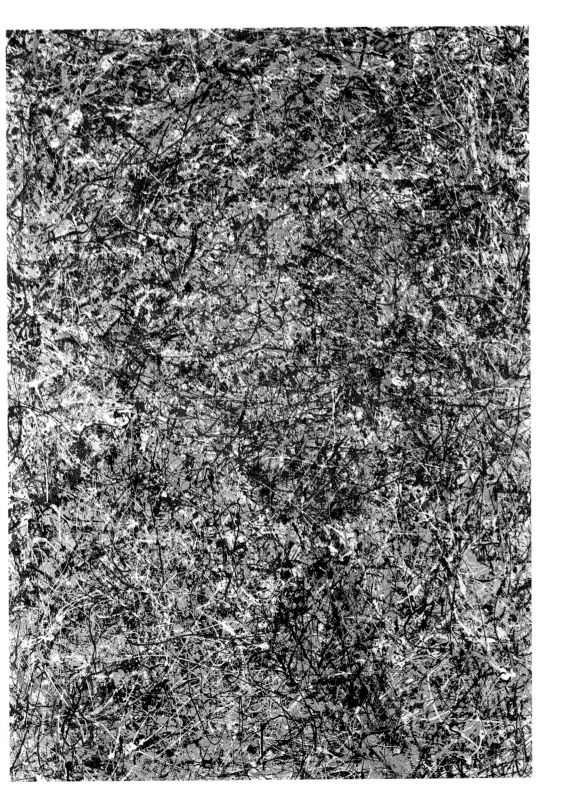

history of the group as a "monstrous stylistic *détente* between the two supposedly antagonistic parts of a mutually reinforcing cultural pair," the paintings of this series purported to show that "expressionistic" pictures could be produced otherwise than by using expressionist technique: Art and Language used drawings and stencils for their "expressionism," in whose abstract patterns an image of Lenin can sometimes (just) be made to appear. The scandalous compatibility of American abstraction and Soviet realism was intended to break open a central taboo of 1950s formalist Modernism while yet resisting any affirmative proposition other than an ironic or even comic one.

As is now clear, the revival of painting in the early 1980s was already under way for several artists in the recession-hit 1970s, and not all of it was aligned with the dubious assumptions of the *transavantgarde*. Further, it is clear that Art and Language's earlier Conceptualism had sought to contest the premises of Modernism on the ground of art itself, not outside it. Both Art and Language and Richter claimed that revised conditions for painting were being set. Charles Harrison wrote of the V.I. Lenin series: "Now that the possibility of painting as a form of practice had emerged for Art and Language out of the legacy of Conceptual art...the history of painting itself was open to recovery and revision...The *culture* of painting, it seemed, could now be critically addressed *by* painting." Harrison was drawing attention to the argument that, after the "end of painting" in the 1960s, painting had to be "second-orderish," not merely a reflection on the condition of painting from outside, but engaged with the nature of painting and its historical and critical condition *from within*. In the wake of Minimalism and Conceptualism, no artistic decision could be free from what another sympathetic observer, Thomas Crow, called "the burden of historical and theoretical self-consciousness." Painting would now have to become, in Harrison's words, "as complex in the receiving and describing as in the making."

Yet such a version of modernism-after-Modernism could hope to appeal only to those for whom a tiny number of postwar artists and critics (say, Pollock and Greenberg) were canonical. For others, especially artists trained away from the clamour of the debate about Modernism conducted in the English language, that canon never existed anyway, certainly not in an absolute form. Many women cared nothing for a theoretical position that bore the hallmarks of masculine agonising about the art of other men. Nor was the dry, academic tone of the debate calculated to appeal to those untrained in philosophical

36. SIGMAR POLKE *Measurement of the Stones in the Wolf's Belly and the Subsequent Grinding of the Stones into Cultural Rubbish*, 1980-81. Mixed media on fabric (plaster and/or acrylic modelling paste, acrylic painting used as paste, iridescent mylar on felt and synthetic fur), 6' x 3'10½" (1.8 x 1.2 m). Art Gallery of Ontario, Toronto.

criticism. For these artists, at least, the nuances of recuperating a better Modernism were an irrelevance.

Something called "post-Modernism"

One kind of work which attempted to find a way beyond the orthodoxies of abstract Modernism leant not so much towards irony as towards the perceived pluralism and heterogeneity of the mass media. Sometimes dubbed "post-Modernism" owing to its embrace of eccentricity, historical pastiche, and its rejection of high cultural seriousness, such painting attracted artists to whom official Modernism was constraining and doctrinaire. Two of the most prominent painters in the use of mixed and media-derived imagery were the German Sigmar Polke and the American Julian Schnabel. The problem for criticism was whether a distinction could be drawn between instances of stylistic heterogeneity that were passive and conformist, and those that could be said to raise challenging questions about the world in which they were made.

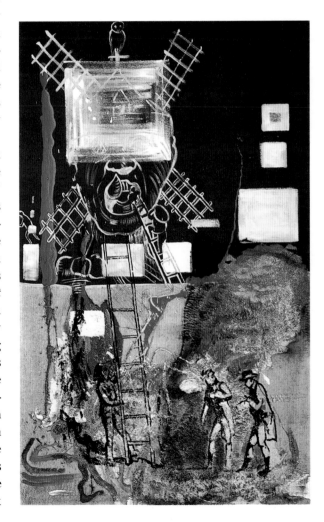

Sigmar Polke first exhibited in Düsseldorf in 1963 as part of the group termed "Capitalist Realism." Throughout the later 1960s his paintings inverted existing consumer images in apparent defiance of the tendency among German artists to perpetuate tired versions of Surrealist abstraction or *art informel*, which he viewed as a Parisian import. What Polke now practised was a critical re-working of cultural effects, taking as his source material images from the mass media, film, or historical culture, and degenerating them through deliberate mistreatment. In a series of paintings from the late 1960s and 1970s, Polke used surfaces that later became scandalous in the work of Julian Schnabel – black velvet, leopard skin and the like – in order partly to travesty the fetishised surfaces of Modernist painting (FIG. 36).

Polke has always taken a wry attitude to explanations of his work, yet beneath the cynicism and despair is the belief in layering imagery, in change and in the flow of time. "You have to look first...you have to watch [the paintings], take them to bed with you, never let them out of your sight. Caress them, kiss and pray, do anything, you can kick them, beat the daylights out of them. Every picture wants some kind of treatment – no matter what." Although in his work of the 1980s Polke seemed to drift into nature-mysticism, he had already done enough oblique and counter-cultural painting to establish himself as an archetype of the resistant, quizzical, and non-conformist artist – perhaps the essential, playful, post-Modernist.

The contrast is with Julian Schnabel, who in the early 1980s was encumbered with a large international reputation despite a low, or at least ambiguous, critical standing in the art world. Schnabel had had his first one-man show at the Mary Boone Gallery in New York early in 1979; later in the same year he exhibited some "plate" paintings – paintings incorporating broken crockery – examples of which were included in both *A New Spirit in Painting* and *Zeitgeist*. Schnabel's paintings of the 1980s, most of them very large, are characterised by profusion and a rough-and-ready mixture of sources and styles, derived from Texas "Funk" which Schnabel had absorbed in Houston as a student. These works looked reckless and confusing. They contained, apart from smashed crockery, bits of wood and other props

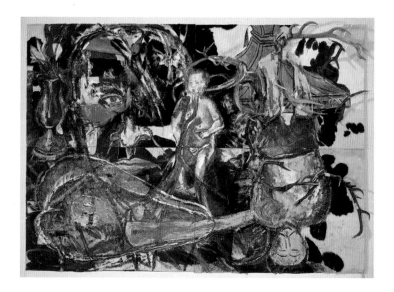

37. JULIAN SCHNABEL
Prehistory: Glory, Honor, Privilege, Poverty, 1981. Oil and antlers on pony skin, 10'3" x 14'10" (3.2 x 4.5 m). Saatchi Collection, London.

The title and scale of this work evoke epic yet conflicting narratives of claustrophobic density, which a supportive critic described as "writhing, pulsating images [whose] effect is one of suffocation, excess, and decay."

attached to unconventional surfaces such as velvet, linoleum, or synthetic fur. The "flatness" of the base surface was interrupted by a variety of levels and protruding objects, in this instance antlers (FIG. 37). Quotations from old-master paintings existed alongside inconclusive or semi-finished passages that seemed not to cohere. Schnabel's images – made to seem collage-like, banal, or sometimes infantile – first appeared as challenging "aberrations" in an art world which was now ready for a new and marketable style.

The critical reaction to Schnabel was disarmingly mixed. On one level, his most controversial paintings served as a focus for an already burgeoning art-world debate about authorial originality and intention: which of Schnabel's many styles were "truly" his? The question seemed to imply that the unified "author" in art had died, and with him (it was usually "him") the coherence of the idea of an authentic creative manner. Those who assessed Schnabel's significance in these terms claimed him as a representative of the tendency towards eclecticism and vagrant historicising known as post-Modernism. Others placed him within Expressionism. Schnabel had admired the mosaics by the Spanish architect Antonio Gaudí (1852-1926), in the Park Güell in Barcelona and had wished to "make a mosaic also, but one that wasn't decorative." "I liked the agitated surface" he remarked in a 1987 interview; "it sort of corresponded to my own taste... These paintings really are not about aggressive surfaces, but about an imagistically focused inarticulateness, which shows itself in agitation." Schnabel spoke too of his "anxiousness...the sense that things aren't right." "I want to put something in the world that can communicate this in a concentrated, shorthand way, that finally becomes explosive." Other critics accused Schnabel of sacrificing his art to an overweening personal ambition. They charged him with replaying mass-media effects and post-Modernist simultaneities without reaching for the critical judgements and priorities that those effects and simultaneities demanded. For a time, Schnabel was an *enfant terrible* whom nobody could pin down.

Discussion about the role of painting in a media age was furious and fast. While Douglas Crimp and the *October* writers were urging the inevitable "end" of figurative, expressive painting, other voices were attempting to locate painting's place in an essentially photographic world. The young painter and critic Thomas Lawson argued in *Artforum* in 1981 that "the work of the pseudo-expressionists [he is referring partly to Schnabel] does play on a sense of contrariness, consistently matching elements

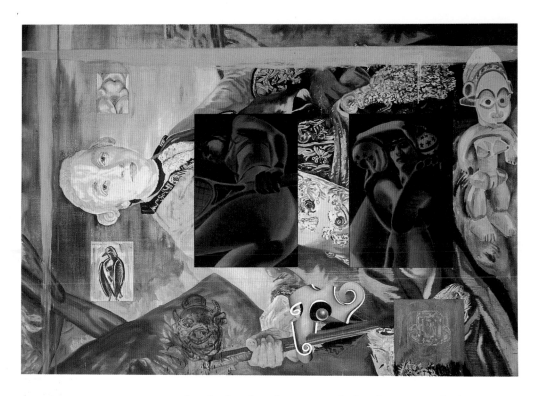

38. DAVID SALLE
Lampwick's Dilemma,
1989. Acrylic and oil on
canvas, 7'8" x 11'3" (2.4 x
3.4 m).

The "dilemma" of Salle's
title seems to refer to the
classic children's tale by
C. Collodi, in which
Pinocchio's errant
schoolfriend Lampwick
suggests a journey to the
Land of Fun, where there
are no schools or books and
the days are spent in play.
Once there, however, they
discover that those who
engage in endless fun turn
into donkeys. In this
painting may be seen a
"play" of images, including
an African mask, an
historical figure holding a
staff, and a fragment of a
painting by Lucian Freud.

and attitudes that do not match, but it goes no further...a *retardataire* mimeticism is presented with expressionist immediacy."

Lawson's preference was for the strategy of the New York painter David Salle, first seen in a solo show in 1980 and again at the Mary Boone Gallery (with Julian Schnabel) in 1981. Salle's paintings, Lawson observed, consisted of images placed next to or on top of one another in what looked like unplanned, disinterested combinations (FIG. 38). They looked immediately stylish, observed Lawson; yet "the images Salle presents this way are emotionally and intellectually disturbing. Often his subjects are naked women, presented as objects. Occasionally they are men. At best these presentations of humanity are cursory, off-hand; at worst they are brutal, disfigured...meaning is intimated but tantalisingly withheld...they are dead, inert representations of the impossibility of passion in a culture that has institutionalised self-expression." For Lawson and others on the "left," Salle's intuitive eclecticism, though often seen as destabilising, could at times descend into decoration or mere diversity.

Lawson's cautious defence of Salle was part of a more general argument: in preference to abandoning painting wholesale for photographic strategies in ways that could be dismissed as yet another avant-garde gambit, artists could square the circle by allowing painting itself – the medium from which an engagement with photography was least expected – to trade in the photographic and photo-based image. "It is perfect camouflage," wrote Lawson, whose own paintings of the time looked unswervingly at media images from the front pages of the *New York Post* (FIG. 39). "We know about the appearance of everything, but from a great distance...Even as photography holds reality distant from us it also makes it seem immediate, by enabling us to catch the moment. Right now a truly conscious practice is concerned above all with the implications of that paradox." The stage was set for a re-evaluation of painting squarely within the context of the appropriated photographic motif.

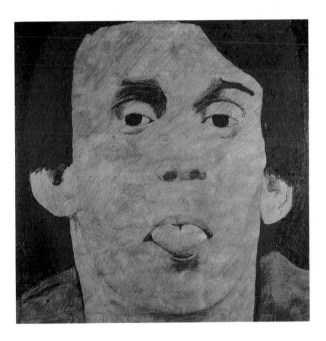

The critical framework of the early 1980s welcomed that appropriation as potentially parodic and hence subversive of the mythology of Modernist painting, with its obsessively crafted surfaces and its posture of authenticity. On the other hand, the critical Modernists would be seen as stopping short of ironically celebrating mere vapidity or "bad taste." Painting, in the wake of Conceptualism, had to be difficult rather than entertaining, oblique rather than condescending, to one side of already known categories: it needed to be "as complex in the receiving and describing as in the making." A corollary – one that undoubtedly damaged the critical reputations of Salle and Schnabel – was that art that became instantly popular with museums or in the market-place was unlikely to have substantial critical depth. Painting could afford to adopt an ironic mode – to be painting, but also something else. But it should remain wary lest that irony evaporate into mere sarcasm or camp.

39. THOMAS LAWSON
Burn, Burn, Burn, 1982.
Oil on canvas, 4' x 4' (1.2 x 1.2 m).

The distinction proved vitally important. Camp had been the prevailing hallmark of the Chicago school of "bad" painting led by Ed Paschke and Jim Nutt in the 1970s. The years between 1982 and 1985 were a period which in New York suddenly produced "East Village" art and which in both America and Europe produced "graffiti" art, along with new kinds of sculpture and various other accommodations to street art and life. The East

Village (the area south of 10th Street between Broadway and Tompkins Square) had been inhabited by artists before. Now, a combination of ethnic restaurants, clubs, small galleries, and exotic retail outlets continued to support a generation of younger artists already estranged from the career networks of up-town galleries and magazines, to produce a brief explosion of garish and transgressively styled works that had consequences for discussions of what it meant to be in some strong sense "avant-garde."

East Village art depended for its appeal directly upon what its most eloquent supporter, Walter Robinson, called "the unique blend of poverty, punk rock, drugs, arson, Hell's Angels, winos, prostitutes and dilapidated housing" that was the social and economic legacy of a forgotten inner-city neighbourhood. Replaying the profusion and disorder of real street life, East Village artists, supported by cheap-to-run galleries with exotic names – Fun, Civilian Warfare, Nature Morte, New Math, Piezo Electric, Sensory Evolution, Virtual Garrison and the like – threw caution to the winds in an orgy of attitudinal and technical excess. Copying and pastiche became a hallmark of East Village art in ways that were supposed to signal a hedonistic widening of the sources of pleasure and an irreverent taste for such unfashionable historical styles as psychedelia and Op art. Works by George Condo and Peter Schuyff, shown at Pat Hearn's gallery, recaptured Surrealistic motifs out of Salvador Dali, René Magritte, and Yves Tanguy. Patti Astor's Fun Gallery, from its beginnings in late 1981, held openings celebrated as "minifestivals of the slum arts," with rap music and break-dancing, and works by Jean-Michel Basquiat (a one-time collaborator of Andy Warhol), Fab Five Freddy, Keith Haring, Kenny Scharf, Les Quinones, and others. Nature Morte and Civilian Warfare showed photo-based work (Gretchen Bender, Richard Milani) and so-called "expressionistic" painting (Huck Snyder, Judy Glantzman) respectively. The Gracie Mansion Gallery was a focal point: the ensembles of Rhonda Zwillinger and Rodney Alan Greenblat were popular (that is, admired by East Village types), self-parodying, cheap, and self-consciously kitsch. Other such locations proliferated.

Perhaps only Mike Bidlo's assault on the conventions of "authorship" produced genuinely paradoxical results. At first sight his transcriptions – copies of poor quality reproductions of Brancusi, Morandi, Kandinsky, Léger, Schnabel, and Warhol's factory, done to scale – seem to be little more than low-grade Pop art revelling in wackiness and irony for all it is worth. A

40. MIKE BIDLO
Picasso's Women, 1988. Exhibition at the Castelli Gallery, New York.

For this show Bidlo worked through most of Picasso's paintings of women, from the Blue Period to Mougins. Since Bidlo's paintings are re-invented from low quality reproductions and hence falsify the registration, colour, and textures of the originals (even though painted the same size), they are strictly neither copies nor fakes, but a kind of mimicry.

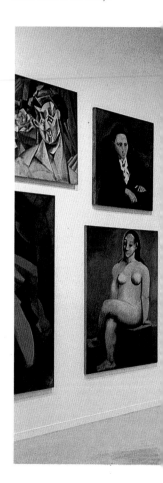

Bidlo installation at the P.S.1 Gallery in 1982 recreated Jackson Pollock's notorious drunken gesture of peeing in Peggy Guggenheim's fireplace. At most, Bidlo's works raised questions about the relationship of copy to original, and hence about the wider notion of Modernist "originality" and its relation to the operations of taste and cultural consumption. At the least, they provided cheap copies of very expensive paintings for the market (FIG. 40).

For a while, East Village art seemed to promise the final defeat of "high" Modernist seriousness and its traditional masculine orientation. Certainly, the establishment of commercial exchange networks outside the axes linking up-town museums and established dealers seemed to promise an escape-route for younger artists looking for a break. But the heyday of East Village art was brief. Left-inclined critics tired of its dominant tendency to reduce all symptomatic phenomena – urban graffiti, debased design, marks of squalor or disorientation – to grounds

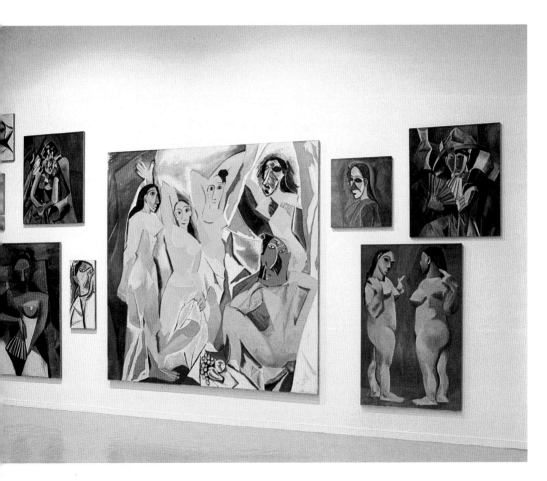

of celebration and/or indifference. To some, the East Village preoccupation with the media (Kenny Scharf is an example) was itself a sign of alienated consciousness that had abandoned any attempt critically to examine the world that produced it. A third argument was that the East Village avant-garde was part of, rather than an antidote to, the general levelling of sexual, regional, and cultural difference. East Village art was accused of replacing those signal differences with the culture industry's artificial, mass-produced, generic signifier for "Difference" in a motley of empty diversity and puerilism.

The latter position, of *October*'s Craig Owens, is important for suggesting the concept of avant-garde to which most East Village artists and comparable artists elsewhere simply failed to measure up. The argument was that the classic European avant-garde had struck up a position of real ambiguity between an educated and cultured middle class, from which many of the avant-garde were deserters, and various sub-cultures on the city's margins which they did not entirely join – for Daumier, Degas, and Manet, in nineteenth-century Paris, these had been ragpickers, prostitutes, street entertainers. In contrast, the East Village adventurers had adopted something akin to a fashion posture that was not only self-advertising and commercially successful ("a miniature replica of the contemporary art market" was Owen's least flattering description), but was precisely incapable of evoking ethnic or sexual "difference" as a culturally resistant force. It now stood to genuinely avant-garde practice not to replicate but to dislodge an institutionalised avant-garde production model. Counterposed to the East Village "enfant-garde" stood the Political Art Documentation/Distribution (PAD/D) group, whose productions were typically neither commercially marketable nor paintings (FIG. 41).

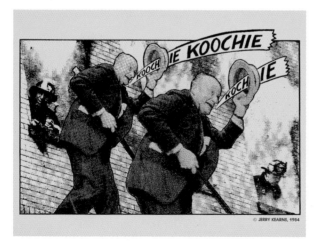

41. JERRY KEARNS
Koochie, Koochie, Koochie: Project Against Displacement, 1984. Printed offset poster, 18 x 24″ (45 x 61 cm). For PAD/D's *Not For Sale* show, New York.

The debate about the viability of parodic painting in the early 1980s became an international phenomenon. In France, where President François Mitterrand, newly elected in 1981, embarked upon a course of cultural investment on a grand scale, painting was well represented by the young Gérard Garouste, who practised a kind of banal mannerism derived from Picasso, de Chirico, and Tintoretto

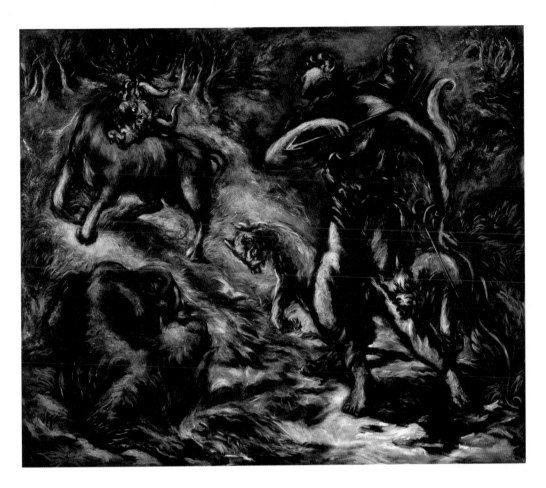

(FIG. 42). Garouste emphasises that painting after Conceptual art was bound to seem strange at first. "After Buren," he has said, "originality no longer existed...We have to return to the original system of our Latin culture and see what comprises the system of painting and invest all the archetypes with new meaning." Quickly absorbed into a rapidly growing international mainstream, with a support-base in the German galleries, Garouste drew upon classical narrative painting – a Modernist heresy – but unstraightforwardly. "When I make the myth of Orion, it's not the fact of having taken Orion from Greek mythology that matters, but of drawing on him through mythology that comes from the depths of our culture." The distinction between the "primitive" and the inauthentic in Garouste becomes almost nil.

In East Germany the Czech-born Milan Kunc produced works whose deliberate banality was meant to stand for the impossible, absurd interface between West European avant-gardism and the prevalent conditions of cultural collapse in the

42. GÉRARD GAROUSTE
Orion le Classique, Orion l'Indien, 1981-82. Oil on canvas, 8'5" x 9'10" (2.5 x 3 m). Musée National d'Art Moderne, Paris.

"Banality interests me," says Garouste. "It's a question of playing with what is called classical painting, as if that were the language of painting. And starting with that language I am writing a novel...I see myself as part of the generation which cut short the whole game of Modernism."

Communist bloc (FIG. 43). Kunc's cartoonery and nihilism – on a par with the Chicago school of the 1970s or the contemporary work of the Dutch artist, Rob Scholte – is not to be admired, but read as a symptom of an existential state. In saying that "modern art was over and done with by 1930," that "art since then has been post-Modern," Kunc meant to signal the inevitable degradation of all styles by repetition and over-use. Yet his own paintings play the "kitsch" gambit straight, as if nothing can be salvaged from low culture except a good joke.

At another extreme, Ken Currie, from Scotland, elicited particular critical sympathies. The most interesting of a group of Glasgow painters heavily touted in the early 1980s, Currie painted scenes of working-class heroism and trade-union solidarity, but at the price of importing some old-fashioned narrative, pictorial devices. He was greeted by some as a "realist" capable of extolling the virtues and identifications of a traditional, but declining, political culture. Close inspection of his manner suggests however that he too may be engaging in a kind of parodic repetition with a difference. His harsh, glaring colours, sulphuric atmospheres and surly male workers repeat only some aspects of 1930s proletarian realism. Currie's *People's Palace* murals (FIG. 44) have been claimed for a Brechtian tradition of contradiction and complexity (they show women in a male political environment,

43. MILAN KUNC
Venus, 1981-82. Oil on canvas, 5'3" x 7'11" (1.6 x 2.6 m).

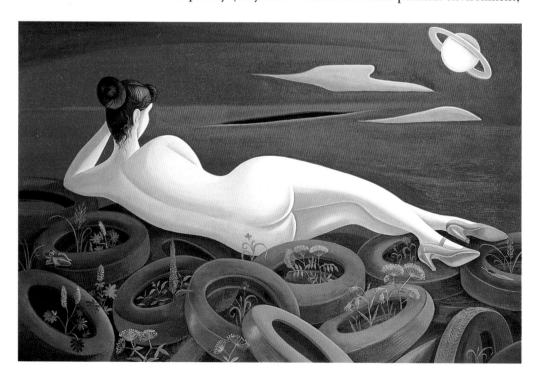

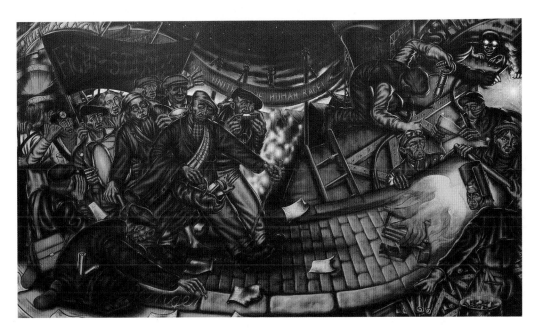

ordinary workers in an international political theatre). Others believe that they present an illusionistic realism of the typical of the sort described by the Hungarian Marxist critic, Georg Lukács. Currie has said merely that he wanted his paintings to "speak a democratic language," to make art "about working people for working people," one that is "demystified, popularised and socialised, giving artists the chance to fulfil a useful social function": language which quickly alienated Currie from those who wanted socialist art to be sceptical and reflective, not celebratory. The argument – an important one for painting and for "left" political affiliations in art – turns upon the extent to which the apparent directness of Currie's paintings exhausts their immediate content. Was this art a critique of abstract Modernism from within the figurative and the "popular," or another manifestation of marketable good intentions?

44. KEN CURRIE
The People's Palace History paintings. Panel 6: Fight or Starve...wandering through the thirties, 1986. Oil on canvas, 7'2" x 12'6" (2.2 x 3.8 m). The People's Palace, Glasgow Museums, Scotland.

Painting and "the Feminine"

All of the paintings discussed so far in this chapter have been by men. The suggestion that painting in the 1980s favoured men is inescapable: it in turn associates feminist art with photography, performance, and some kinds of sculpture. But that logic is too simple, as is shown by a range of confident new postures adopted recently by a number of women painters in both America and Europe.

Given the continued association of "painting" with authentic tradition, with maleness, and with Modernist history, it is unsurprising that women artists should seek a way of ending their exclusion from this history by deriving norms of practice from the idea of the feminine as such. This search starts from the premise that "the feminine" exists, and goes on to propose (for example, in the writings of Shirley Kaneda) that "feminine" abstraction has little or nothing to do with vaginal imagery (Hannah Wilke, Judy Chicago) or with craft elaborations (Faith Ringgold, Joyce Kozloff). "Feminine" painting, in this argument, seeks to articulate neglected and even denigrated qualities, but without guilt. It embraces the tentative and the unstable (feminine), rather than the totalised or balanced (male). It welcomes, rather than suffers from, traits such as intuitiveness and passivity. It ties the work's facture to the body (feminine), rather than to the mind alone (male). It insists upon criteria of judgement which accompany paintings one-by-one rather than in general. It tends to the additive rather than the subtractive. It embraces the sublime through sensuousness (feminine) rather than through reduction, geometry or "negation" (all male). It seldom forecloses or completes. It indulges in the eccentric or unprincipled (on principle). Finally, it insists that the production of "feminine" painting derives not from the gender of the painter, but from the values prevailing in the work itself.

By this logic, Philip Taaffe's recent painting can be claimed for femininity because it defies the reductive good taste of "male" art and celebrates arbitrariness and decorativeness as values which, so to speak, have no stable value in the male aesthetic pantheon (FIG. 45). The delicate grids of Agnes Martin are to be claimed for "the feminine" because they open the authoritarian grid of male Modernist architecture, atomise it and render it receptive to quietness and the poetic. In a similar vein, the recent works of Valerie Jaudon superficially resemble Sol LeWitt's structures, but with an attitude that seeks out, rather than avoids, subjectivity and taste (FIG. 46). (Interestingly, recent assessments of LeWitt's work have divided between male critics who find it reductive and theoretical and female critics who see in it a staged abandonment of control as it seeks variety, disorder, and even colour).

According to the premise that expressiveness has been a Modernist male prerogative, the possibilities open to "feminine" expressive painting might initially appear to be restricted. Male expression was always identified with ambition and with the philosophical penetration of "nature" – qualities only males could attain. Yet the claims of the *écriture féminine* ("female inscription") of Thérèse Oulton and Joyce Pensato (FIG. 47) have been to establish channels of viewing, endorsement, and display that value and legitimate the feminine, not as another art-world gambit, but on its own terms and for its own sake. Of course, that aspiration encounters the difficulty that wider social structures still largely define culture as masculine, even if in some sections of the avant-garde the pattern is slowly changing.

It remains moot to what extent "feminine" painting and its sensibilities will be able to impress themselves upon a world still dominated by war, ecological aggression, and the misuse of resources according to a predominantly male agenda: the moral demands of "feminine" painting may seem to go beyond what any artistic medium can sustain. And yet a dialogue of gender upon the very grounds of masculine achievement in art would seem to remain a vital and necessary context.

The dilemma for female and male alike is that paint on canvas *in itself* seems to approach being a source of value. If it is true that the medium remains superior in durability, transportability, and what Walter Benjamin in his 1936 essay described as "aura," then it will follow as a corollary that, at least for escapees from conventional value, other resources and media will become significant primarily in the ways that they depart from it. This is one reason why painting's "return" after Conceptualism was at its most convincing when informed by Conceptualism itself. Or to put it differently, the best recent work in the medium has been not a revival, but a repositioning of painting practice somewhere between its former self and its reflective or philosophical opposites.

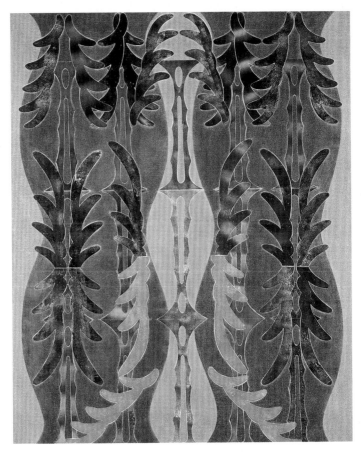

45. PHILIP TAAFFE
Nefta, 1990. Mixed media on canvas, 5' x 4' (1.5 x 1.2 m). Private collection.

Taaffe's open yet self-conscious attitude to decoration – the bane of Modernist formalism – he describes as "pluralistic, completely non-authoritarian, and which doesn't overtly exalt the heroic or the masculine." Taaffe has also said that "painters are really the best philosophers of mass culture...it's more of a critical role than an entertainment posture."

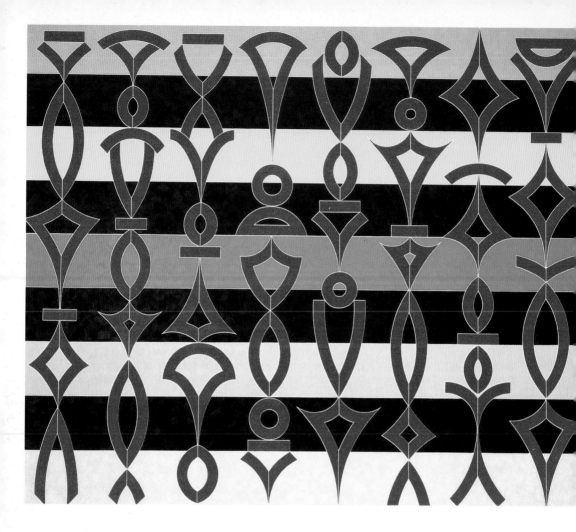

Above
46. VALERIE JAUDON
Ballets Russes, 1993. Oil on canvas, 7′6″ x 9′ (2.3 x 2.7 m).

Jaudon, who in the later 1970s practised pattern painting, has recently injected into her work a series of hieroglyphs that point towards rhythm-within-diversity. She sees this as a social construction, and at the same time, a feminist strategy. "The world is falling apart so rapidly [because] it is a male-constructed world... it's their bridges that are falling."

Right
47. JOYCE PENSATO
Untitled, 1990. Oil on linen, 7′6″ x 6′ (2.3 x 1.8 m).
Collection of the artist.

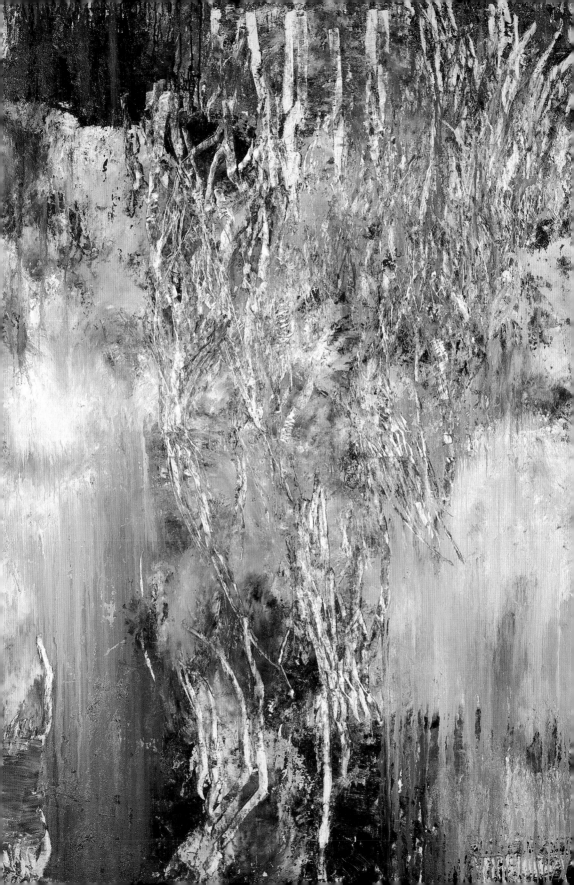

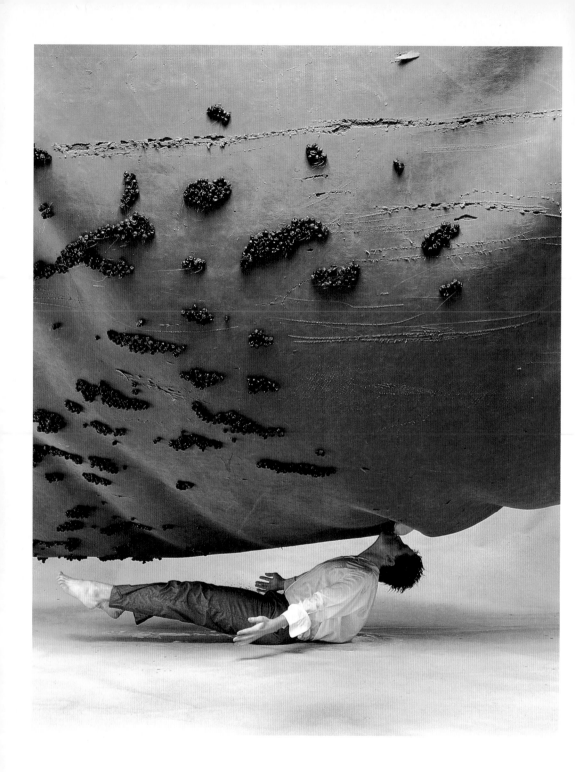

THREE

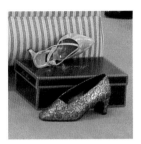

Stolen Forms: 1976-90

48. BOYD WEBB
Nourish, 1984. Unique
colour photograph, 5′ x 4′
(1.5 x 1.2 m). Southampton
City Art Gallery, England.

Such photo-works effect a
contrast between bizarrely
improbable events and the
"reality" medium of the
colour photograph, but on
the scale of the Modernist
oil painting. Increasingly,
Webb has touched on
issues of human survival.
Here, a clothed man under
water is sucking at the
nipple of a whale. The
whale's "skin" is a mock-up
of old rubberised sheeting,
while the nipple is an
Indian vegetable.

I n the decade and a half between the mid-1970s and 1990, an
unusual quantity of aesthetic energy was invested in the
concept of the "ready-made." In 1913 Marcel Duchamp had
taken an ordinary bicycle wheel and mounted it upside-down on
a domestic stool. In 1914 he purchased and exhibited a rack for
drying bottles. In 1919 he took a cheap photographic reproduction of the *Mona Lisa* and added a moustache, a goatee beard,
and a *risqué* pun. All of these objects – like the urinal famously
submitted to a New York exhibition in 1917 – Duchamp claimed
to be art. The "ready-mades" (assisted or plain) allowed him "to
reduce the idea of aesthetic consideration to the choice of the
mind, not to the ability or cleverness of the hand which I
objected to in many paintings." In the 1960s and 1970s the
Duchampian spirit entered Conceptualism. Emphasis was placed
on the choosing of existing objects and phenomena, at the same
time elevating the idea-structure of art at the expense of the
visual alone.

Against that general background, Conceptual art led to
"ready-made" practices in at least three areas of art-making
activity between the mid-1970s and 1990 – photography, sculpture, and painting. The camera, of course, already treats as
ready-made those sections of the world to which it opens its
shutter. The ready-made object-as-sculpture begins from the
premise that a re-presented existing object can be aesthetically
more powerful – given certain assumptions about authorship,
originality, and "presence" – than a newly crafted one. Much of
the more adventurous painting of the late 1970s and 1980s tended
to borrow images from low culture and the mass media and to

relocate them, altered or ironically manipulated, within larger ensembles. It took existing historical styles as re-presentable and made an issue out of the scandal involved.

Photography and Gender

Black-and-white photography was widely used in Conceptual art of the late 1960s and early 1970s as documentation of an event taking place beyond the gallery. In the later 1970s it took only the subtlest changes in artists' attitudes to transform photography from a humble signifier of "not-painting" to a surface of interest and relevance in its own right.

The photograph's "link with reality" was vital. In the Netherlands in the 1970s the work of Stanley Brouwn, Jan Dibbets, and Ger van Elk is representative. In the later 1960s van Elk had worked always with dualities: back and front, left and right, presence and absence. In works like the *Missing Persons* series (1976) he staged photographs which lacked a crucial figure, suggesting the susceptibility of the photo-image to manipulation and falsification – the reverse of what its mechanical contact

49. GER VAN ELK
Lunch II, 1976. From the
Missing Persons series.
Retouched colour
photograph, 31½ x 39″
(80 x 100 cm). Tate
Gallery, London.

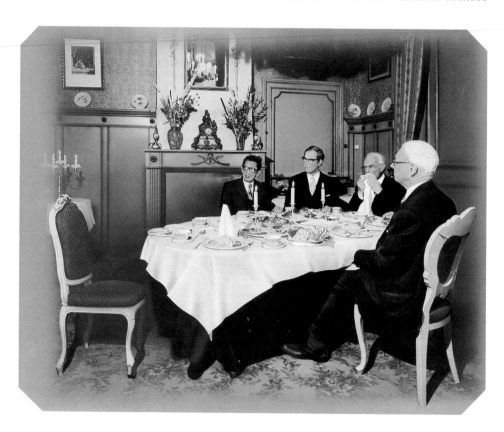

with reality suggests (FIG. 49). Van Elk's output can be read as a morbid reflection on public life; but formally it tries something else, a re-glamorisation of the staged colour-photo as an alternative to the "heroic" media of Modernist painting and sculpture.

Van Elk's counterpart in Great Britain, the New Zealand-born Boyd Webb, made a comparable move from events and actions after the later 1960s, staging surreal scenes that appear at once impossible *and* impossibly real (see FIG. 48). While such works appear to signal a retreat from the tendency to analyse or enumerate in early Conceptual art, they can be seen as a way forward for it too, one that proposed an engagement with clearly fictional or narrative elements. They also betrayed an interest in advertising and magazine photography – the directorial approach to the *tableau*, particularly – which in early Conceptualism had been far from politically *de rigueur*. Both Webb and the Dutch artists are symptomatic of a wider burgeoning of photographic practice in the later 1970s, ranging from the snapshot or the film-still to the magazine cut-out and the found photograph or directorial shot. Artists after Conceptualism were able to subject such photographic types to a variety of analytical critiques.

An important early manifestation of new photographic activity in American art was the show organised by the *October* critic, Douglas Crimp, at Artists' Space in New York in 1977 called, simply, *Pictures*. The artists – Troy Brauntuch, Jack Goldstein, Sherrie Levine, Robert Longo, and Philip Smith – were provided with a critical framework which established the distance of their work from idealist versions of Modernism while placing it within a set of discourses of the "post-Modern." Recent Modernist doctrine, Crimp pointed out, had inveighed against the theatricality of Minimal (and by implication Conceptual) art on the grounds of its dependence on the unfolding, durable time of the physical spectator and its perverse location between painting and sculpture. Yet theatricality (or staging) and "in-between-ness" were the very qualities that he now admired in the work of the Pictures group.

Cindy Sherman was not a Pictures artist, but was closely allied to them. From the late 1970s she presented photographs which, though they looked like film stills, were staged portraits of herself in various thinly concealed guises (FIG. 50). Early feminist readings of Sherman's photos drew attention to ways in which they revealed woman as a

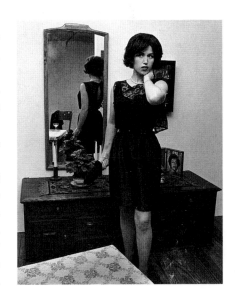

50. CINDY SHERMAN
Untitled Film Still, 1978.
Black and white
photograph, 10 x 8″ (25.4
x 20.3 cm).

cultural construct, a pawn of media interest. Yet for Crimp the question was about the photographic still *per se*. What kind of temporality did this "very special kind of picture" inhabit: the natural continuum of "real" events, or the constructed context of the fictional film? Crimp argued that its condition is that of the snapshot whose location in the real is yet subverted by our knowledge of the photo's origins. "The work's sense of narrative," Crimp wrote, "is one of simultaneous presence and absence, a narrative ambience stated but not fulfilled." Troy Brauntuch, one of the Pictures group, staged historical photo-fragments (of Hitler asleep in his Mercedes, photographed from the back, in one example) in such a way as to evoke both desire and its frustration: the desire to know, to capture and complete the meaning of what an image shows, and the frustration that comes with the awareness that photographic fragments from the past appear more and more as fetish and display, less and less as historical transparency. "That distance," said Crimp, speaking of the gap between the photographic surface and the historical time-slice that caused it, "is all that these pictures signify." About Sherrie Levine's early works, showing silhouettes of eminent statesmen enframing images of a family group, Crimp suggested that they were through and through acts of theft and post-Modernist obfuscation of the question of medium. Both categories of fragment were lifted from other sources: coins on the one hand, magazines on the other, restaged in the form of 35 mm slides, prints, or reproductions of themselves. Their true medium remained all the while unclear.

Levine's work of the early 1980s consisted of re-photographed photographs of well-known works by male artists such as Walker Evans, Eliot Porter, Alexandr Rodchenko, Edward Weston, and others (FIG. 51), as well as watercolour copies of El Lissitsky, Joan Miró, Piet Mondrian, and Stuart Davis, and drawings after Kasimir Malevich. Was this a case of female authorship hiding within a classic male prototype, the complete eradication of the female voice, or its complete return within the credentials of masculine art? Furthermore, the "after" of Levine's titles induced expectations both of distance (in time) and of absence (in space); yet those expectations are confounded, in the act of looking, by the seeming presence of the works themselves. Crimp made the pertinent observation that, due to the importance attached in post-Modernist practice to staging, photo-based art-works, especially simulationist ones, absolutely resist their own photographic reproduction. They demanded (and demand) to be seen.

Yet the requirement of actual visibility was never intended as a return to the "aura" or "present-ness" ascribed to some painting surfaces; nor was that visibility to count towards a spiritual "wit-nessing" of authorial uniqueness or skill. On the contrary, the use of photography by younger artists and (or) refugees from painting in the early 1980s was born of a desire precisely to examine (and by examining to bury) the rem-nants of a predominantly male painting tradition: not only Mod-ernist abstraction, but also the neo-expressionism that was its much vaunted contemporary residue.

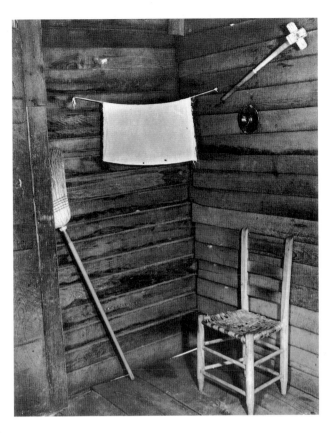

51. SHERRIE LEVINE
After Walker Evans: 7, 1981, Black and white photograph, 10 x 8″ (25.4 x 20.3 cm).

The de-masculinisation of art suggested by the migration into photography at the start of the 1980s coincided with, indeed was stimulated by, a number of impor-tant developments in the field of photographic theory. Texts like Susan Sontag's *On Photography* (1979) and Roland Barthes's *Camera Lucida* (1981, published in French as *La Chambre Claire* in 1980), together with periodicals like *Screen* and *October* from the later 1970s, pushed the analysis of the photograph and the representational process generally – including the contribution and creative unity of "the artist" – to new heights of sophistication. Those debates, and fruitful re-read-ings of classic psychoanalytical texts, such as Freud's essays on narcissism, fantasy, scopophilia, repetition, and fetishism, now stood in a set of authoritative relationships to the practice of art in all media, but particularly to the photograph. Also influential were the writings of Michel Foucault, whose *Discipline and Pun-ish: The Birth of the Prison* of 1977 (more particularly, its cele-brated seventh chapter on "Panopticism") propounded a contro-versial thesis on the relationship between visibility and power. It is probably no exaggeration to say that, in those countries where these texts were debated in the early 1980s, art gained a new energy and ambition of a kind that did not separate the concep-tualisation and the making of art, but made them almost one.

In this regard, the writings and work of Victor Burgin have proved seminal. Burgin, who figured prominently in European Conceptual art of the period 1968-73 and had used photography in his parodic visual-verbal "poster" works of the later 1970s, now proposed a revaluation and revision of the thus far inconclusive Modernist theory of the photograph. "Photography's triumphs and monuments are historical, anecdotal, reportorial," Clement Greenberg had written in 1964. "The photograph has to tell a story if it is to work as art, and it is in choosing and accosting his story, or subject, that the artist-photographer makes the decisions crucial to his art." Greenberg's account here ran counter to the wider Modernist doctrine of self-definition in the practice of each medium; it bypassed the work of "classic" modern photo-artists such as Alfred Stieglitz, Man Ray, and Rodchenko, each of whom had, in his own manner and local context, attempted to establish photographic practice outside the parameters and institutions of the easel picture. John Szarkowski, Director of Photography at the Museum of Modern Art in New York, had for his part identified "The Thing Itself," "The Detail," 'The Frame," "Time," and "The Vantage Point" as aspects of a formalist approach. For him, as for Greenberg, the

52. VICTOR BURGIN
The Office at Night, 1985. Mixed media, 3 panels, 6' x 8' (1.8 x 2.4 m).

The subservient female office-worker from a 1940 painting by Edward Hopper appears re-inscribed in a new network of relations arising from vision itself, including the voyeuristic role of the viewer, the woman's imagined reactions to that gaze, and the inherent fascination exerted by the photo-surfaces themselves.

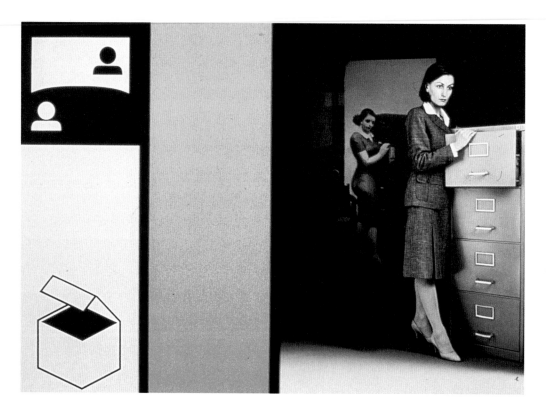

meanings of the photograph derived largely from the properties of the thing photographed.

Such theory badly needed overhauling. Burgin went back to the Soviet debate of the 1920s on "social photography," while drawing heavily on psychoanalysis. He complicated Freud's basic analysis of "the look" into active (scopophiliac) and passive (exhibitionistic) components by adding to it Jacques Lacan's emphases on the narcissistic *mirror-phase* (the early moment of identification with the self by a mirror or other means) and on *objectification*, in which "the look" becomes characteristically gendered (male), and social (a question of power). Burgin's position was that in so far as a photograph records a moment of looking (that of the photographer) and a moment of being looked at (that of the objects or persons shown), it becomes not only a representing surface but a site of multiple relations of empowerment, submission, gender, surveillance, identification, and control. In his *Office at Night* series (FIG. 52), Burgin mobilised the voyeuristic functions of the photograph while at the same time drawing attention to its very distinctness from other systems of representation. He further proposed that other sign-systems, however banal, could function alongside the photograph in use in such a way as to direct, excuse, and articulate that fetishistic regard.

Not all practices of the photographic "moment" of the early 1980s were as conceptually refined as Burgin's. While in Europe photographic art tended to be reflective, allusive, and sensitive to theoretical niceties, in America the immersion of the artist within a fast-moving media environment tended to generate more openly assertive analyses of power.

When Barbara Kruger first came to critical attention in 1981 after a career in graphics and commercial art, it was as an artist who addressed large questions – relations between women and the patriarchy and the alienating blandishments of the consumer world – in ways that required not only voyeuristic identification with aspects of an image, but reflection on a series of verbal messages directed accusingly at men. In *Your Comfort is My Silence* (FIG. 53), the pronouns "your" and "my" mark out gender identifications that are inescapable: the viewer is either the accusing or the accused. The structural simplicity of Kruger's work has made it attractive to publishers and publicity-conscious galleries; yet the work recognises that the viewer needs both politics and a gender in order to confront the work adequately at all. Kruger's work became a touchstone for many feminists who looked for direct, no-nonsense politicised art that took its direction from an

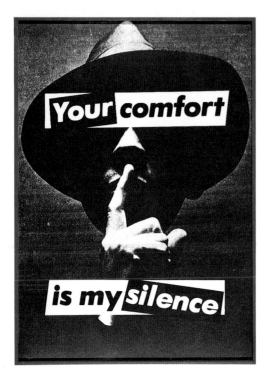

53. BARBARA KRUGER
Your Comfort is My Silence,
1981. Photograph with
added text, 4'8" x 3'4" (1.4
x 1 m). Private collection.

earlier and fabled montage tradition – the pre-1939 German work of John Heartfield and Hannah Höch.

In the combative Western art world of the early and mid-1980s, one that utilised the rampant market mechanism while continuing to indict that market's typical processes and forms, the crucial question became not only who was doing critical art, but how? Were particular "appropriations" comment-free or essentially interrogative in style? When Hal Foster published his influential *The Anti-Aesthetic: Essays in Postmodern Culture* (1983), he drew a distinction that for a while became canonical in discussions of post-Modernist montage or the eclectic mixing and appropriation of forms: "One may support post-Modernism as populist and attack Modernism as elitist, or, conversely, support Modernism as elitist – as culture proper – and attack post-Modernism as kitsch...In cultural politics today, a basic opposition exists between a post-Modernism which seeks to deconstruct Modernism and resist the status quo and a post-Modernism which repudiates the former to celebrate the latter: a post-Modernism of resistance and a post-Modernism of reaction." Proposing to seek out and delineate what Foster called a "post-Modernism of resistance [that] arises as a counter-practice not only to the official culture of Modernism but also to the 'false normativity' of reactionary Modernism," the contributors to *The Anti-Aesthetic* sought to re-connect the aesthetic and the cultural to the wider field of communications, architecture, audiences, and museum culture.

For example Craig Owens, in his contribution "Feminists and Postmodernism," made a proposal that was already latent in the photographic work of some women artists, and that had itself grown indirectly out of Conceptualism. Bringing together the notion that post-Modernism constituted a crisis of traditional cultural authority with the realisation that the traditional viewing subject was generally assumed to be self-possessed, unitary, and masculine, Owens concluded that the feminist critique of patriarchy was precisely the keystone of a resistant post-Modernism. The idea that Modernist artistic "mastery" had usually meant signs of artistic labour – agitated brushwork or sculptural objects in heavy steel – led Owens to the proposition that something akin to a photographic feminist art was the quintessential post-Modernist form. The early works of Sherman, Kruger, Levine, Martha Rosler, Mary Kelly, and Louise Lawler suggested a post-Modernist strategy that, in "investigating what representation does to women (for example, the way it invariably positions them as objects of the male gaze)," answered both to the demands of gender *and* to the need for a cultural space other than the traditional phallocentric one. "The existence of feminism," Owens wrote, "with its insistence on difference, forces us to reconsider."

Conceptual art and feminism were not the sole engines of photo-appropriationist art. A benchmark figure in the debate was Walter Benjamin, whose 1936 essay on the impact of photo-reproductive methods upon culture had by now been widely reprinted and read. Now, however, there was a new concern: the ever renewable image-technologies and the ever higher levels of glamour being injected into the commercial and entertainment spaces of the 1980s. In the face of such an onslaught, artists might have been forgiven for quitting the scene. But the significance of the photographic environment was just then being articulated by the influential, if ambivalent, figure of the French sociologist and cultural theorist, Jean Baudrillard. Baudrillard's early books, *For a Critique of the Political Economy of the Sign* (1972) and *The Mirror of Production* (1973), had had more impact on academic Marxist theory than on art. The publication of *Simulations* in 1983, however, placed Baudrillard at the centre of the New York art world (he became a contributing editor to *Artforum* the following year). In a section of the book called "The Precession of Simulacra," he advanced the suggestive but paradoxical thesis of a *hyperreal* that has no "real" beneath it. "Abstraction today," wrote Baudrillard, in reference to thought and language as much as to art, "is no longer that of the map, the double, the mirror or the concept. Simulation is no longer that of a territory, a referential being or a substance. It is the generation by models of a real without origin or reality: a hyperreal [which is] henceforth sheltered from the imaginary, and from any distinction between the real and the imaginary, leaving room only for the orbital recurrence of models and the simulated generation of difference." The idea of an erosion of priority between the original and the copy – the "precession" of simulacra – Baudrillard explained by analogy. "The territory no longer precedes the map, nor survives it. Henceforth, it is the map that precedes the territory."

54. JEAN BAUDRILLARD
Venice, California, 1989.
Colour photo, edition of 15,
dimensions vary. Collection
of the artist.

By aligning the edges and
colours of some objects
with the overlap and
disjunction of others,
Baudrillard's photographs
throughout the 1980s and
early 1990s proposed
the visible world as a kind
of two-dimensional
continuum, as if constituted
as a montage against the
pull of its three-
dimensionality.

The hyperreality thesis was endlessly discussed. In its weak version, distantly echoing the German philosopher, Immanuel Kant, it said that objects are unknowable apart from their representations. In its stronger and more contentious form, it said that at a certain stage in civilisation objects had collapsed into, even came to coincide with, their representations. Applied to the contemporary media environment, the thesis was taken to imply that the "real" that supposedly lay behind television and advertising imagery no longer existed. Baudrillard's prose seemed both to diagnose and to promote a bleak acceptance of a kind of ecstatic reduction of experience in the face of a much accelerated media and commercial world.

Baudrillard's sense of an imploding reality corresponded to a widespread belief in the art world at the time that saw the mass media as gargantuan and out of control. As the New York writer Edit deAk put it in an *Artforum* discussion of 1984: "Reality has long been a shifty bastard, a gigolo, a flash of enchantment, a fairy, a desire, the richest internal lining of the 'nothing' we have been talking about. Let's not pretend we live in terms of it." On another level, Baudrillard's writings and his own practice as a photographer (FIG. 54) positioned Europe as the old world in which things were still analysed, pondered, and felt, in distinction to America, especially New York and Los Angeles, which had become fabled centres of specifically cultural "affects" constituting a whole "ecstasy of communication," in which public and private, object and subject, truth and falsehood, collapsed into what Baudrillard called "a single dimension of information."

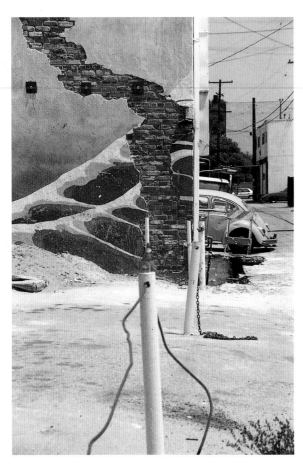

What was finally distinctive about simulationist art and its theory – simulation literally copies an antecedent object or image in the same medium – was how closely they were bound together, at least for a time. Simulationist art and photography suited one another because the photograph simulated the real in the very act of representing it. The Duchampian ready-made suggested how the photograph might function radically as art. For all that, Baudrillardian "simulation" was unable to solve the question of resistant versus reactionary post-Modernism. It took no account of gender, and seemed implacably opposed to any but passive forms of consumption in the commercialised city. Indeed, Baudrillardian "hyperreality" appeared to some to be part of the problem, rather than its solution. Its application in the field of sculpture, for example, can be directly compared.

Objects and the Market

It was possible to characterise the position of sculpture around the middle of the 1970s in terms of a division of aims. Minimal and Conceptual art had been predicated on the idea of the art object's renegotiation of its privileged sites of display and modes of approval. By the mid-1970s it was recognised that a major shift had occurred in the criteria by which a made three-dimensional entity could be classified as art. Despite a minority who still maintained that sculpture should concern itself with direct physical properties of mass, outline, shadow, relationships of parts, and volume – the Modernist view – it was increasingly argued that no entity, however apparently random or unpromising, could automatically be disqualified from, or fail to actually be, art: lines worn in the ground, empty boxes, filing cabinets, ordinary tables and chairs, even documentary photographs of physical activity elsewhere.

But the debate was growing repetitive, even sterile. Both Conceptual art and orthodox Modernism came to be perceived by younger sculptors as theoretical impasses obstructing the making of new work. A reversion to a level of engagement with elements of mass culture was one immediate result. The crucial change, from materials to real objects, became visible in both Europe and North America in about 1977 or 1978: it occurred first in Europe and surfaced in North America as the working-out of a relationship to the new market in consumer goods.

This vital shift can be described as a reinvesting of the forms of Conceptual art with narrative or social meaning. In his student works of the early 1970s, the British artist Tony Cragg had depended upon placing and stacking found materials in formal patterns. After moving in 1977 to Wuppertal in Germany, Cragg made several floor-pieces out of remnants of

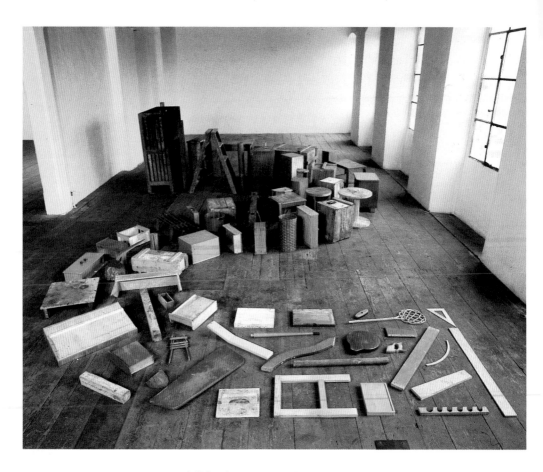

55. TONY CRAGG
Mesozoic, 1984. Mixed
media. Installed at the Ticci
Russo Gallery, Turin.

Cragg has said: "I liked the...
unpretentiousness in Minimal
art, and the intensity that
looking at the work needed.
But there was too much
geometry, too much reliance
on the natural material
quality, on big natural
processes, without new ways
of dealing with them. And so
the crucial question became
one of finding a content...I
want to place [materials] and
give them meaning."

real-life objects: toy plastic cars, or wooden fragments arranged
in the shapes of larger three-dimensional structures depicting
axe-head, boat, or horn (FIG. 55). Both the content and the manner of this return to iconography can be related to the British
Punk revolution of around 1977 to 1979, which utilized unwanted
materials in fashion, and raw protest sounds in music. Some of
Cragg's pieces were openly ideological – notably the wall-pieces
in which plastic fragments were used to form massive policemen
or riot troops battering demonstrating crowds. Anti-authoritar-
ian "meanings" were suddenly back as sheer illusion, rather than
as exercises in materials alone.

A prescient show of 1981 entitled *Objects and Sculpture*, held
simultaneously at the Institute of Contemporary Arts in London
and at the Arnolfini Gallery in Bristol (featuring Cragg, Bill
Woodrow, Edward Allington, Richard Deacon, Anthony Gorm-
ley, Anish Kapoor, Brian Organ, Peter Randall-Page, and Jean-
Luc Vilmouth) extended and consolidated this novel use of urban
materials. It was followed by a display at the British Pavilion at

the 1982 Venice Biennale, and by a rapid succession of shows in Berne, Lucerne, and elsewhere. Guided in its early stages by the Lisson Gallery in London, it was clear that the "new British sculpture" was making a series of aesthetic claims which underpinned its evident curatorial appeal.

Bill Woodrow, also a student in the Conceptualist heyday of the late 1960s and early 1970s, produced assemblages of discarded domestic machinery and other objects, reassembled according to a montage aesthetic, while still utilising the pedestal-free placing on the gallery floor that had been shared by Modernists (Anthony Caro) and anti-Modernists (Robert Morris and Donald Judd) alike. Developing from works such as *Hoover Breakdown* and *Five Objects* of 1979, in which simple objects were taken to pieces or disposed, dysfunctionally altered, on the floor, Woodrow now cut one object out of another in such a way as to supply all parts of the resulting tableaux with references to a lived-in domestic world (FIG. 56). They are made by performing work on remaindered objects, themselves suggestive of quotidean wear-and-tear, with a sculptor's analytical skill.

The third member of the Lisson Gallery group, Richard Deacon, has achieved precisely such an extension of Modernist syntax in what has amounted at times almost to a narrative mode. Deacon's originality as a sculptor has been, in the first place, to use highly dubious ready-made materials, such as linoleum, leather, galvanised steel sheeting, and laminated wood (predominantly DIY or high-street products) and to join them by glueing, riveting, or bending in a craftsmanly, even virtuoso, manner. Second, Deacon has enlarged miniature forms of the body, such as the eye or the ear, in a manner exactly opposite to that of traditional Modernist sculpture, whose scale and imagery, always external and public, were generally intended to coincide. Third, like Woodrow and Cragg, Deacon has felt no hesitation in enriching his already heterodox materials and techniques with a vein of scatological humour, transgressing Modernist high seriousness with a playful mixing of imagery and forms.

Much of Deacon's sculpture "refers" to the human or animal body, yet without courting an unambiguous or non-ironic relation between the sculpture's form and its title. The wayward

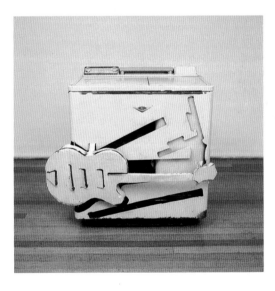

56. BILL WOODROW
Twin Tub with Guitar, 1981. Washing machine, 30 x 35 x 25" (76 x 89 x 66 cm). Tate Gallery, London.

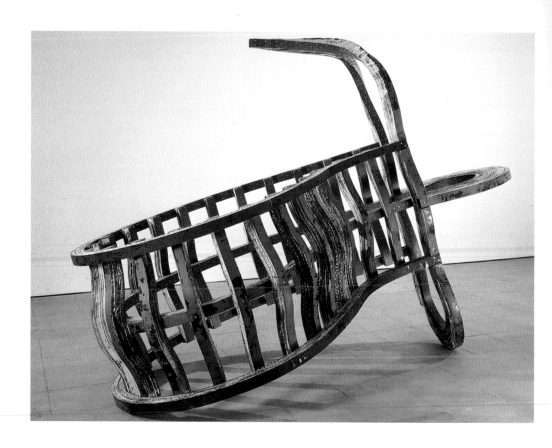

57. RICHARD DEACON
Fish Out of Water, 1987.
Laminated hardboard with
screws, 8′ x 11′6″ x 6′3″
(2.5 x 3.5 x 1.9 m). Saatchi
Collection, London.

yet precision-made loops of a work like *Fish Out of Water* (FIG. 57) manage to be narratively and materially complex at the same time as being in some more familiar sense an impeccably sculptural work. Others members of this generation such as Jean-Luc Vilmouth, Shirazeh Houshiary, and Richard Wentworth, or the younger Edward Allington, Alison Wilding, and Julian Opie have, perhaps unfairly, been perceived *en masse* both as the Thatcher period's contribution to European sculpture and as the counterpart of the Scottish painting "revival" further north.

But what of the work's critical power? As a generalisation, it may be said that Deacon and Cragg have sought a revised relationship to the image by using existing objects and surfaces as significant in themselves – essentially the strategy of Pop. From 1983 onwards, for example, Cragg made a series of pieces that exploited the textures and patterns of formica, plastic, and DIY goods. In these pieces he placed tables, bookcases, cupboards, and material off-cuts in conjunction, and covered these surreal assemblages with banal, deliberately down-market textures (FIG. 58). Cragg voiced his concerns in 1986: "to live in a world that

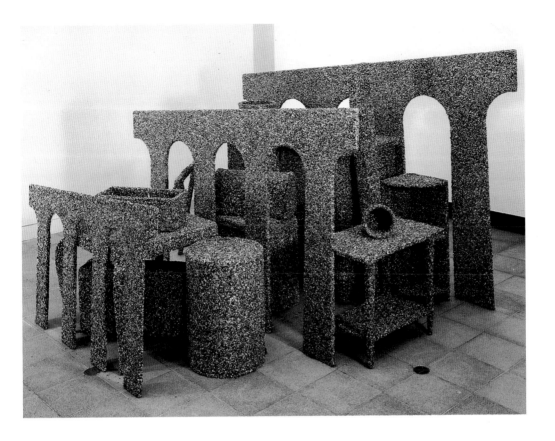

has become predominantly artificial and man-made...I would define myself as an extreme materialist...Art has to do with a claiming of new territory out of the non-art world into the art-making world." This is tantamount to claiming, as the Cubists did, that all objects, however humble, are suffused with cultural signification. It is an attitude which contrasts strikingly, for example, with the impetus behind the metal sculptures of the British sculptor Anthony Caro, who after being championed by Clement Greenberg in the 1960s had by the 1980s become regarded as a beacon of high Modernist endeavour. To Modernists, the work of Caro and his school was quintessentially sculpture before it was anything else: it was taken to express its values through the medium of its syntax alone, particularly what Greenberg's ally Michael Fried had called its "openness and its lowness" – the basis of alleged "correspondences" to gesture and the human body.

The work of Cragg and Deacon was precisely parodic of such late-Modernist heroics. It pleaded for a wholesale descent from the look and feel of enduring "high art" to the use of

58. TONY CRAGG
Aqueduct, 1986. Plastic and wood, 11'4" x 11'4" x 5'5" (3.5 x 3.5 x 1.7 m). Installation at the Hayward Gallery, London.

"I don't want nostalgia," Cragg has said. "I don't want to make an art that sticks, bogged down, hanging on to a natural world that we've lost our grip on anyway. But equally I don't want to make an art which has a horrible futuristic quality about it." The results can be compared to de Chirico's painting from his later, derided period, also undergoing re-evaluation at the time.

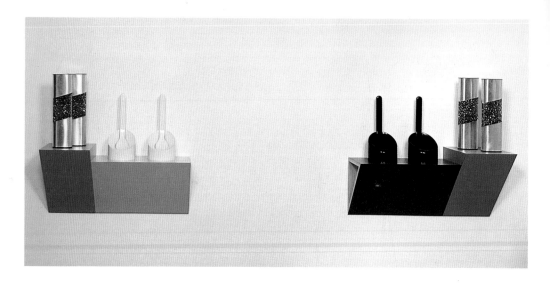

59. HAIM STEINBACH
security and serenity, 1985.
Plastic laminated wood
shelf with "GemLites" and
plastic toilet brushes, 30 x
31 x 13" (76 x 78 x 33 cm).
Private collection.

In Steinbach's words: "I'm
interested in how we
perceive objects to be
grotesque or fashionable,
or, yet, fashionable and
grotesque, as in punk; how
attraction, revulsion and
compulsion are put into
object-forms and rituals.
Archaeologists dig up the
culture of others...I want to
capture the picture of the
history of the present."

domestic materials, non-legitimate surfaces, and the construction of flimsy, non-permanent structures – a switch from serious to non-serious, from Modernist to post-Modernist, from masculine to non-masculine. Yet the attempt to render galvanised iron or commonplace washing machines aesthetic *could* be registered as complicit with a 1980s economic and social policy that was obsessed with encouraging consumerist attitudes to almost all objects and services. Assigning status to plywood or formica *could* be taken as a sort of cheerful play in territory that the new social policy tended to remainder: essentially the materials and methods of an earlier style of upward mobility, that of 1960s and 1970s Britain.

Yet this revived interest in ready-made objects and surfaces was not confined to Great Britain alone. On the other side of the Atlantic a group of younger artists was simultaneously working out the terms of deployment of Duchampian concepts in the form of an explicit interest in commercialism, consumerism, and taste.

The Israeli-born New York artist Haim Steinbach, for one, had for some years purchased junk-store objects and brought them into the gallery. His installation at Artist's Space in New York in 1979, entitled *Display No. 7*, consisted of objects arranged on shelves that ran continuously with the magazines and brochures displayed at the receptionist's desk. In the early 1980s Steinbach evolved a formula for which he became mildly celebrated: the arrangement of newly purchased from-the-store artifacts in duplicate or triplicate on triangular Minimalist shelves (FIG. 59).

It is a measure of the speed of change in the New York art world that Steinbach's interests as an artist can be very precisely distinguished from those of the Pictures group already mentioned. The Pictures group, especially Sherrie Levine, Troy Brauntuch, and Richard Prince, can be said to have undercut, or evaded, the standard strategies for reading art images: questions of production and reception had become, for them, critical questions. By contrast, Steinbach and his peers appeared to parade an openly celebratory attitude towards commercially produced objects at a time when the very status and meaning of the commodity was an urgent issue in the wider culture.

Yet Steinbach's "shopping" sculptures of the mid-1980s were never about the distinctions between good taste and kitsch, between "good" objects and "bad." Launched upon the same consumer culture from which they derived (New York), within the framework of an international exhibition circuit newly primed for experimentation with objects, it was the very irrelevance and collapse of those distinctions that formed the primary content of the work. "There is a renewed interest in locating one's own desire," said Steinbach in a New York discussion staged by the magazine *Flash Art*, in 1986; "there is a stronger sense of being complicit with the production of desire, what we traditionally call beautiful seductive objects, than being posi-

60. ASHLEY BICKERTON
Le Art, 1987. Silkscreened acrylic, lacquer on plywood with aluminum, 34½" x 6' x 15" (87 cm x 1.8 m x 38 cm). Saatchi Collection, London.

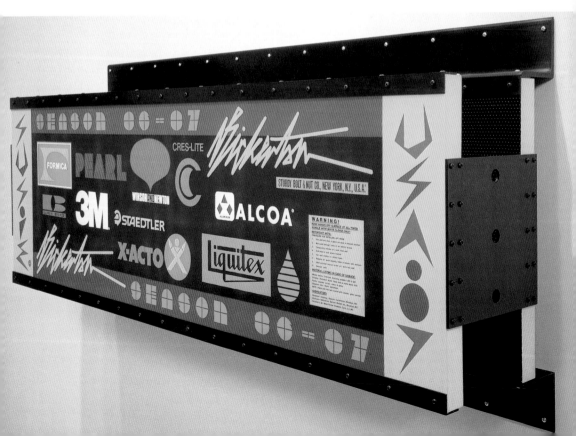

tioned somewhere outside of it. In this sense the idea of critical-ity in art is...changing."

Steinbach's colleague, Ashley Bickerton, also opposed the orientation of the Pictures Group. He described its work, in the language of Marshall McLuhan, as a "cool approach to a hot medium." "Pictures was after a particular deconstruction or breakdown of the process of the corruption of truth, whereas... we are utilising that process of corruption as a poetic form, a platform or launching-pad for poetic discourse in itself...This work has a somewhat less utopian bent than its predecessor." The surfaces of Bickerton's works carry the corporate logos of the companies involved in the various stations of their operational life, from storage and shipping to reproduction and display. "Through the last few decades [the art object] has been ripped off the wall and twisted through every conceivable permuta-tion," Bickerton has said, "yet back to the wall it insists on going. So be it, on the wall it shall sit but with aggressive dis-comfort and complicit defiance." Thus a work like *Le Art* of 1987 (FIG. 60) asks to be seen as gathering up a series of commercial logos and endorsing the power of corpora-tions in a (knowingly) politically incorrect way. Refer-ring to the tendency of avant-garde art to end up "above a sofa," Bickerton wrote that his wall-mounted art "imi-tates the posture of its own corruption ...attempting to forward the question of precisely where conflict exists in this morass of ideal, compromise and duplicity."

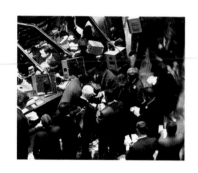

61. Stockbrokers hurrying to complete transactions on the New York City Stock Exchange in 1991, at the end of a decade of rapid but unstable expansion in Western markets.

Arguably, such off-the-peg "radicalism" brought the condition of the art-object perilously close to that of the style accessory. Certainly the realisation that shopping sculpture was finding favour with curators and galleries throughout the West came as a blow to those artists who still har-boured "left" ambitions amid the conservative cultural politics of the mid-1980s. Bickerton's tone is often defeatist: "we're all riding the monster train and we can't get off," he says. His and Stein-bach's attempt to share rather than deconstruct the consumer's viewpoint can be aligned with the "boom" mentality of rapid but shallow growth, of leverage-broking, asset-merging and deregula-tion (FIG. 61). The distance of these ready-mades from the utopian moment of 1967-72 was by now extreme. Or it was worse. Very little writing outside of *October* was proposing a counter-cultural posture. There was much talk of the "end of history" and the effective collapse of all choices into those of the shopping-spree. "Politics is a sort of outdated notion," said the painter Peter Halley in the same discussion; "we are in a post-political situation now."

Perhaps the most that could be claimed for the new American commodity-art was that it contained a sort of pragmatic acknowledgement of the failure of classic models of socialism, both in Eastern Europe and the West. Indulging in a kind of indecent open season on the cornucopia of Western over-production, it revelled in certain kinds of identification and desire and seemed to announce a moratorium on puritanical abeyances and proscriptions identified more easily with the "left." The pleasures, rather than the frustrations, of consumption were now apparently to be placed centre-stage.

Probably no one more wilfully invited the disapproval of his specialised or general public in this regard than the New York artist Jeff Koons. Koons openly embraced a number of attitudes that had hitherto been regarded as virtually taboo. One was a readiness to extend, severely, the operations of the Duchampian ready-made to embrace a range of consumer products comprised almost exclusively of kitsch. Koons's earliest works, such as the *Inflatable Flower and Bunny* (FIG. 62), lent validity to cheap plastic adornments, apparently without embarrassment and certainly

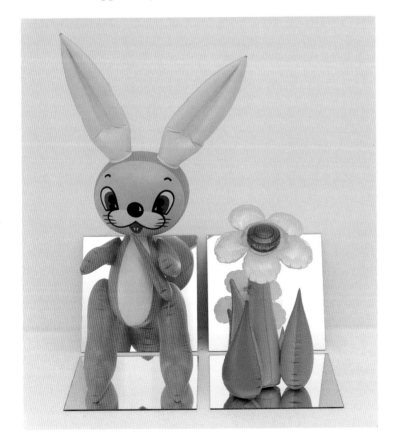

62. JEFF KOONS *Inflatable Flower and Bunny (Tall Yellow and Pink Bunny)*, 1978. Plastic, mirrors, and Plexiglas, 32 x 25 x 18" (81 x 63 x 45 cm). Collection Ronny Van De Velde, Belgium.

Low-art values have remained important to Koons from the time of these early pieces. "Banality is one of the greatest tools that we have," Koons has said. "It is a great seducer, because one automatically feels above it; and that's how debasement works...I believe banality can bring salvation right now."

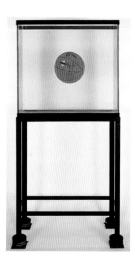

63. JEFF KOONS
One Ball Total Equilibrium Tank, 1985. Glass, steel, sodium-chloride reagent, distilled water, and basketball, edition of two, 5'4³/₄" x 30³/₄" x 13¹/₄" (160 x 93 x 33.7 cm). Collection Dakis Joannou, Greece.

without what Brechtian theorists had called *estrangement* (the corruption or critical distancing of the image). Mute yet self-announcing, these ephemera were innocently presented in all their appalling, yet fascinating, allure.

In the intervening period Koons has sought to "sell" himself as a hustler and salesman type through art magazine ads, interviews, and reminiscences about his entrepreneurial past (he was for a time a commodity broker on Wall Street). His posture has been, perhaps, that of a popular entertainer or clown. Commenting on his early work, together with the *Vacuum Cleaner* pieces of 1980-81 and the *Tanks* works of around 1985 (FIG. 63), Koons has said that "anyone can come to my work from the general culture...Almost like television, I tell a story that is easy for anyone to enter into and on some level enjoy...I purposely always try at least to get the mass of people in the door [but] if they can go further, if they want to deal in an art vocabulary, I hope that that would happen...I do not, however, rule out transforming the object's content in order to reveal certain personality traits that have always been within that object." There was even a salesman's attempt at iconography: "The basketball refers to its traditional role in lower-class communities of being a vehicle for upward mobility...It took on another meaning when encased in the tanks: it was cellular, womb-like, foetus-like." In speaking of the "sparseness and emptiness" of the work, Koons also claimed a relationship to Minimal art. Yet in the mid-1980s his work attracted the scorn both of "left" critics, who disparaged its complicity with the market as "repulsive" (Rosalind Krauss) or who complained of its uncritical fetishism of the object which "ingratiates rather than disrupts" (Hal Foster), and of those on the critical "right," who found his enthusiasm for market values no better than frivolous.

Koons took part in two important group shows in 1986, *Damaged Goods: Desire and the Economy of the Object* at the New Museum of Contemporary Art in New York and *Endgame: Reference and Simulation in Recent Painting and Sculpture* at the Boston Institute of Contemporary Arts, in which he was championed as having posed some unsettling questions. First, what seemed to distinguish Koons's work was not the Duchampian ready-made, nor a primary interest in kitsch, but rather a reversion to kinds of taste and attention identifiable with that "low" suburban culture that "left" culture-theorists since Theodor Adorno (1903-69) had tended to revile. Shiny porcelain mantle-piece sculpture, garish evocations of pets, film stars, religious sentimentalia, gawky teenage toys, and the rest – not to mention

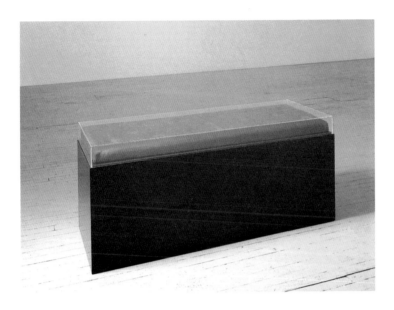

64. TONY TASSET
Sculpture Bench, 1986-87.
Painted wood, leather
cushion, Plexiglas, 22 x 55
x 19" (55.8 x 139 x 48 cm).

In anther variation on the
original Minimalist
aesthetic, Tasset simulates
the bench on which
museum visitors sit. Looking
both like and unlike the
bench whose position it
occupies, it both resists and
attracts the viewer's
puzzled museal gaze.

photo-pieces of mock-erotic couplings between Koons and his
then wife, the Italian porn star, Illona Staller – became rapidly
identified with his name. The incorporation of Koons's work on
the side of "high" art, in such shows as MOMA's controversial
High and Low: Modern Art and Popular Culture (1990), merely
served to compound the dilemmas posed by his graceless style.
Second, within an art system in which fame was a sign of artistic success, who could deny that Koons's fame was not a pointer
to other anxieties, not least those concerning the relationship of
the market to virtually all art?

In general the critical question was how far the "appropriated" object could counterpose itself to the overtly commercial
context from which it came. Koons's works remain problematic:
the notion that the redisplay or evocation of consumer objects
could provide an effective critique of commodity culture was at
best utopian in the market zeal of the 1980s: aside from the aesthetic arguments, the two sides in any such contest could be said
to remain grossly unequal in financial and cultural power.

It comes with a sense of relief, then, to find that the commodity-art genre has proved capable of greater formal and conceptual sophistication. When the Chicago artist Tony Tasset
transformed the visitors' stools at the Chicago Museum of Contemporary Art into a wall-relief, as part of a series of works in
which elements of museum-viewing – benches, stools, display
cases – were made identical with the art itself, some interesting
perplexities arose. In his *Sculpture Bench* of the same year (FIG. 64)
Tasset devised a paradox: between an object which simultane-

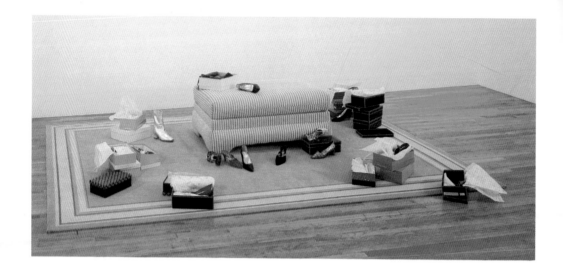

ously asks to be used and also requires attending to as art. The bench's perspex cover serves further to complicate the sculptural coding of the work (i) by transforming it into a box, Minimal-art style, (ii) by showing that it is not to be sat upon but looked at, and (iii) by seeming to "protect" the work in the manner of a museum showcase. On which level was one to attend to the work? How could the artist's collusion in the very museum system he sought to critique be brought to resolution?

Sophistication of another kind marks the work of the Swiss artist Sylvie Fleury, who has recently adopted a very different *persona* from Steinbach or Koons – that of the wealthy female shopper who is consumed by, rather than in command of, her desires. In a series of exhibitions of the early 1990s, Fleury has literally gone shopping for expensive feminine adornments from leading designers in Paris and New York. She has frequented elegant hotel lobbies to observe the promenading *haut monde*. She has then brought her purchases into the gallery and displayed them, in and out of their boxes, in the spirit of a fictional celebration of the "shop-to-drop" mentality of the rich and alienated (FIG. 65). The New York critic Elizabeth Hess has summed up Fleury's message nicely: "She suggests that most people don't (or can't) go shopping to buy; they go to fantasize about the shapes of other people's lives. The slippers scattered across the gallery belong to Madonna or Cinderella. If the shoes become metaphors for the invisible body, the imperfect body that we are continually told needs fixing, then the ottoman becomes a psychiatric couch, leading us to consider this massive neurosis. It's a conspiracy against women that is irresistible."

Painting and Appropriation

The revived painting tradition discussed in the last chapter was also subject to the pressures and rewards of "appropriation," both in Europe and America. The great example of an appropriationist painting attitude is Andy Warhol, whose use of existing commercial and media images in the early 1960s set a beacon for others to follow. Artists who learned from Warhol, though from a basis in Conceptual art, included the Pictures group member Jack Goldstein, whose acrylic paintings of the early 1980s stepped ingeniously backwards to examine a concern of an older tradition, namely the sublime. The source for each painting was a photograph: first, of distant views of tracer trails, airborne fighters, bomb-bursts, and descending parachutists hurtling through space (FIG. 66) and, subsequently, very large paintings of microscopic phenomena presented in the lurid colours of the digitalised image. Goldstein's photographic engagement with the very distant and the very small evoked what one commentator, in reference to the simultaneous intensity and distancing effect of contemporary media, called "a flattening of history, an instantaneous contemporaneity which we experience day by day in the world of electronic information."

In an important respect this tendency of Goldstein's is characteristic, for the general aura of "pastness" in art of the 1980s was often, paradoxically, attributable to a concern for the very recent. The kind of abstract painting frequently tagged "Neo-

66. JACK GOLDSTEIN *Untitled*, 1980. Oil and acrylic on canvas, 3 panels, overall 8' x 15' (2.4 x 4.5 m).

The writer Fulvio Salvatori said: "When I discovered the paintings of Jack Goldstein I immediately associated them with the Polyptych of Ghent, the *Mystic Lamb* of Jan van Eyck: at first sight two different things. The *Mystic Lamb* shows the moment just before the outburst of the Apocalypse when time is held back and life is an endless instant."

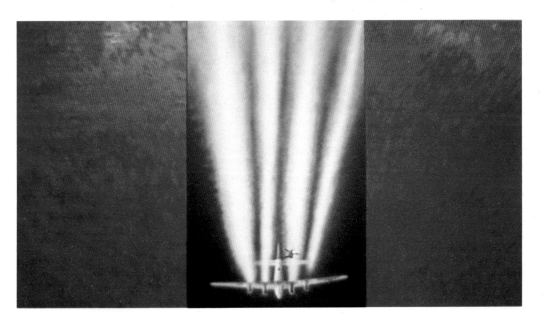

geo" in the art press of the mid-1980s is one example. Neo-geo was claimed by its supporters to subject the basic conventions of geometric abstraction – the square, the grid, and the strip – to re-readings which looked cynically at qualities such as "inspiration," "genius," and, above all, "metaphysics." In place of Modernist intensity and spiritual expression was to be offered depersonalised, post-Modern allegory embedded in existing languages of form. Thus the works of the New York painter Peter Halley, from the early to mid-1980s, originated in an attempt to raise Minimalism to a plane of explicitness about social and industrial life.

Impressed by Foucault's *Discipline and Punish: The Birth of the Prison*, Halley proposed taking *geometry* as a metaphor for coercion and confinement, as well as for reductive form. In the early 1980s he completed a set of paintings related to the forms of jails or jail-like structures, using a Constructivist or Minimalist idiom. Mimicking, on a large scale, the visual spaces found in video games and computer graphics, Halley also deployed bright, commercial colours and a rough, artificial texture. "The cell is a reminder of the apartment house, the hospital bed, the school desk – the isolated end-points of industrial structure," Halley has

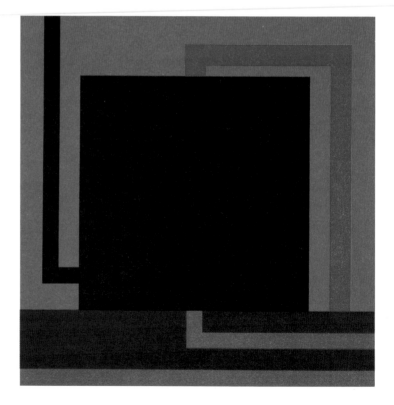

67. PETER HALLEY
Asynchronous Terminal,
1989. Day-Glo acrylic,
acrylic, and Roll-a-Tex on
canvas, 8'1¼" x 6'3" (2.4 x
1.9 m). Private collection,
New York.

Of the Abstract
Expressionists whose
paintings had the scale of
his own, Halley once said
that "they were sure that
what they were doing could
have meaning on a world
philosophical/political stage
...the glow in their work, as
well as the emptiness of it,
relates to social issues."

written; "the 'stucco' texture is reminiscent of motel ceilings. The Day-Glo paint is a signifier of 'low-budget mysticism.'"

What is curious about Halley's position is that other examples of his paintings, visually comparable to these, have been read as evoking widely divergent aims. Halley himself related how the publication of Baudrillard's *Simulations* in 1983 made possible an extension of Foucauldian theses on power to a very different realm of theory – one which we may see as contradicting Foucault's drift. Halley now saw his paintings as structures that did not so much refer to, as present in reflective form, qualities of urban consciousness in the late capitalist city (FIG. 67). "Conduits supply various resources to the cells," he said.

Electricity, waste, gas, communication lines and, in some cases, even air, are piped in. The conduits are almost always buried under ground, away from sight. The great networks of transportation give the illusion of tremendous movement and interaction. But the networks of conduits minimalise the need to leave the cells...Today [he is writing in 1986] Foucauldian confinement is replaced by Baudrillardian deterrence. We sign up for body-building at the health club. The prisoner need no longer be confined in jail. We invest in condominiums. The madman need no longer wander the corridors of the asylum. We cruise the interstates.

In this formulation Halley's "enrapture by geometry," his "building of the linear that characterises modernity," is presented as a kind of spatial equivalent of Baudrillard's "hyperrealisation." Combining pessimism with elation, a sense of ending with a mood of transcendence, the paintings suggest ways in which the practice of art sought to keep pace with theory, around 1983-88, but at the cost of some credibility to both.

They also serve as a reminder how, in the high days of "post-Modernism," the ebbing of the idea of single master narratives knocked stuffing out of the quest for coherence or truth in particular doctrines. Theory became packaged, multivalent, and at worst impressionistic. It could be taken up or put down: mixed, layered, or selectively ignored. Baudrillard's theses on "hyperreality" and "simulation" can be read as symptoms as well as theories of the media-effect; mere consequences of the urban anxieties of his milieu turned back upon theory itself. His thinking is now less fashionable than it was.

The more enduring facet of American painting of this period may be its attempt to find a relationship to history. As is suggested by the relation of Halley's work to Minimalism and

68. ROSS BLECKNER
Architecture of the Sky III,
1988. Oil on canvas, 8'10"
x 7'8" (2.7 x 2.3 m).
Collection Reinhard
Onnasch, Berlin.

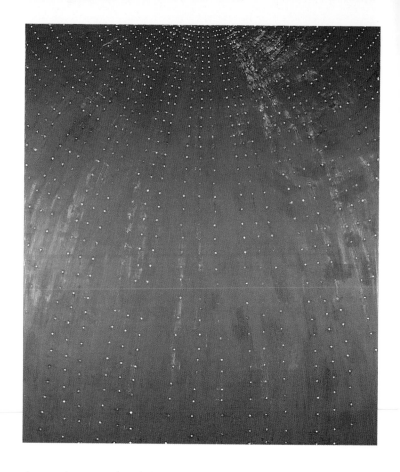

abstraction, much of the more interesting art of the Neo-geo phase needed a relation to previous painting in order to be read as art at all. Halley, writing now as a critic of his friend, Ross Bleckner, in *Arts Magazine*, pointed to a relation with Op art of the 1960s, less as an act of reverence as in recognition of a failed and short-lived experiment – from the period of the artist's own youth – that history had largely passed by. "Op art is chosen [by Bleckner]," Halley says, "as a telling symbol for the terrible failure of positivism that has occurred in the post-war era, for the transformation of the technological, formalist imperative advanced by the Bauhaus into the ruthless modernity preached and practised by the post-war American corporation, of the transformation of the aesthetic of Mies and Gropius into the Hoola Hoop, the Cadillac tailfin, into Tang and Op art. How did this occur?" But it is also the case that Bleckner doubles his preparedness to learn from bad art (and the bad culture that supported it) with a bizarre investment in the spiritual significance of light – the radiating patterns that structure his paintings of the time (FIG. 68). It amounts to saying, as Halley does, that Bleckner presents the "disturbing aspect of irony and transcendentalism coexisting in the same body of work."

Sherrie Levine's Neo-geo works, the stripe, checker-board and knot paintings that were first exhibited in New York in late 1985, may be seen as succinctly announcing a move from "appropriation" to "simulation." Following the *Photographs After* series, Levine had gradually reintroduced copies of Lissitsky, Mondrian, Malevich, and others already mentioned. "Where as an artist could I situate myself?" she had written of this phase. "What I was doing was making explicit how this Oedipal relationship artists have with artists of the past [i.e. wanting to kill them] gets repressed: and how I, as a woman, was only allowed to represent male desire." But a new interest in optical painting was also emerging. In a work of 1984, Levine had "reproduced" Malevich's epochal *White on White* as yellow on white: interpretable perhaps as a turn away from idealism and mysticism to a form of deprecating transcription. Shortly afterwards she produced plywood panels whose knot-hole plugs were painted gold; she used casein instead of oil and framed the panels with glass in the manner of a museum display (FIG. 69). Like Halley's paintings, the works contain unstable references to older art, while yet draining out the formal and emotional appeal that was normal in the tradition. It is a kind of endgame art. Levine's most recent works, sculptures which re-present modern masterworks by Constantin Brancusi or Duchamp – even Brancusi done after the manner of Duchamp – continue the illusion of repeating Modernist male gestures, but according to a feminising, post-Modernist logic.

Within European painting, "appropriation" took many forms, not all of them addressed to the consumer or media worlds in the New York manner. The Yugoslav artist Braco Dimitrievic had until 1975 been involved in the documentation of passers-by on the street, among other projects. But in that year he published a book, *Tractatus Post Historicus*, which looked squarely at the situation of art in what he variously called the

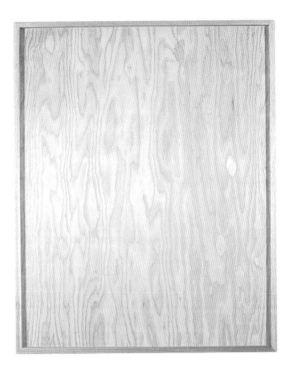

69.   SHERRIE LEVINE
Large Gold Knot: 2, 1987.
Metallic paint on plywood,
5' x 4' (1.5 x 1.2 m).
Collection Martin
Zimmerman, Chicago.

Describing these works as "distillations," Levine suggests that, unlike Modernist art, they "do not give you that kind of satisfaction: the closure, balance, harmony. There's that sense of things being all there, all served up, that you get from classic, formalist painting. I wanted the ones I was making to be uneasy. They are about death in a way: the uneasy death of Modernism."

70. Braco Dimitrievic
Triptychos Post Historicus
or *Repeated Secret*, Part I:
The Little Peasant, Amadeo
Modigliani, 1919; Part II:
Wardrobe painted by Sarah
Moore; Part III: Pumpkin,
1978-85. Mixed media,
6'7½" x 3' x 2'3½" (2 m
x 91.5 cm x 70 cm). Tate
Gallery, London.

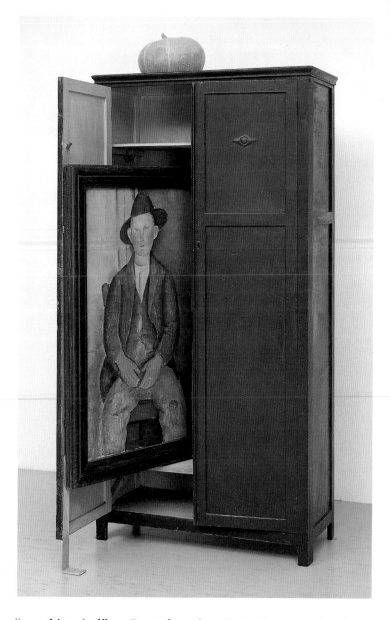

"post-historical" or "post-formal-evolution" phase. That latter phrase summarises a common perception among the first Conceptualist generation: that traditions from Duchamp and Malevich finally converged in the period of Fluxus and Minimal art, after which culture had had to "begin again." Dimitrievic's *Triptychos Post Historicus* art-works standardly combined three sorts of object: an old or Modernist "masterpiece," another, ordinary object, and a vegetable or piece of fruit (FIG. 70). "I did not want to add anything to the accumulation of styles and formal innovation," Dimitrievic has said, but "to use the museum as a studio." "In the set-up of the *Triptychos* something of the painting's aura reflects on the triviality of objects, pulling them out of anonymity. Instead of looking at them with our usual indifference we start deciphering their meanings or search for layers in their unknown existence – the fate of their producers or one-time owners." In line with structuralist thinking made popular in the 1970s, the *Triptychos* works extend a long-standing concern for the relativity of judgements of value. "If one looks down at Earth from the Moon," Dimitrievic has said cryptically, "there is virtually no distance between the Louvre and the Zoo."

Such appropriative strategies, tied to particular philosophical concerns about painting, may be placed alongside others from Eastern Europe. In the Soviet Union of the 1980s, information arrived relatively freely from America and other points west: neo-Conceptualism, East Village art and simulationist strategies were known and understood, even if their economic and social contexts were not. It was the East Village example and its aftermath – or the return to montage aesthetics in American post-Modernism more generally – that stimulated the so-

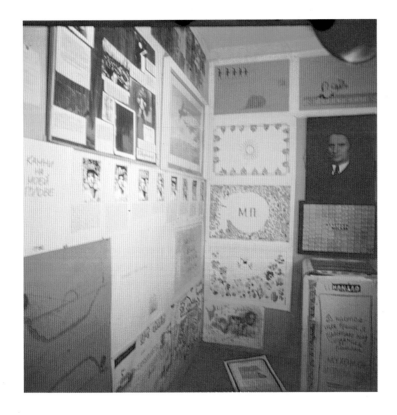

71. THE MUKHOMORY GROUP
First Apt-art Exhibition, 1982. Apartment of Nikita Alekseev, Moscow.

The exhibition comprised seventeen artists from four principal groups: the Mukhomory (Sven Grundlakh, Aleksis Kamensky, Konstantin Zvezdochetov, Sergei and Vladimir Mironenko), the group known as S/Z (Vadim Zakharov and Viktor Skersis), the husband-and-wife team of Anatoly Zhigalev and Natalia Abalakova, and the Collective Actions members, including Andrei Monastyrsky.

called "Apt-art" concept in Russia. Apt-art took the form of showing art in private apartments, and began in 1982 with a show by the Mukhomory group and others in the flat of Nikita Alekseev. The participants were not concerned with pure painting: they assembled urban detritus and old posters to produce camp tableaux in parody of the coarse texture of late Soviet life. Apt-art became a sort of environmental *bricolage*, dependent upon a "complete saturation of available space" (Sven Grundlakh) or "an avalanche of texts, inscriptions and posters" (Anatoly Zhigalev). Sarcastic and colourful, these crowded installations radically undermined the distinction between art and life, and to thoroughly paradoxical effect. While art was removed from the gallery, a new gallery was created for it in domestic space: above the sink, across the ceiling, in the fridge (FIG. 71).

Apt-art was neither incantatory or shamanic, as Collective Actions had been; rather it attended to the social and political. Like some East Village artists, the Mukhomory group claimed to have gone beyond plagiarism in a spirit of desperate comedy: they claimed mockingly that "the elimination of private property, as Marx argued, signifies a complete emancipation of all human feelings and characteristics." What lay behind such clowning was the intuition that the separation between private and public in the USSR had led artists inexorably to a posture of empty quotation of existing mass culture rather than to purposeful engagement with it. In Russia, such despairing quotation was enough. Apt-art was denounced by the authorities for being "anti-Soviet" and "pornographic," whence its organisers switched briefly to outdoor events (Apt-art "*en plein air*") before it folded completely.

Yet the impulse to quotation remained. Yurii Albert, who took part in many Apt-art events, demonstrated one version of Soviet appropriation aesthetics in his painting *I Am Not Jasper Johns* (FIG. 72), which stylistically duplicated a painting of Johns, but with the letters of its title in Cyrillic script. The work is in a clear sense duplicitous. In deploying the style of Jasper Johns to say that its author is not Jasper Johns, it looks detachedly at language only to play with the viewer's recognition of the double-bind which this posture requires. Having absorbed most varieties of Western Conceptual art and theory, Albert claimed to be making paintings "about possible 'conceptual' art-works in the spirit of early Art and Language." "Imagine," he said, "a member of Art and Language who, instead of doing serious work, tells everyone he is getting ready to do it, but who never brings his proposals to fruition. Instead, he stops halfway, gets out of it with jokes, and in the final analysis doesn't really understand the problems he is trying to solve...As soon as the possibility of serious research arises, I stop."

Albert holds *both* that "our entire activity is nothing but ritual gestures, metaphors, hints, and winking at each other around art," *and* that "this may be regarded, if you like, as the emancipation of art, liberation from causes and effects, just as man in the secularised world makes an ethical choice, expecting neither salvation nor punishment." Placing his art within the tradition of Russian formalism, Albert compares canonical works (such as those by Johns) to points in three-dimensional space, with traditions, analogies, and "influences" conceived as the multiple lines between them. "These connections are more important than the works themselves," Albert said. "I immediately try to draw lines, and not to distribute more points. My latest works are only a positioning in artistic space; outside of it they have no value."

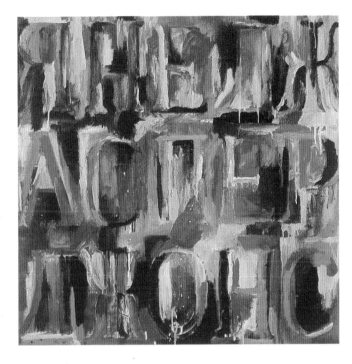

72. YURII ALBERT
I Am Not Jasper Johns,
1981. Oil and collage on canvas, 31½ x 31½" (80 x 80 cm). Private collection, Philadelphia.

Like other artists across the international spectrum – Bertrand Lavier from France or Andreas Slominski from Germany might be mentioned – some East Europeans demonstrated that not everything termed "appropriation" needed to be crassly complicit with those forms of economic organisation that work to oppress us. The replaying and quotation of existing art, in particular, made for contexts free of just those suspect marks of "originality" that an unflinching Modernism has wanted to call its own. Replacing expression with sophisticated coding in order to engender self-reflective awareness in the viewer, single or multiple reference to other representational codes has become the lifeblood of innovative culture. And this is to indicate, once more, that ascending to the meta-language may be a necessary (but perhaps not always sufficient) condition of a contemporary avant-garde.

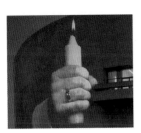

FOUR

Art within the Museum: the later 1980s

73. SUSAN SMITH
*Green Metal with Red
Orange*, 1987. Oil on
canvas with found metal,
4′5½″ x 4′1¾″ (1.3 x 1.2 m).

T wo phenomena of the later 1980s, taken singly, tell us
much about the cultural dynamics of the retrenchment
years. The first was the massive expansion in the infra-
structure of art: the elevation of the curator-showman-impre-
sario, the expansion of the business agenda, and, most impor-
tantly, the building of many new museums of contemporary art.
Even a selective list is a long one. In France, after the opening of
the Pompidou Centre in Paris (1977), well-appointed provincial
centres opened at Bordeaux (1984, extended 1990), Grenoble
(1986) and Nîmes (1993). The Museum of Modern Art in New
York was expanded in 1984. Great Britain had new spaces at the
Whitechapel (1985) and the Saatchi Gallery (1985), both in London, and at the Liverpool Tate (1988). New museums opened in
Los Angeles – the Temporary Contemporary (1983) and the
Museum of Contemporary Art (1986) – in Tokyo (1987), Madrid
(1990), and other locations. While private galleries boomed and
then bust towards the end of the decade, the public museums
were increasingly to encourage and simultaneously to meet a
growing demand for works of avant-garde art. High-profile
curators commanding large exhibition budgets, often bolstered
by corporate sponsorship, became a professional elite with considerable local fame and commensurate international power. The
question became whether the counter-cultural impulse of the
post-1960s avant-garde, under any description, could survive its
own rapid institutionalisation.

The second phenomenon was the surviving Conceptualist and Marxist traditions in Europe, which continued to uphold an avant-gardist outlook in which art could contest the expanded institutional network even as it used and was used by it. We have already seen how, following artists such as Richter and Polke, the question was whether painting could complicate the *reception* of art, make the surface look like more than a painted analogy for something. In sculpture, a key issue had been whether the leads provided by Beuys or Manzoni or Duchamp might be resumed. If the danger for painting had been uncritical versions of neo-expressionism, sculpture's difficulties arose from a highly unstable boom in the art market that coincided historically with the trading practices and the fashionable lust for goods characteristic of the Reagan and Thatcher years. The critical reception of that work had split into (at least) two. Dealers and museum people were generally delighted with the reappearance of goods-as-art; yet left-inclined critics saw in the less successful appropriation art varying degrees of accommodation to the combined forces of Mammon and alienation. This is consistent with, indeed leads towards, the judgement that the best such work – Deacon, Burgin, Tasset, Fleury, Levine – treated that accommodation with extreme caution.

The latent tension between advanced art and the expanded museum structure received its most intelligent elaboration in a vein of work, founded at some distance upon Conceptualism, that took its presence in the museum as part and parcel of its unfolding significance. Such work divided, more or less, into two types: that which by repeating an earlier strategy became innocuous (even servile) within the framework of the international art network; and that which strove to mobilise that network's redefinition and even its contestation. The first category might include Carl Andre, Richard Long, Jan Dibbets, Joseph Kosuth, Ed Ruscha, John Hilliard, and Gilbert and George. Within the second and smaller category would fall those artists pursuing engaged or critical practices relatively discontinuous with, even illegible with regard to, past patterns.

Culture Itself as a Subject

An example and symptom of the revived Marxist anti-aesthetics of the 1980s was the successful excavation and revalidation of the Situationist International, an organisation founded in France in 1957, which published the journal *Internationale Situationiste* between 1958 and 1969 before being finally dissolved in 1972.

The Situationist International had included among its members, at different times and on different footings, Guy Debord, Asger Jorn, Ralph Rumney, and Timothy Clark. Debord's book, *The Society of the Spectacle* (1967, first English edition 1970), had claimed that "the spectacle is the moment when the commodity has attained the 'total occupation' of social life...it is the self-portrait of power in the epoch of its totalitarian management of the conditions of existence." Situationism went beyond an analysis of the commodity-as-fetish and its artistic counterpart, the ready-made, to embrace a refusal of concepts of "art" and "the museum" in any but their most evacuated and scurrilous forms. Derived at some distance from Dada and Surrealism, Situationism was in effect an attempt to destabilise and "make strange" existing culture by means of ironic graphics and cartoons which sought to rupture social signs and conventional meanings. Two of its major concepts were *détournement*, or the theft and revitalisation of pre-existing aesthetic elements, and *dérive*, defined as "a mode of experimental behaviour linked to

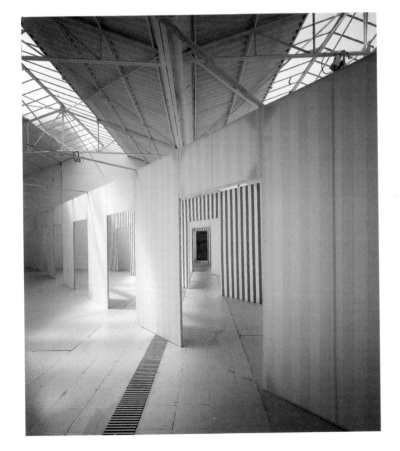

74. DANIEL BUREN
Photo Souvenir...*Ce Lieu D'òu (This place whence)*..., work in situ, Gewad, Ghent, 1984. Wood, striped linen. Collection of the artist.

"Most art produced today is totally reactionary and reinforces social reaction," Buren said in an interview in 1987. Yet the artist saw his work as having adapted to this change rather than capitulated to it. Still all but unavailable to public or private collectors, it continues to defy description in spite of its repetitive formats.

the conditions of urban society, a technique of transient passage through varied ambiences," implying an attitude of openness to urban spaces and contexts structured by solo or collective passage through the city's attractive or repulsive places.

The revival of Situationism as a museum phenomenon around 1989 invited inevitable charges which the original anti-aesthetics of the movement had by then reached its terminal phase, as recollection and/or nostalgia. Yet its significance lay in its re-evocation of the spirit of protest after a 20-year interval. Its original effects had included not only Fluxus, but anarchist affiliations such as the Dutch Provos, the American Yippies, Punks, Mail Art groups, and a later Canadian variant termed Neoism. Situationism's revival helped keep alive the possibility of a critical reading of cultural institutions such as the exhibition and the museum itself. And it is this critique that has distinguished the work of a number of artists who, while never themselves Situationists or members of allied groups, had had some contact with, and sympathy for, original Situationist activity: Daniel Buren, Marcel Broodthaers, Mario Merz, and Art and Language.

Daniel Buren, for example, strove to maintain his strategic posture in the face of the general de-politicisation of art in the

75. NIELE TORONI
Exhibition at the Galerie Buchmann, Basle, 1990. Foreground: 3 hanging papers in blue, green, and yellow, 10'2" x 14¾" (3.1 m x 37.5 cm); rear: 2 canvases painted in red acrylic, 9'8" x 6'6" (3 x 2 m), on a wall painted in red acrylic; all No.50 brush at 11¾" (30 cm) intervals.

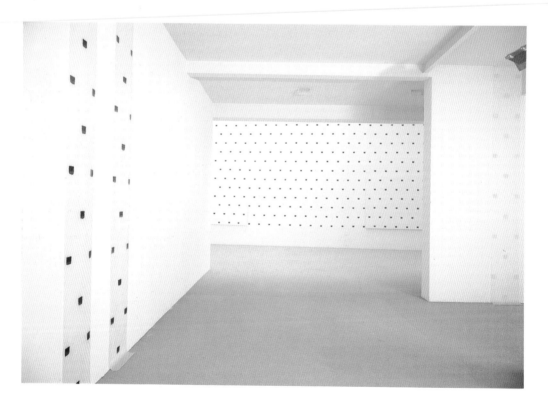

later 1980s. Buren's work has been accused of declining into a signature, a mere sign of radical intentions. Yet his projects, though now often highly decorative, continue to demand of the viewer a subtle form of reflection on art's relationship with its institutional setting. Of a construction made in 1984 for a site in Ghent (FIG. 74), Buren offered only a series of negations:

> Though all of the elements of the piece are in fact elements of traditional painting, it is not possible to say that what we are talking about here is painting. Further, although all of these elements are built to stand in a site, we cannot say that what we are talking about here is sculpture. And if all these elements create new visions of and volumes for a space, we still cannot say that this is architecture. And even though the entire apparatus can be approached as a decor that reveals both sides of itself depending on the movements and positions of visitors, so that they become actors in a play without words, this nevertheless does not allow us to say that what we are talking about here is theatre...what the work *does* have to do with is what it does.

The falling-off of the final part of Buren's statement will be taken by some as symptomatic of the difficulty in preserving radicalism from an almost irresistible descent into mere style. Yet take Niele Toroni, for instance, whose elegant yet reductive painting-installations have for nearly three decades consisted of even-spaced dashes of paint as a means of "bringing painting to view" (FIG. 75). Since 1967 each one of Toroni's installations has been done by applying patches of paint with a No.50 brush at 11³/₄ inch (30 cm) intervals according to the dictionary definition of the word *application*: "to put one thing on another so that it covers it, sticks to it or leaves a mark on it." Early statements issued by the artist (with Daniel Buren, Olivier Mosset, and Michel Parmentier)

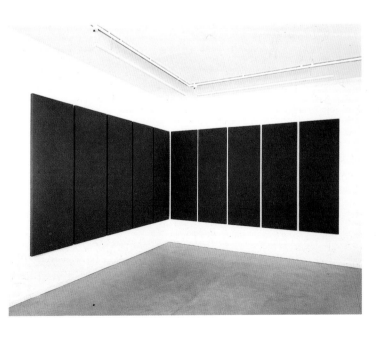

76. ALAN CHARLTON *"Corner" Painting*, 1986. Acrylic on cotton duck, 10 parts, each 7'9" x 26" x 1³/₄" (2 m x 67.5 cm x 4.5 cm) with 1³/₄" (4.5 cm) spaces between. Musée Saint Pierre Art Contemporain, Lyon.

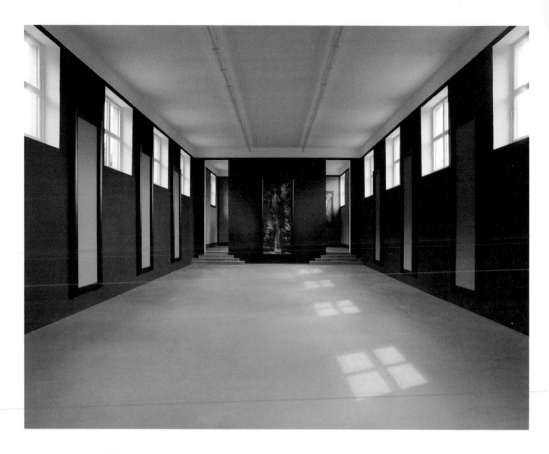

explained that "because painting is a game, a springboard for the imagination, and spiritual illustration...*we are not painters*." Toroni has more recently said that "my job is not to displace, but to paint; to try to do paintings without a state of mind...and to hell with fashions!" As with Buren, such affirmations make use of repetition precisely to avoid the embrace of the non-art world that the work originally sought to critique. Indeed, such repetition is intended to *be* that critique.

Reference might also be made to Alan Charlton, whose "grey" paintings have constituted the working-out over more than two decades of an idea first developed in the late 1960s. Like other painters of his generation with whom he has exhibited – Buren, Robert Ryman, Brice Marden, and Agnes Martin – Charlton determined early in his career to make paintings which were private, personal, "where somebody couldn't tell you what to do...that's when I decided that I had to make my own rules up. I found I could make a painting which nobody could tell me was right and nobody could tell me was wrong ...from the beginning I knew all the things that I didn't want in

77. GERHARD MERZ
Dove Sta Memoria (Where Memory Is) (Room 3), 1986. Installation at the Munich Kunstverein.

Attracted always to the nostalgic but critical projects of Giorgio de Chirico and Ezra Pound, Merz's post-Modern incunabula resonate with the forgotten violence of European history. For Merz's Munich project, a suite of oppressively coloured rooms stages images of death from the Renaissance to the Holocaust. A silk-screened version of Cima da Conegliano's *Saint Sebastian* here functions in the manner of a chapel altarpiece.

the painting." Those things have notoriously included internal composition, colour, and what Charlton calls "intricacies of craftsmanship." A formula once set down is followed remorselessly. Charlton has produced paintings with slots, square holes, channels; in series, teams, or parts; equal, rectangular, and grey (FIG. 76). Taking standard-width timber he builds outwards from its sizes and proportions, towards the intended context of display. "Many of my conditions or rules were not just unique to how to make a painting," Charlton has said; "they were in a sense a foundation for how I was going to live my life and the paintings in a way just followed those foundations." He means, in effect, that they were about their own means of production and display. They were "about equality and the equality sometimes happens in the way I think about making the art...from the concept of making the painting, to building the painting, to painting the painting, to packing the painting, to seeing to the transport of the painting, to seeing how the layout of the catalogue is, to seeing to the day-to-day activities of the studio: all those qualities for me are completely equal...It is about reality."

There is a correspondence between the determined austerity of Charlton's project and a series of works made during the 1980s by the German artist, Gerhard Merz, which are best described as installation paintings: monochrome colour-field paintings with vast, overbearing frames, positioned as if they were part of, rather than merely installed in, particular gallery or museum spaces. Normally requiring whole suites of rooms, Merz's environments relate formally to Constructivist, Suprematist, and Minimalist predecessors while casting severe doubt – imparted by a generically arid format – upon their containing spaces. While works of the early 1980s took the form of installations interwoven into the texture of existing art-historical museums, more recent installations have taken the architectural format of the modernist gallery as the point of reference. For the *Dove Sta Memoria* (*Where Memory Is*) project at the Munich Kunstverein in 1986 (FIG. 77), Merz took a silk-screened image of a Renaissance *Saint Sebastian*, Otto Freundlich's sculpture *The New Man*, pilloried by the Nazis' *Degenerate Art* exhibition in Munich in 1937, and an image of bones and skulls, and placed them in what then became a series of oppressively empty memorial chambers, perfectly symmetrical and tomb-like. In such cases, the high architectural style of authoritarian culture is Merz's immediate concern. His installations insert themselves into those legitimated spaces as a disruption and critique of the privileged historical knowledges they purvey.

A different attempt to address the culture of the recent past was made by the group Art and Language between 1985 and 1988 with the paintings known as *Index: Incidents in a Museum*, a number of which were first shown together in Brussels in 1987. By this time Art and Language had the strong support of the critic and historian Charles Harrison, who became virtually a spokesman for the two artists of the group, Michael Baldwin and Mel Ramsden. The three had persistently raised questions about the managerial and curatorial aspects of the "Story of Modern Art," but had not previously taken on the space of the archetypal Modernist art museum. In the *Index* paintings it was Marcel Breuer's Whitney Museum of American Art on Madison Avenue, New York.

The paintings of this series are characterised by a series of visual and conceptual paradoxes, mostly irresolvable. Incompatibilities of scale, size, support surface, perspective, and mode of address unsettle even the minimally inquisitive viewer (FIG. 78). The colours of *Incident VIII* are, strangely, those of analytical Cubism, while the text is a murder mystery derived from an opera libretto, written earlier by the group, about Victorine Meurent, the model Manet used for his *Olympia*. Much of the force of the painting springs from a distinction between the spectator *in* the painting (whose notional presence is implied by

78. ART AND LANGUAGE *Index: Incident in a Museum VIII*, 1986. Oil and alogram on canvas, 5'9" x 8'11" (1.7 x 2.7 m). Private collection, Belgium.

The *Incident* paintings, in Charles Harrison's words, "represent in allegorical form the spectator's activity as structured within the imaginary museum...Shifts of size and scale open the processes of reading to a dialogue of values and competence...As a reader of the text which *Incident VIII* presents [the murder story], the spectator in the painting is caught up in a drama of conflicting significations."

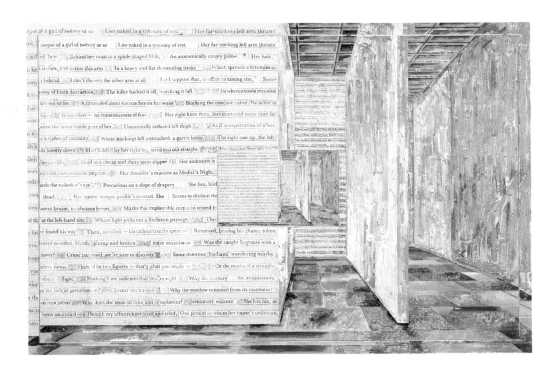

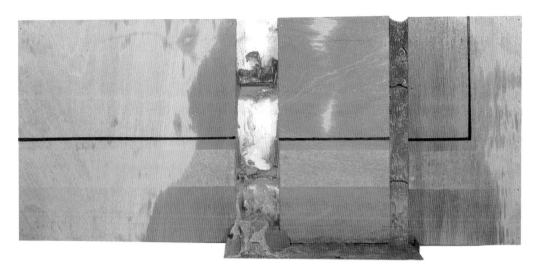

79. TERRY ATKINSON
Grease-Mute Shelf, 1988.
Hardboard on 1½″ (3.8 cm)
baton, metal shelf, and
grease, 4′7″ x 2′ x 6⅔″ (139
x 61 x 17 cm).

the painting) and the spectator *of* the painting. Harrison wrote that "it is arguable that...competently to view *Incident VIII* is to be able to become, in imagination, the reader of the text on a museum wall − and not simply the reader of the text on the surface of the painting...What is read *in* the painting threatens to disqualify that which the painting is seen *as*, while the conditions of the painting's being viewed as a painting tend to remainder the findings of the imaginary reader." He further proposed that "what is required if the spectator is to be critically engaged is that reflection upon the uncertainty involved be at some level a form of reflection upon the culture of the Modern. In so far as the paintings succeed...the conditions of consumption and distribution of modern artistic culture are taken into them and reflected back as formal effects...Unreassuringly, the painting works at the viewer."

Charlton, Merz, and Art and Language could be said to be among the most determined of those attempting to dislodge the orthodox certainties of the producer and the viewer of art. To consider the work of the painter and object-maker Terry Atkinson is to begin to make a wider statement about a dominant European way with materials and their relation to cultural seriousness. At various times close to Art and Language, Atkinson's work has veered more to the disarmingly evasive than to the theoretically correct. In a little-noticed show entitled *Mute* that toured Copenhagen, Derry (Northern Ireland), and London in 1988, Atkinson made some works generically grouped under the concept of *grease* (FIG. 79), presented as contributions to an investigation into concepts of *disaffirmation* and *negation* that had

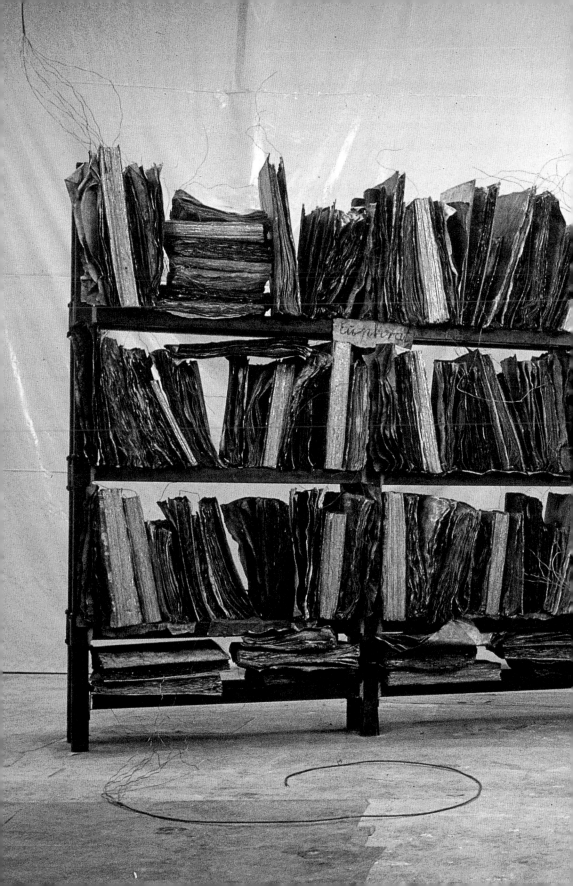

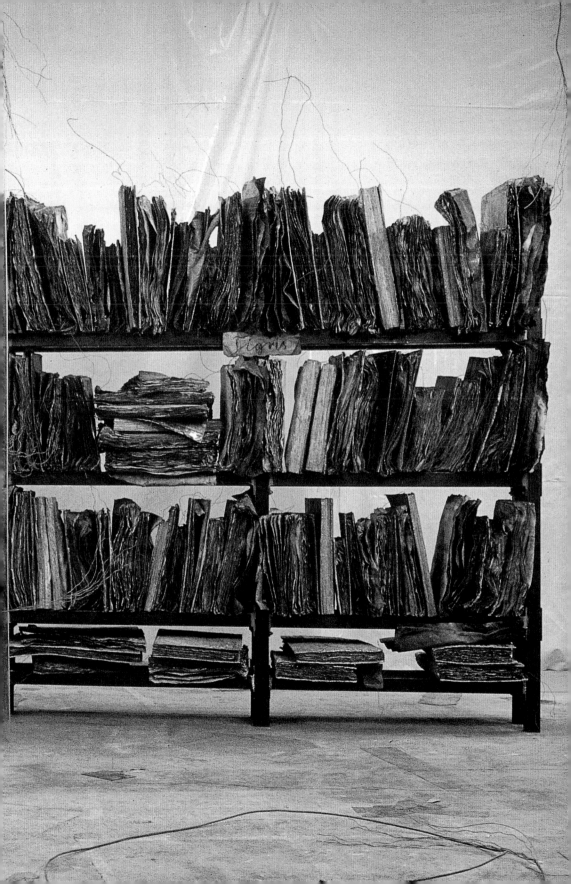

80. ·ANSELM KIEFER
High Priestess, begun in
1985. Approximately two
hundred lead books in two
steel bookcases, with glass
and copper wire, 14′ x 26′
x 3′ (4.2 x 7.9 x 1 m).

Too heavy to lift or
manipulate by a mortal
audience, the elements of
Kiefer's library remain
largely mute as to their
contents. In fact they
contain photo-images of
clouds, desolate
landscapes, rivers, deserts,
industrial waste: also
human hair and dried peas,
as well as blank pages. Both
the material of the work and
its allusive contents can be
read as elements of a
contemporary alchemical
experiment.

been proposed as necessary to inventive new practice by the art historian, Timothy Clark. "By 'practice of negation,'" Clark had written some years earlier, "I mean some form of decisive innovation, in method or materials or imagery, whereby a previously established set of skills or frame of reference – skills and references which up till then had been taken as essential to art-making of any seriousness – are deliberately avoided or travestied, in such a way as to imply that only *by* such incompetence or obscurity will genuine picturing get done." Clark had gone on to give a list:

> deliberate displays of painterly awkwardness, or facility in kinds of painting that were not supposed to be worth perfecting; the use of degenerate or trivial or 'inartistic' materials; denial of full conscious control over the artifact; automatic or aleatory ways of doing things; a taste for the vestiges and margins of social life; a wish to celebrate the 'insignificant' or disreputable in modernity; the rejection of painting's narrative conventions; the false reproduction of painting's established genres; the parody of previously powerful styles.

Atkinson sought, in this spirit, to produce art "that had mistakes, feints, gaps in it." The grease-paintings were disaffirmatively sarcastic about grease, but also about themselves. Among the grease-analogies assembled by Atkinson we find this statement: "Using grease: (1) The material of the avant-garde greasers, (2) Grease – the new material, (3) Grease as the repository of the potentially oppositional. Chortle! (Be serious now! Grease is entering the portals of serious art histories of the social referent), (4) Grease as a disaffirming material – will it ever dry?" Pointing both downwards to the world of the car mechanic and upwards to the "oiling of careers, the greasing of art," the metaphor transforms the art-objects from a set of worthy, abstract expressions into a mordant joke at the expense of art, from the inside.

It is in Germany alone, perhaps, that the fertile lessons of Conceptual art have become infused with portentous historical themes. Like other artists whose origins lie in the later 1960s, Anselm Kiefer, has built on those foundations an art of extraordinary ambition and complexity. Often identified (mistakenly) with the German painting revival of the later 1970s and early 1980s, Kiefer can be more tellingly viewed as a maker of objects and environments: books, particularly, have preoccupied him since controversy first surrounded his *Occupations* documentation of 1969, in which he presented photos of himself in symbolic locations producing parodies of a Nazi salute. Here lay a key to a preoccupation of Kiefer's that he has obsessively elaborated since. Yet the artist has denied a primary interest in history painting or its revival. He begins rather with Minimalism and Conceptual art – two ideas that he says "need completion with content" – and with a concept of history that sees it as "like burning coal...it is material...a warehouse of energy." Unlike most other contemporary artists, ancient history and symbolism are for Kiefer contemporaneous: "history is for me synchronous, whether it is the Sumerians with the Epic of Gilgamesh, or German mythology." In a major book-project of the mid-1980s, Kiefer used both Minimalist form (the shelving) and Conceptualist process (the enumeration of parts) to give articulation to a massively heavy library made of some two hundred lead books, filled with evocative images from geology, architecture, landscape (FIG. 80). The material itself is laden with ancient lore. "Lead has always been a material for ideas," he has said. "In alchemy, it was the bottom level among the metals in the process of extracting gold. On the one hand, lead is dense and linked with Saturn, but on the other it contains silver, and alludes to...a spiritual plane." Determinedly averse to the usual types of art-world publicity, Kiefer has repeatedly indicated that his concerns are mythical, synthetic, and even gnostic. The lead library of *High Priestess (Land of Two Rivers)* – its secondary title refers to the two rivers of ancient Mesopotamia – in this sense combines material and idea, knowledge and its secret origins, base historical matter and a spark of redemptive hope.

The high moral tone of Kiefer's impressively labyrinthine reflections approaches a limiting point, however, in terms of the kinds of seriousness normally permitted to avant-garde art. What Clark called "genuine picturing" has more often been approached through play with the materials and orthodoxies of Modernist art, as a cipher for the larger historical process. There are the abstract paintings being made in New York by Susan Smith, for example, who on one level devises a montage of urban detritus (found metal, plaster-board, and the like) with Minimalist painted canvases, while on another level seeming to want a more complex dialogue between the resonances of the artistic surface and those of non-art, or waste (see FIG. 73, page 105). Can spectators of the work tread in the aesthetic footsteps of Piet Mondrian or Ad Reinhardt *and* enter the mentality of the *bricoleur*, even a Duchampian, at the same time? Can spectators reconcile their instinctive reverence for the sensitively brushed monochrome surface with the uncomfortable presence of a piece of discarded masonite found on a street corner? Those are questions of the kind that Susan Smith likes to generate.

But the motif of interrogating the museum-space directly has proved persistent. Louise Lawler's photo-work in America has looked sceptically at the "aura" of Old Master and Modernist works and has tried to displace that aura with views that focus not upon the "masterpiece" but upon its supposed epiphenomena. In the early 1980s Lawler took high-definition photos of picture-edges, frames, and captions to give a new shape and articulation to the viewer's attention. "I am showing what they are showing," Lawler said of such works. "Painting, sculpture, pictures, glasses and words on painted walls furnishing the same material experience: my work is to exchange the positions of exposition and voyeurism." In one work, Lawler photographed an archetypal Stella painting of his Protractor series, not as you see it on the museum wall, but as it appears reflected in the polyurethane varnish beneath.

It may be possible to deduce from these examples that within the larger project of engendering self-consciousness in the viewing subject, American work has tended to the well-mannered formats of previous American painting, while European work has tended to lop-sidedness, anti-formality, humour, awkwardness, and (in a spirit of self-mockery) deliberate absence of poise. Much European sculpture, to take another important category, tended in the later 1980s towards the broken, the bathetic, and the reduced.

Installation as Decay

Several factors helped to keep alive a culture-critique in Europe based on concepts of decay. One was the *arte povera* inheritance of recovering (hence aestheticising) materials discarded by nature or manufacture: wood and metal, junk and mass media fragments. A second was the Fluxus aesthetic of randomness and the scandalous negation of "art." A third, perhaps, has been the survival of the spirit of European existentialism of the 1940s and 1950s: moods of cynicism and despair, and their conversion into a quest for "revolutionary" seizures in art that might re-animate past conflagrations: those of 1789, 1848, 1917, and 1968.

A position somewhere between the United States and Europe is represented by the painter and sculptor John Armleder, who was born in Switzerland and works in both Europe and New York. Armleder's roots as an artist lay in Fluxus, in chance systems of the kind made famous by the composer John Cage, and in performance. Armleder came to attention in the early 1980s with "appropriated" abstract paintings and, to even better

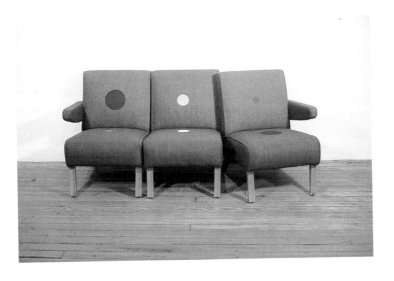

81. JOHN ARMLEDER
Furniture-Sculpture 60,
1984. Three seats, wax, and
acrylic on cloth, 31" x 6'2"
x 35" (0.8 x 1.8 x 0.9 m).
Collection Daniel Newburg,
New York.

For his first New York show Armleder scoured the pavements and thrift stores of Manhattan and Brooklyn for pieces of found furniture, only to return many pieces to the street after the show. The re-representation of obsolete furniture styles with Minimalist or Suprematist painting here constitutes a tryptich, with "spots of increasing diameter painted in the centre of each seat, the same series inverted on the backs."

effect, with furniture-sculpture in which items of second-hand furniture were scavenged from the street, assembled in tableaux, and painted with Suprematist forms before being returned to the streets after the show (FIG. 81). "There was a large sofa sawn in two halves by its aged owner," says Armleder, "which enabled us to be able to get it up easily, the gallery being at that time in the apartment where John Gibson was living. He was very grey-faced at having to live in the company of this rotting furniture for the duration of the show." In formal terms these tableaux looked like an ironic playing with conventional migrations of paintings into real space. Yet Armleder's Fluxus inheritance suggested to him a strategy of "playing at being a decorator" in the spirit of what he called "cynical devaluation of the enterprise [of art]." In claiming to dissolve the distinction between rubbish and art, Armleder mobilised an aesthetic gambit that has become central for many artists of this tendency: an exploitation of the disused and overlooked as a pretext for philosophical and aesthetic speculation on the expectations and values of art itself.

The gambit runs from the "presentation" of rejected objects and artifacts at one extreme through to full-blown installation art at the other. An accompanying formal shift has been a switch from minimal to maximal expression; another has been a move from specialist to generalist attitudes to art's traditional hierarchies and media. In each case, the project has been one of severe problematising of what it means for a cultural space to be perceived as a container for the category "art."

A group of post-Fluxus artists in Germany in the later 1980s exemplify this posture precisely. Variously dubbed "model-

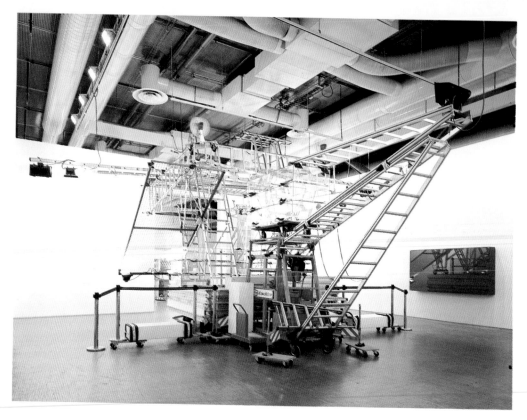

82. REINHARD MUCHA
Calor, 1986. Work made *in situ* for an exhibition at the Centre Georges Pompidou, Paris.

makers," "scene-setters" or "presentation artists," they have been preoccupied with a post-Constructivist assemblage aesthetic, taking everyday objects or fragments and positioning them off-handedly in real space. Hubert Kiecol and Klaus Jung have taken their cues from architecture. Wolfgang Luy and Reinhard Mucha, in Düsseldorf, have manipulated materials according to the particularities of a chosen site. In Mucha's recent work a mixture of useless showcases, ladders, and *passé* office-furnishings culled from the environs of the exhibition site have ended up as makeshift structures in real space (FIG. 82), but without coalescing into a "good gestalt" (compare in this respect Woodrow and Cragg). Mucha's pieces have been both utterly ordinary and nightmarishly complex; yet they are not illustrative, and seem not to point beyond their own origins and resources. Mucha's "staging the stage," to use his own phrase, can be seen as an extension of the founding impulse of modern sculpture from Brancusi onwards, tinged with nihilism and a radical desire for impermanence.

Mucha's objects have proved as determinedly anti-artistic, in the better tradition of Beuysian philosophy, as the contemporaneous work of a group of seven artists: Gisbert Huelsheger, Wolfgang Koethe, Jan Kotik, Raimund Kummer, Wolf Pause, Hermann Pitz, and Rudolf Valenta. For their exhibition *Räume* (*Spaces*) of 1978 they re-articulated the spaces of a disused Berlin warehouse using nothing other than the debris of the building itself. "No one can say where the art begins," wrote Pitz of the arbitrary-seeming ensembles inside. "Who did that scribbling on the wall? An artist? Who drove these nails into that particular order on this wall? An artist? Who broke the window over there? Who painted the line on the floor? Who is it here who's looking out of the window?" The show gave expression to a manifesto statement that "the art object alone is no longer important. The object can document an attitude." The group known as Büro Berlin that developed in 1980 under the guidance of Kummer, Pitz, and Fritz Rahmann – joined occasionally by Tony Cragg and others – extended this attitude to all manner of urban detritus however marginal or unpromising. It took to another kind of limit the idea that "the quality of a work of art consists...in the structure of its realization not being concealed," to quote Büro Berlin's essay *dick, dünn* (*thick, thin*) of 1986. Fritz Rahmann's project for the *Lützowstrasse Situation* exhibition in 1979 remains exemplary (FIG. 83). He collected up the debris of twelve other projects and disposed the pieces frankly yet informally like the set of disused fragments they were. Restaging the material remnants of the exhibition site directly as the work itself, Büro Berlin predicated itself through the early and mid-1980s on precisely *not* being the "neue wilder" grouping of

83. FRITZ RAHMANN
Lützowstrasse Situation 13, 1979. Wall paint, remains of Situations 1-12, water.

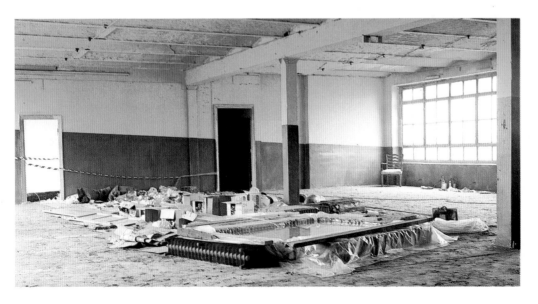

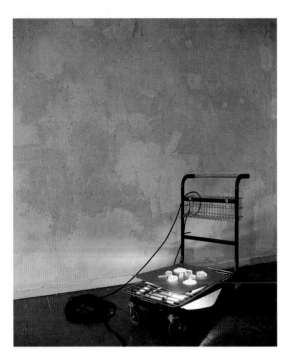

84. HERMANN PITZ
Out of Infancy, 1989. Nine
resin casts, aluminum,
lamp, caddie, 3'2" x 3'4"
x 23" (0.9 x 1 x 0.6 m).
Collection of the artist.

Pitz takes non-cultural
objects and parades them
provocatively in a new
setting. Particularly
unsettling is the position of
this tableau on its own
wheels, suggesting a breach
of perhaps the oldest
convention of sculpture,
that it does not move.

Rainer Fetting, Middendorf, and Salomé. Anarchic and sometimes scarcely recognisable as art, Büro Berlin evaded, and were in turn usually evaded by, the promotional machinery at work on their more marketable neighbours. Though the group was formally dissolved in 1986, most of the artists have since continued to work on their own (FIG. 84).

The desolate or materially damaged forms taken by much of the work of this German generation, many of them born near the end of World War II and reared in a period of rapidly increasing material prosperity, can be related to Theodor Adorno's remark that "after Auschwitz, lyric poetry is no longer possible." Far from associating itself with the tortured *angst* of an expressionist past, the best work of the younger Germans was art precisely in not being "art"; aesthetic only in not performing "aesthetically," pleasurable only in completely renouncing "pleasure."

Thus Joseph Beuys's pupil from Düsseldorf, Imi Knoebel, moved from devising Dada-like arrangements in the later 1960s and 1970s to making installations of low-grade wooden panels that were painted (frequently face down), stacked, or disposed on wall and floor surfaces according to the poetry of an existing room. Some of Knoebel's works echo childhood incidents: a series of triangular plywood panels from the mid-1980s recalls the window through which he watched the burning of Dresden as a five-year-old boy. A 1980 room installation for a Ghent museum, reinstalled subsequently in several other museums, combines order, chaos, geometry, and informality in an arrangement that manages to stop short of completeness or finality (FIG. 85). Storage, accumulation, deference to pioneer Modernists and a refusal of sensuous declaration all inhabit Knoebel's work. "Beuys showed Knoebel a way to free non-objectivity from design," one critic usefully wrote in a essay of 1987; "the look of an art...is far from its whole story."

What was also distinctive about Germany in the later 1980s (as before) was the existence of several artistic centres, each with its own cultural traditions through the post-war period. One of these was Cologne. In the 1950s Cologne had been the home of

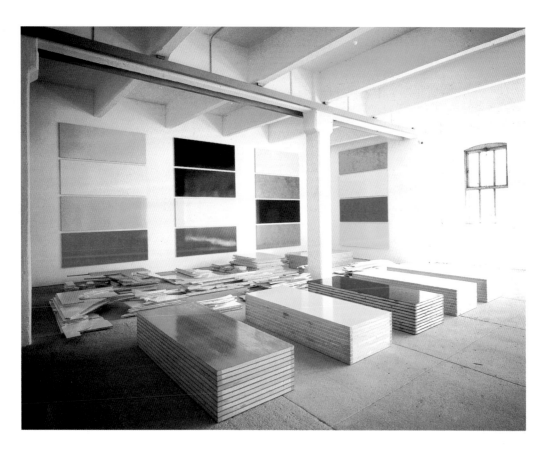

a kind of abstract painting, associated with Ernst Wilhelm Nay and Georg Meistermann, that had attempted to break free of National Socialist proscriptions on the modern. Subsequently associated with Fluxus, experimental music (John Cage, Nam June Paik, Karlheinz Stockhausen, and David Tudor) and the "de-collage" aesthetics of Wolf Vostell, the Cologne art community by the later 1980s had begun to codify its differences from other cities. The stance of the original Mülheimer Freiheit artists is a case in point. Walter Dahn now began to describe his earlier activity as "playing with" Expressionism, rather than – as was loudly proclaimed at the time – plumbing spiritual depths directly. Jiri Georg Dokoupil, too, swayed by the childlike, cerebral, and distanced posture of a precursor like Sigmar Polke (who frequently exhibited in the city), came to view the much-vaunted neo-expressionism of the early 1980s as a strictly bad-faith, role-playing product.

Hence a more ironic and complex attitude came to engage Cologne artists like Martin Kippenberger, Werner Büttner, and the painters Markus and Albert Oehlen. In his shows towards

85. IMI KNOEBEL
Ghent Room, 1980. Lacquer on plywood, 459 parts in varying sizes. Installation at the Dia Center for the Arts, New York, 1987-88.

Originally shown in Ghent in 1980, this room installation has been reconstructed in Kassel, Winterthur, Bonn, New York, and Maastricht. Varied according to the dictates of each space, the stacked and hung panels resonated with echoes of founding Modernism – from Malevich to Marden – under the aegis of a deceptive informality learned from Beuys.

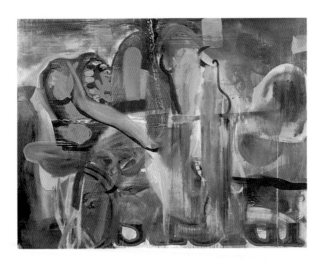

86. ALBERT OEHLEN
Fn 20, 1990. Oil on canvas,
7′ x 9′ (2.1 x 2.8 m).

the end of the decade, Albert Oehlen confronted a dilemma that was central to any avant-garde: the dilemma of how to "go on" with an art that had been ritually pronounced dead many times; how painting *at that moment* could survive as more than a nihilistic or repetitive fetish. What emerged from Oehlen in the later 1980s was not *belle peinture*, but scurrilous and defeatist mark-making that knew that the power of painting to make descriptive images was by then a lost cause (FIG. 86). Adopting a despairing attitude to questions surrounding the social function of painting – and particularly deriding the work of Otto Dix – Oehlen has nevertheless evolved a particular conceptualisation: "I try for example to force the concept 'mess' or 'crap' or 'out of focus' or 'fog' onto the observer. My goal is to see that he can't help having the word 'mess' in his head." Provisional and mute, his works speak of irresolution on a grand scale. Yet it is the making plain of that irresolution within the painted surface that marks Oehlen's as an aesthetic rather than as a merely nihilistic project.

In German sculpture of the period a sense of chaotic aggression was conveyed by the sculpture-installations of the Berlin-trained Olaf Metzel. His contribution to the *Skulpturenboulevard* show in Berlin in 1987 consisted of a pile of police crash-barriers heaped up at a major junction of the Kurfürstendamm, steadied by concrete blocks at its base, and with a supermarket trolley hanging teeteringly near its top (FIG. 87). Always deploying an iconography of wreckage, of ruined machinery and apparatus, of violent rupture and collapse, Metzel – who has since lived and worked in Munich – has come close to converting *bricolage* into overt political symbolism.

The paradox is that German art of this appropriately bitter kind has evolved against the backdrop of comprehensive critical publicity at the hands of journals like *Art* and *Kunstforum International*, and a massive proliferation of museum-building for the display of contemporary art. In the train of Philip Johnson's Kunsthalle at Bielefeld (1966) and Mies van der Rohe's Neue Nationalgalerie in Berlin (1968) have followed the Wilhelm-Hack Museum Ludwigshafen (1979), the Städtische Museum

Mönchengladbach (1982), the Städtische Kunsthalle Mannheim (1983), the Museum Bochum and the Staatsgalerie Stuttgart (1984), the Kunstsammlung Nordrhein-Westfalen Düsseldorf, the Ludwig Museum Cologne (1986) and MOMA Frankfurt (1991), to name only the most prominent (FIG. 88).

In the context of such an expansion of the machinery of display, it becomes pertinent to ask whether the new German avant-garde did not encounter the danger of becoming co-opted by those very values which their work at some level seemed to want to resist: the pursuit of art as recreational pleasure, the elaboration of a national culture, and the entrenchment of patriarchal management. There is an old implication here: that an avant-garde both needs, and needs to resist, the art-historical and managerial competencies of the museum curator. But that question

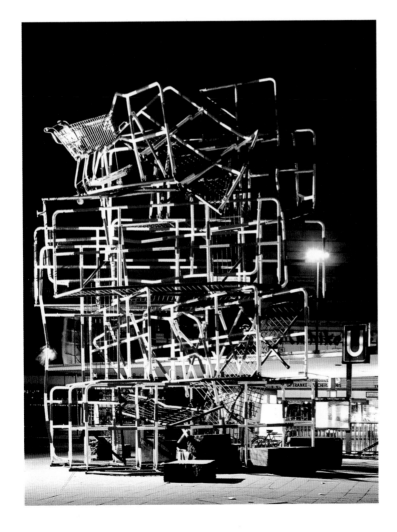

87. OLAF METZEL
13.4.1981, 1987. Steel, chromium, concrete, 37'7" x 29'5" x 22'9" (11 x 9 x 7 m). Installation at the Kurfürstendamm/ Joachimstaler Strasse, Berlin.

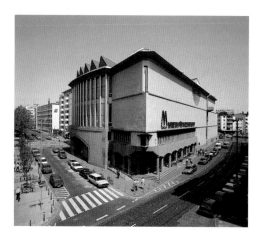

88. The Museum of Modern Art, Frankfurt. An innovative series of spaces designed by Hans Hollein and completed in 1991, the new museum in central Frankfurt stands as a symbol of the city's banking prosperity in the 1980s.

too is ideological. In whose interests do curators act? On behalf of what gender, class, and ethnic constituencies does cultural management function? The problem is one of identifying the steps by which each party performs its elaborate, ritual-like negotiations with the ideals and aspirations of the other.

The Curator's Part

The re-emergence of large-scale international curatorial projects at the end of the 1980s served to complicate the question still further. A key event was *Metropolis*, a huge showcase of German and American trends of the 1980s mounted at the Martin-Gropius-Bau in Berlin in 1991 by Christos Joachimedes and Norman Rosenthal, two of those who had promoted the much-advertised "return to painting" of 1981. Now, "painting" itself was the missing term: *Metropolis* claimed that Warhol, Beuys, and Duchamp – a diplomatic blend of American, German, and French progenitors – were the vital figures. "A feature of art in this century is the imaginary pendulum swinging between Picasso and Duchamp," Joachimedes suggested; "if 1981 was Picasso's hour, Duchamp's time has come in 1991." The geographical idea was that "in the image of art presented today, there are two obvious points of culmination drawing events to themselves like magnets: New York, and the area around Cologne." Yet as in other mega-projects of the recent past, the curatorial eye remained fixated on male artists of already secure reputation, which then functioned to stimulate the international dealer network without burdening it with local differences, questions of gender, or inconsistencies of aspiration or allegiance. Curatorially moulded for rapid projection into the space of art journals, criticism, and even tourism, *Metropolis* postulated a seamless international continuum linking Europe (even Eastern Europe) and America of a far simpler kind.

The relation of Rosemarie Trockel's paintings and objects to those of the Duchamp-Beuys-Warhol axis is at least partially clear. Trockel had trained at the Werkkunstschule in Cologne in the late 1970s and had had contact with the ironic tendencies of the Mülheimer Freiheit group of painters in that city – Walter Dahn, Jiri Georg Dokoupil, Pieter Bommels, and others – who in their work combined historical and social referents with a series of eclectic, quotational styles. The most celebrated early result of this background was Trockel's computer-knitted paintings and objects of the mid-1980s, which by incorporating heavily loaded motifs such as the hammer and sickle, the *Playboy* symbol, the Wool-mark and other commercial signifiers, managed at once to load an immediately gendered surface with a menacing sense of the familiar gone askew (FIG. 89). Following an affinity for the work of the French *Documents* group of the later 1920s – it had included Georges Bataille, Michel Leiris, and others – Trockel towards the end of the 1980s resumed an appetite for a kind of "ethnographical surrealism" in which objects with social-sexual and "magic" connotations were placed tantalisingly in vitrines (a format perfected by Beuys). For *Metropolis* itself Trockel contributed a series of works which extended a dialogue with Mini-

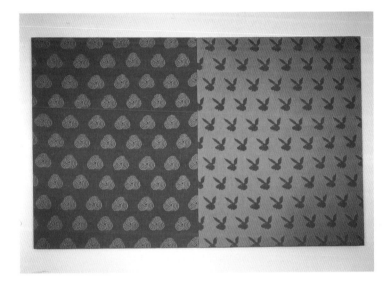

89. ROSEMARIE TROCKEL *Untitled*, 1988. Machine-knitted wool, 2 panels, overall 6'7" x 10'6" (2 x 3.2 m).

malism by enriching an elementary geometrical plan with the forms of a cooker surface, complete with four circular hotplates, the whole being raised from the horizontal to the vertical in a parody of the Cubist still-life picture. A Duchampian "ready-made" joke, a Warholian play with the banal, and often a Beuysian fascination for the atavistic, are all to be found in such work.

On the other hand, Katharina Fritsch had already made it clear that she wanted "to have nothing to do with the ideas of Beuys or with Warhol's factory." Fritsch had scandalised the good citizens of Münster, a Catholic town in Westphalia, by exhibiting a six-foot-tall, yellow, plastic Madonna in the centre of the town's pedestrian precinct in 1987. In the same year, she had exhibited a life-size green elephant mounted on a large oval

90. KATHARINA FRITSCH
Red Room with Howling Chimney, 1991. Colour, sound from tape. Installation at the *Metropolis* show, Martin-Gropius-Bau, Berlin.

Fritsch has made it clear that she "never exhibits ready-mades." She likes to free objects or environments from their usual significances, working instead with a sculptor's attention to exact dimensions and placing. Asked about the evacuation of content, Fritsch replied: "My works are neither icy nor cold, just precise."

pedestal in the Krefeld Museum. She generally makes objects from moulds, implying repeatability. "You will find that my works are always symmetrical...it's very important that they be exact." "I don't aim for expressiveness," she says. "That is a concept that I find too spongy, too vague...I don't want to force myself onto things but to let them grow on me and show me the clarity of the things themselves." For *Metropolis* Fritsch showed *Red Room with Howling Chimney*, a monochrome space in which chimney sounds could be heard (FIG. 90). Concerned less with iconography than with symmetry and precision, her structures or installations eliminate emotional resonances or particular associations, as if their significance consisted in their sculptural values alone – what Fritsch calls "exemplary form without ideological meaning."

Functioning simultaneously as a showcase for advanced tendencies in art at the end of the 1980s and the beginning of the 1990s, and as a simplifying, banalising account of them, *Metropolis* demonstrated several of the paradoxes of representing visual culture on an international scale that have still not been resolved and perhaps can never be satisfactorily overcome. Perceived bias, the tendency on the part of particular high-profile curators to omit or over-emphasise certain types of work, must be set against the fact that – as recent theoretical work in the arts also insisted – there can be no "final" or "truthful" representation of a culture that does not undermine its claims to finality or truth by betraying its origins and local concerns. No global perspective can exist in an age of many perspectives; no single knowledge-system has the power to dominate all others.

And yet specialism in the arts, as in other fields, continues to exert strong claims upon competence and sophistication which is unlikely to be found in the common weal. Many of the major museum shows of contemporary art in the period have wrestled with both sides of this paradox. Shows like *Bi-National: American and German Art of the Late 80s*, which exchanged work between Düsseldorf and Boston in 1988-89, or *Magiciens de la Terre* in Paris in 1989, not to mention the continuing *Documenta* series in Kassel, or the Venice Biennales, all vigorously assert the possibility of an international (even global) cross-section while conceding to institutional or critical tendencies that marshal necessarily selective expertise.

No amount of juggling with the claims of "other" constituencies such as minority cultures, geographically remote groups, emergent power-bases and critically experimental genres is likely finally to perfect the ways in which art is represented in a world of multi-national commercial interests, image-enhancement sponsorship, and competitive governments. The ways of cultural power will remain as elusive as they are important. On one side of the equation will be a continued attempt to maintain a "high" visual culture which does not altogether fall back into commerce or the values of family entertainment. On the other hand, important misrepresentations look likely to remain. What the cases of Trockel and Fritsch point to symptomatically is not only that neglect of women's art in the period has been endemic – *Metropolis* contained men to women in proportion of 93 per cent to 7 per cent and quickly acquired the tag *machopolis* – but that radical art could enter public visibility in the last ten or fifteen years only on condition of being often mis-described and misunderstood.

The Power of the Photograph

The question has been particularly complex for photographic art. Innovative photographic practice of the last decade or more has been both philosophically important for its re-examination of the medium's potentialities, yet at the same time highly agreeable to the curatorial mind. Its interrogation of the image *per se* and its leverage upon representation as a concept have been ambitious and impressive. It has extended the critique of basic picturing practices that had been begun but left undeveloped in earlier Conceptual art.

Recent work by the Düsseldorf artist Thomas Ruff has proved identifiable as a single, repeated idea: large colour photographs of friends or acquaintances (or architecture, or corners of the night sky) which are devoid of formal rhetoric, dramatic lighting, or nuances of arrangement (FIG. 91). Reinvesting energy in the lost art of portraiture, but against the grain of glamour photography, advertising, and publicity, Ruff has claimed that "most photos we come across today aren't really authentic any more – they have the authenticity of a manipulated and pre-arranged reality." He says of his own photo-pieces

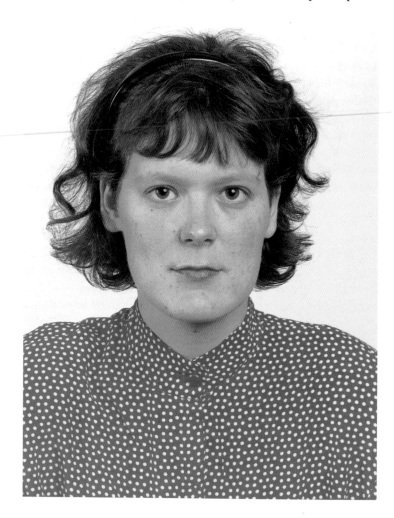

91. THOMAS RUFF
Elke Denda, 1989. C-Print
on Plexiglas, 6'8" x 5'2"
(2.1 x 1.6 m).

that they "have nothing to do with the person any more...I'm not interested in making a copy of my interpretation of a person." Called simply *Portraits*, these works conceal clues to the subjects' status, age, occupation, or character (we know only they are all friends or acquaintances of the artist) while appearing superficially lifelike. The series presents the paradox that the increasing stripping-away of portraiture's conventions reveals less and less of their notional subject, not more and more. The corollary, that representing personhood requires formulae and conventions, would have been taken for granted had Ruff's medium been painting. That it appears true for photography as well comes as a shock, given the assumed relationship of indexicality between the photograph and the world.

A further instance of Ruff's interest in the "defeat" or "confusion" of representation is that he has shown several of his *Portraits* side by side, so that his subjects take on the look of specimens for classification. In discarding "direct" representation in favour of a Zen-like repetition of the almost arbitrary, Ruff follows the precedent of his Düsseldorf Kunstakademie teacher, Bernd Becher, and his wife, Hilla. Yet the work of Ruff is to be distinguished from that of original serialists like the Bechers by the more thorough-going fetishisation and particularisation of the former: it approaches the standards of technical perfection found in advertisements for some better commodities. But, like the Bechers and other Conceptualists, Ruff appears to demonstrate that the photograph is inexorably a construction and never a neutral sign.

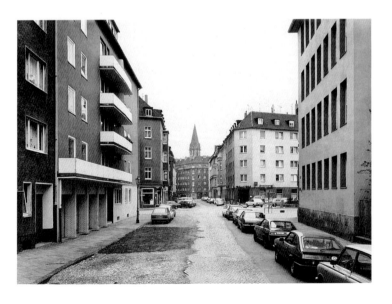

92. Thomas Struth
Düsselstrasse, Düsseldorf, 1979. Black and white photograph.

93. CHRISTIAN BOLTANSKI
*Chases High School:
Graduating Class of 1931,*
1987. Photographs, metallic
boxes, bulbs. Castelgasse,
Vienna.

For the installation in
Vienna in 1987, of which
this is a detail, Boltanski
took a photo of Jewish
students in the Chases
Gymnasium in Vienna in
1931, re-photographed and
enlarged details, and
mounted them under the
glare of a table lamp in the
format of an altar to the
dead. "What I want to do is
to make people cry," says
Boltanski, against the grain
of much contemporary
work. "This is difficult to
say, but I am for an art that
is sentimental."

Another of Bernd Becher's Düsseldorf students, Thomas Struth (who began his studies under Gerhard Richter), may also be said to toy with the paradoxes of photographic particularisation. Struth's views of city streets and buildings direct the eye to aspects of the urban scene that to normal, functional perception are invisible: contingent arrangements of parked cars, open and closed windows, architectural perspectives, and conjunctions of street furniture. These urban scenes are seldom populated (FIG. 92). One sees miraculously empty streets whose very ordinariness makes the observer feel he should apologise for being there. Unlike Ruff's photo-portraits, Struth's works seem to supercharge the photographic surface with the marks of accident and history, meanings that only cities can generate and only the camera can see.

This recent explosion of photo-based art is a development whose ramifications extend far. Replacing the traditional large-scale painting with a coloured surface of comparable size and scale, the photo-art of an entire generation – Andreas Gursky in Germany, Clegg and Guttmann and Mike and Doug Starn in the United States are to be included – has come safely to occupy (but not fundamentally to redefine) the museum and gallery spaces that Conceptualism once aspired radically to refigure. Once cool and minimal, photo-art has recently become not only visually "hot" and maximal, it has converted the anti-establishment gesture of 1960s art into a more measured, more philosophical critique. In the process, the art museum has become a space, not of contestation, but of speculation about representation and reality itself.

The tendency has been geographically widespread. The work of the French artist Christian Boltanski has been concerned since the early 1970s with the evocative power, not of the thing itself, but of the photographic record of the thing as a fallible index of the memory-process. Continuously absorbed since his early Conceptualist days by the image of the archive – of personal effects, of ordinary objects enumerated in all their banality –

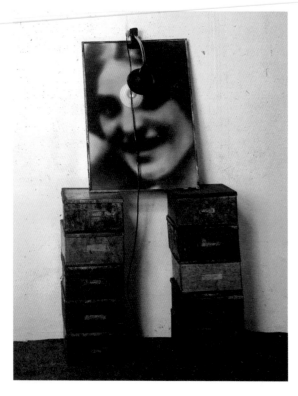

Boltanski has in his recent work used the installation format to pile up nostalgically charged photo-information arranged in the manner of the forensic laboratory, detective-agency workroom, or archive of missing or dead persons (FIG. 93). Claiming particular affinity with the projects of Tadeusz Kantor and Anselm Kiefer, Boltanski has said that he bases his work on cultural memory. "I am for an art that is sentimental," says Boltanski. "The task is to create a formal work that is, at the same time, recognised by the spectator as a sentimentally charged subject." As with Kiefer, these subjects have been moments of loss in European history, such as the Holocaust, the artist's own childhood, the exterminations of World War II, but above all with the sense of transience conveyed by the photo-archive itself. Roland Barthes's words in *Camera Lucida* might almost apply. "The life of someone whose existence has somewhat preceded our own encloses in its particularity the very tension of History, its division. History is hysterical: it is constituted only if we consider it, only if we look at it – and in order to look at it, we must be excluded from it...I am the very contrary of History, I am what belies it, destroys it for the sake of my own history." Yet, as Barthes also tried to show, the contemplation of a photograph can seemingly cut across that division and make the historical once again poignant and full of resonance.

A not dissimilar preoccupation has exerted a hold on a generation of photo-artists in Moscow who, working in relative isolation and with inadequate equipment, have made plentiful use of found photos, visual jokes, montage techniques, and performance. They deserve wider recognition. Following the work with found snapshots by the Ukrainian Boris Mikhailov, Vladimir Kupreanov and Alexei Shulgin have gathered photographic remnants from the days of the old Communist state and have crumpled, veiled, parodied, or electronically rotated them in the manner of mischievous children let loose in a disused archive. In their case it is the state as origin of the "real" in representation that has come under stern yet jocular review.

No technique or tradition of representation has proved immune from revision from within the photographic camp. The most acute of the new photo-Conceptualists may be the Vancouver-based artists Ian Wallace, Rodney Graham, Ken Lum, and Jeff Wall. Wall creates in meticulous detail events that only happen for the camera, though they have all the look of scenes which the camera just happened to observe – incidents in the workplace, accidents on the street, moments of interaction between types from different classes. Wall presents these scenes in large-scale cibachrome transparency, back-lit in display cases of the kind used in expensive street advertising. They are intended by Wall to be a kind of "painting of modern life," an accumulation of compressed yet symptomatic detail from the social mix (FIG. 94). In common with the work of Ruff and Struth, the apparently extreme mimeticism of Wall's works gets betrayed, in effect, precisely by mimeticism itself: the precision of the staging results in pictures of a sort, but one that proves dependent on highly complex orderings of the photographic sign in relation to its general and particular referents. Wall has said that "it is the overall value of the content of the image, not to mention the sensuous experience of beauty in the image, that validates anything critical in art, anything in art which dissents from the established form of things and their appearances." Going so far as to embody sympathy for a pictorial tradition that pre-dates modern art, Wall's work can be seen as a resumption of that manner by means of a kind of Conceptualist negation of Conceptualism itself.

What wider tactics are being pursued within this neo-neo-Duchampian framework for photo-based art? The artists concerned seem to acknowledge that the bad dream of Conceptual art was (and still is) over-rapid assimilation by the market and a drift into the open arms of the museum curator eager to mount spectacles of "radical" art: in effect, confrontational culture for the culture-tourist. For them it remains an active question whether, in a period marked by political retreat from the emancipatory moment of the later 1960s and early 1970s, the glossy and well-presented photo-object can extend and commemorate many of the ideals that were then made current: ideals of relative independence from the gallery and market system, a flexible, even transgressive, posture vis-à-vis the spaces and contexts of the work, and a desire to engage dialogically with the competent viewer's response.

A Kind of Publicity

The widespread regendering of art – if such it can be called – wrought by photography's recent assault on the male arena of painting, is one fragment of evidence that it can. The public projections of the Polish-born New York artist, Kryzysztof Wodiczko, may be another. Wodiczko's technique of taking a public monument, building, or urban site and projecting onto it images which displace its customary public meanings (military commemoration, monument to culture or business or honour)

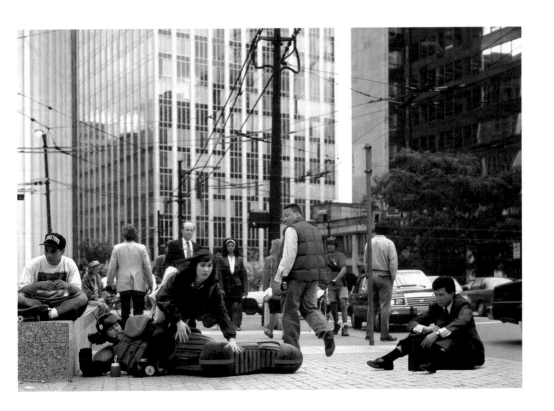

94. JEFF WALL
The Stumbling Block, 1991.
Cibachrome transparency,
fluorescent light, display
case, 7'6" x 11' (2.3 x
3.4 m). Marian Goodman
Gallery, New York.

Returning to a tradition of
representation attacked by
New Left orthodoxy in the
late 1960s and 1970s, Wall
not only reinstates modern-
life scenes of typical events
and behaviour, but
questions that orthodoxy's
other premise, that all
picturing was necessarily
capitalist or "on the side of
the dominant."

may be exemplary. Projecting the hand of Ronald Reagan across
the "chest" of the AT&T building in New York in 1984, or a
swastika onto the centre of the classical pediment at South
Africa House in London in 1985, or proposing in 1986 that the
Lincoln statue in Union Square, New York, "carry" a crutch,
are representative. The artist has said in relation to these projects
that "in today's contemporary real-estate city, the mercilessly
dynamic space of uneven economic development makes it
extremely difficult for city-dwellers and nomads to communicate through and in front of the city's symbolic forms...Not to
speak through the city monuments is to abandon them and to
abandon ourselves, losing both a sense of history and the present." Of course, the formidable difficulties of commission and
permission necessary to Wodiczko's projections are to be
counted amongst their meanings. It is also both unsurprising and
telling that the museum of art itself, in its role of store-house,
support-base, and filter of older and contemporary culture,
should become a target for Wodiczko's recent works (FIG. 95).

"Taking art to the streets" may sound romantic, even com-
munity-minded. Yet, as even the dismal recent debate about
"public" art suggests and as Wodiczko's projects demonstrate,

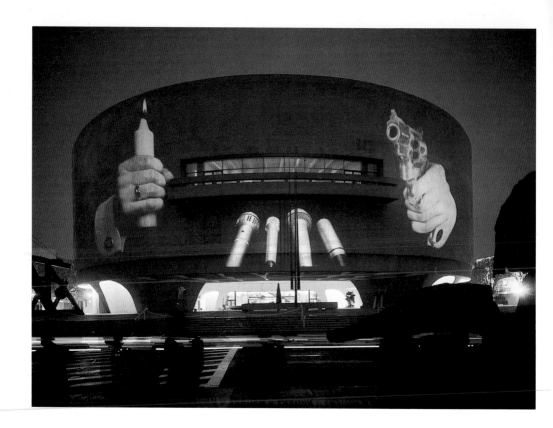

95. KRZYSZTOF WODICZKO *Projection on the Hirschhorn Museum, Washington, D.C.*, October 1988. Hal Bromm Gallery, New York.

Wodiczko's technique of using xenon-arc projectors to re-signify public monuments takes the museum as its inevitable extension. The images projected on to the Hirschhorn Museum present a contradiction in three parts: a candle that shines in the dark and thus illuminates, a gun that threatens, and a microphone-bank that speaks of both publicity and power.

there can be no such category that does not at the same time launch wider questions about the public space, about the posture and politics of audiences, and about the kinds of controversy which avant-garde art itself is scheduled to provoke. The desire of architects or city administrators to embellish otherwise unappealing buildings, especially, is anathema to the most challenging public art. On the contrary, the most vivid recent projects in city environments have been designed to challenge habitual urban behaviour, even to promote counter-thinking about the fabric of the city itself.

From the later 1960s the American sculptor, Richard Serra, has been working both in the studio and the gallery with extremely heavy lead and steel plates, propped against each other or precipitously juxtaposed. As Serra has said in interviews, the aesthetic function of such pieces, though deriving formally from Minimalism, was to reflect attention upon the nature of the physical spaces which they occupy. "What I'm interested in is revealing the structure and content and character of a space and a place by defining a physical structure through the elements that I use...it has more to do with a field force that's being generated, so that the space is discerned physically rather than optically." "Sculpture," said Serra in 1980, "if it has any potential at all, has the potential to create its own place and space, and to work in contradiction to the spaces and places where it is created. I am interested in work where the artist is a maker of an 'anti-environment' which takes its own place or makes its own situation, or divides or declares its own area."

Applied to the city arena, the statement may be easily related to Serra's *Tilted Arc*, commissioned in 1979 and installed in 1981 in New York's down-town legal and administrative centre, Federal Plaza (FIG. 96). Following its installation a New York judge, Edward Re, immediately whipped up public controversy over the piece until, at a public hearing in 1985 led by the Government Services Agency's New York administrator, William Diamond, polarising statements were made in public both for and against the *Arc*'s removal on the grounds that it disrupted the "normal" functioning of the plaza. Though non-specialist opinion was ranged against the sculpture (it was "the ugliest outdoor work of art in the city," according to the *New York Times*' Grace Glueck), persuasive and (in sheer numerical terms) overwhelming support was adduced by the city's artistic and intellectual community. Rosalind Krauss pointed out the sculpture's capacity to externalise vision: *Tilted Arc*, she said, was "constantly mapping a kind of projectile of the gaze that...like the embodiment of the concept of visual perspective, maps the path across the plaza that the spectator will take. In this sweep which is simultaneously visual and corporeal, *Tilted Arc* describes the body's relation to forward motion, to the fact that if we move ahead it is because our eyes have already reached out in order to connect us with the place to which we intend to go." Benjamin Buchloh pointed out that Serra's work was in historical line of that of Picasso, Brancusi, Schwitters, Tatlin, and Lissitsky, who were once vilified by the Nazis but were now installed at the Museum of Modern Art – that its intended philistine desecration was an example of "mob rule in culture." Douglas Crimp argued that Judge Re's complaint of loss of efficient security surveillance demonstrated that at base in the GSA were fears that the social life of the Plaza would become suddenly unstable and uncontrolled. Notwithstanding, the hearing panel voted four to one to relocate the sculpture and, despite a flurry of law-suits from the

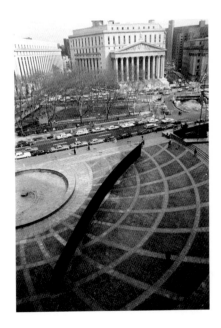

96. RICHARD SERRA
Tilted Arc, 1981. Cor-ten steel, 12' x 120' x 2¹/₂" (3.6 m x 36 m x 5.1 cm). Federal Plaza, New York City (removed).

sculptor, during the night of 15 March 1989 the work was dismantled and removed unceremoniously to a government parking lot in Brooklyn.

A concept of the counter-monument has also animated the much younger British sculptor Rachel Whiteread, whose reputation until recently rested upon a series of gallery pieces consisting of paradoxical "negative" volumes formed by reproducing in wax or plaster the spaces between or behind objects: the volume behind a cupboard or inside a bath. Her much-discussed public project, *House*, formed by spraying concrete throughout the inside of a condemned house in East London, thus stood out from the surrounding wasteland both as a monument to the interior life that it once enclosed, and as a telling symbol of the violence done to communities by contemporary urban planning (FIG. 97). *House* survived for a few weeks after the destruction of the immediate neighbourhood until it

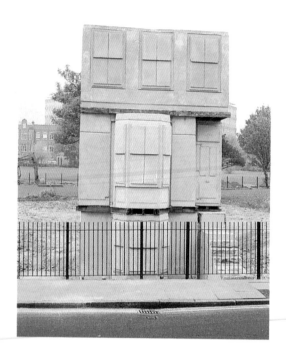

97. RACHEL WHITEREAD *Untitled (House)*, 1992. Metal armature and concrete. Grove Road, East London (demolished 1994).

too, was ritually destroyed by local political interests amidst a roar of conflicting publicity.

The German artist Jochen Gerz has also risked negative publicity with a series of monuments in public places that, like the ill-fated *Tilted Arc* and Whiteread's *House*, relocate the thought-process of the studio in the spotlight of journalistic awareness. Gerz had been a poet, a Conceptualist, and a prolific producer of photo-and-text pieces during the 1970s – a genre he continues today. But in 1984, for the city of Hamburg, Gerz was commissioned with his Jewish wife, Esther Shalev-Gerz, to complete a *Monument Against Fascism, War and Violence, and for Peace and Human Rights*. It was finally completed in 1986. From the outset it was clear that the piece could not be a mere message or propaganda image: instead, the artists devised a 40-foot (14.6 m) hollow aluminium pillar covered with lead, on whose lower section passers-by could make an inscription with a steel point. Periodically the pillar was lowered into the ground and a new surface exposed, until being entirely buried except for its top surface at the end of 1993. Meanwhile, the column was covered with graffiti of all shades, including erasures, complaints, messages of hope and desperation. The *Hamburger Rundschau* characterised the resulting marks of "approval, hatred, anger, and stupidity" as "a fingerprint of our city applied to the column." In a later project conceived at the interface "between the real and its reproduction," Gerz executed with the help of students from the Ecole des Beaux-Arts in Saarebrücken a *Monument Against Racism*. It consisted of names of Jewish cemeteries inscribed on the undersides of the paved cobbles of an ordinary square (FIG. 98). The monument was lent added trenchancy by being situated below Saarebrücken Castle, once a Gestapo headquarters but now a local museum. In both projects, Gerz withholds representation as such, or rather buries it. He enumerates by naming; yet he also wants to perpetuate the "violence of naming" as a function of the public monument. Insisting at Saarebrücken on both horizontality and

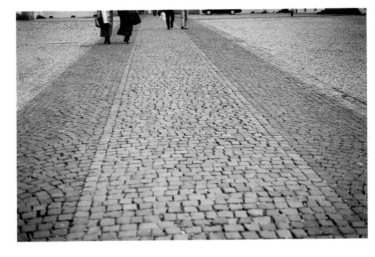

on the "absence of presence" – both hallmarks of the Conceptualist art-work – this particular counter-monument attracted fierce political controversy before becoming a kind of tourist site despite itself.

A heavy dependence upon writing and upon horizontality is a shared preoccupation of the American artist, Jenny Holzer. Holzer came to public art after a brief phase as an abstract painter, though she remembers reading *The Fox* as a student, and realising that not all art need be heroic, or sublime, or an object. Enrolling in the Whitney Museum's Independent Study Programme in 1976-77, Holzer recalls how she was handed a voluminous booklist – unreadable through sheer size – which stimulated the production of a series of one-line written statements hovering somewhere between philosophical profundity and folksy wisdom that she came to call "Truisms": "A LITTLE KNOWLEDGE CAN GO A LONG WAY," "CHILDREN ARE THE CRUELEST OF ALL," "ABUSE OF POWER COMES AS NO SURPRISE," and the like, which she ordered alphabetically and paraded anonymously on posters throughout New York. Courting affinities with advertising and public service announcements, in a tone

98. JOCHEN GERZ
2146 stones – Monument Against Racism,
Saarebrücken, 1990-93.
Photograph by Esther Shalev-Gerz.

By night, Gerz and his students lifted cobbles in small batches, replacing them with fakes while the real ones were inscribed with the names of cemeteries, to a total of 2146. Carried out clandestinely, the work was nevertheless officially sanctioned after a debate in the local parliament, while the square itself was renamed *Square of the Invisible Monument.*

both effortlessly pragmatic and frighteningly official, the series launched a welter of further projects in which Holzer, like the Conceptualists before her, forged images principally out of words.

Like most public artists alive to the possibilities of Conceptualism, Holzer has migrated from the urban space to the gallery and back, as if only thus could contact with an avant-gardist crucible or testing-ground be sustained. In a sequence of messages beamed from a Spectacolour board in Times Square, New York, in 1982, suggestive truths such as "FATHERS OFTEN USE TOO MUCH FORCE" OR "TORTURE IS BARBARIC" were purveyed to an extensive, if passing, audience. For the American pavilion at the 1990 Venice Biennale, Holzer designed a series of rooms clad sumptuously in marble, in which flanking benches, also in marble, carried inscriptions, while LED (light-emitting diode) displays on the walls summoned up in several languages the aura of a quiet devotional space for a minority celebrant clientele (FIG. 99). Despite enormous media attention and an apparently eclectic audience for her signs, what has been at issue in the more specialised critical appraisal of Holzer's work has been the extent of her familiarity with the traditions and possibilities of epigraphy. The critic Stephen Bann has compared Holzer

99. JENNY HOLZER
Venice Installation,
American Pavilion, Venice
Biennale, 1990. Photograph
by David Regan.

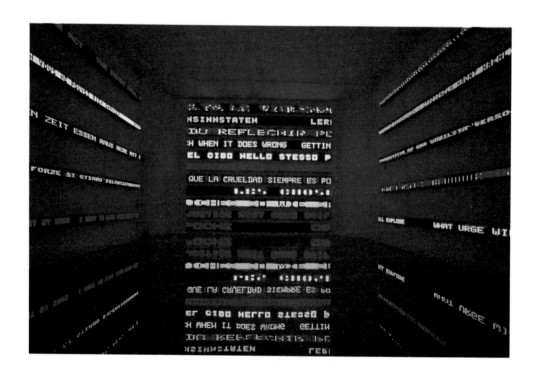

unfavourably with the Californian painter Ed Ruscha, and the Scottish sculptor Ian Hamilton Finlay, and has questioned the extent to which the spread of her epigrammic style to T-shirts, limited-edition LED sign-boards and inscribed sarcophagi in effect undermines and banalises the ambitious reanimation of public space which her better works promote. What cannot be denied is that the range of Holzer's syntax has been considerable, veering from the terse philosophical one-liner to the vernacular graffito-type throwaway, from the authoritative-sounding public announcement to commercial signage, from headline journalism to gossip. In this sense if in no other, her projects have drawn attention to the anecdotal power of language as a ubiquitous feature of the contemporary public realm.

All these projects are marked by the artist's need to abandon traditional materials of memorialisation or representation and to proceed as if only new techniques and locations will suffice for the kinds of subtle dissent of which the most powerful contemporary art is capable. Certainly, the idea of the counter-monument gives the lie to the notion that 1960s radicalism has withered and died. The critique of institutions implicit in the best recent work has removed from serious question whether art objects inevitably fall prey to museumisation or the market process. The impulses born of Conceptual art, to keep one step ahead of the acquisitive hand of power and to resist becoming the mere "good taste" of the culture industry, have continued to animate a sort of vestigial counter-culture even as it offers itself up to inevitable capture by power itself.

The contradiction of post-Conceptual radicalism in a new home – the vastly expanded museum network for contemporary art, managed by curators bent on reconciling subversive aesthetic intentions with public awareness and approval – is an undeniably rich one, in whose capacious scope a high proportion of the most challenging contemporary art has come to realisation. Yet in the early 1990s a vital shift began to occur, one that posed challenges to the Duchampian or Conceptualist tradition. First visible in 1985 or earlier, this shift has taken the form of an unexpected return to overt reference, iconography, and symbolism; further, it has attempted to attune itself to issues of race, ethnicity, and the body that once lay beyond the institutional setting of art. Always prepared to defy widespread social beliefs and customs, this work – for which "narrative" may be the key formal term – strongly suggests that the Conceptualist tradition may now be subject to pressures of an altogether unfamiliar kind.

Sometimes I come to hate people because they can't see who I am. I've gone empty, completely empty and all they see is the visual form; my arms and legs, my face, my height and posture; the words that come from my throat. But I'm fucking empty. The person I was just one year ago no longer exists; drifts spinning slowly into the sutphere somewhere way back there. I'm a xerox of my former self. I can't abstract my own dying any longer. I am a stranger to others and to myself and I refuse to pretend that I am familiar or that I have history attached to my heels. I am glass, clear empty glass. I see the world spinning behind and through me. I see the sutralness and mundane effect of gesture made by constant repetitions. I look familiar but I am a complete stranger being. All I can see are the familiar selves. I am a stranger and I am moving. I am moving on two legs soon to be on all fours. I am no longer animal vegetable or mineral. I am no longer made of circuits or disks. I am no longer coded and deciphered. I am all emptiness and futility. I am an empty stranger, a carbon copy of my form. I can no longer find what I'm looking for outside of myself. It doesn't exist out there. Maybe it's only in here, inside my head. But my head is glass and my eyes have stopped being cameras, the tape has run out and nobody's words can touch me. No gesture can touch me. I've been dropped into all this from another world and I can't speak your language any longer. See the signs I try to make with my hands and fingers, see the vague movements of my lips among the sheets. I'm a blank spot in a hectic civilization. I'm a dark smudge in the air that dissipates without notice. I feel like a window, maybe a broken window. I am a glass human. I am a glass human disappearing in rain. I am standing among all of you waving my invisible arms and hands. I am shouting my invisible words. I am getting so weary. I am growing tired. I am waving to you from here. I am crawling and looking for the aperture of complete and final emptiness. I am vibrating in isolation among you. I am screaming but it comes out like pieces of clear ice. I am signalling that the volume of all this is too high. I am waving. I am waving my hands. I am disappearing. I am disappearing but not fast enough.

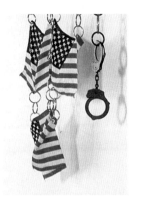

FIVE

Narrating Identity: the early 1990s

100. DAVID WOJNAROWICZ
Untitled, 1992. Silkscreen
on silver print, edition of 4,
38 x 26" (96.5 x 66 cm).

The text on this work
begins: "Sometimes I come
to hate people because they
can't see where I am. I've
gone empty, completely
empty and all they see is
the visual form, my arms
and legs, my face, my
height and posture, the
sounds that come from my
throat. But I'm fucking
empty. The person I was
just one year ago no longer
exists; drifts spinning slowly
into the ether somewhere
way back there."

A change in the practice and theory of art that has occurred in the past few years has involved a re-introduction of the image into made forms. This may sound uncontentious: since all art is at one level image, what significance could the emphasis (or suppression) of the image possibly have? Yet the change in question has confronted the Conceptualist tradition with a profound alternative, based on iconographical enrichment, overt reference to external forms of life, even an illusion of theatre in which the spectator is involved. In calling this impulse "narrative," I refer primarily to its embrace of imagery that originates in mass culture, takes its connotations to the fields of bodily experience, personal and racial identity, and by importing "meaning" directly occludes the strategies of the ready-made in most of its classic or recent forms. The most graphic contrast is with Duchampian art which proposes a critique of ideas of *art* – institutional, authorial, or managerial – by means of devices of art alone.

The Body and AIDS

Narrative art overflows with speech-like activities such as telling, indicating, suggesting. A recent work of the American Robert Gober, for example, though taking a Minimalist, generally circular form, solicits the observer's attention at every turn and by every means (FIG. 101). There is imagery of a dog basket, an absent dog, a sheet on which images of a sleeping white man and a hanged black man appear. The white basket itself is homely and familiar, some three-and-a-half feet (111 cm) across, suggesting a large and perhaps unfriendly occupant. Far from

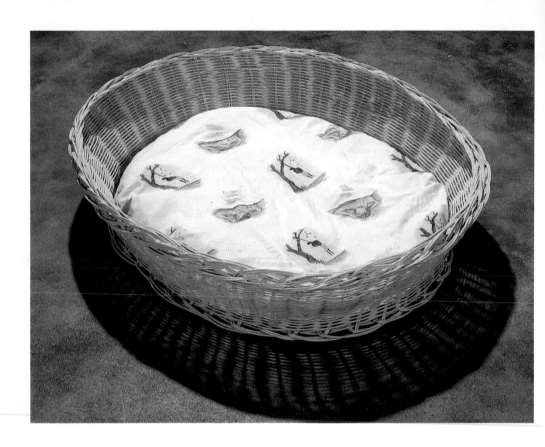

101. ROBERT GOBER
Untitled, 1988. Rattan,
flannel, enamel, and fabric
paints, 10 x 38 x 44″ (25 x
96 x 111 cm). Collection
Jacob and Ruth Bloom,
Los Angeles.

Gober says: "It's such a
good image...because it
yields so many different
responses about what's
happening. And then
something's literally
missing in the story, if you
look at it as a story – and
you kind of have to. You
have to supply that: what
was the crime, what really
happened, what's the
relationship between these
two men."

sparking off a discourse about art as a category, the museum, or
sculpture's past, Gober's work frames associations with violence,
race, America, domesticity, and perhaps death. On hearing that
words like "homely" and "homespun" were being applied to his
work (intended moreover as derogatory, feminised words)
Gober pointed out that this was exactly his purpose. He cites an
entire generation of American women as his mentors: Cindy
Sherman, Jenny Holzer, Barbara Kruger, Sherrie Levine. Their
work is "meaty yet popular, enjoyable yet erudite," he has said.
For him, most male artists provided poor examples to follow.

Gober's deliberate feminising of art through iconography
points to the fact that an effective way to the concept of "narrative" is through the sensibility and self-image of the male gay
community. It is too seldom noticed that the post-Modernist
tradition in America and elsewhere – a tradition kick-started in
the later 1950s by Jasper Johns, Robert Rauschenberg, and Andy
Warhol – was based not simply on differences of life-style, but
on emphatic rejection of male, heterosexual Modernist aesthetics
and the various concepts of "expression" that went with it. Pop

art provided the first camouflage for this post-Modernism, and it was Pop art that Modernist critics roundly condemned. As far back as 1968 Leo Steinberg had said of the "flat-bed" or "all-purpose picture plane" of Rauschenberg and Warhol that it had "made the course of art once again non-linear and unpredictable." It had implied "a change in the relationship between artist and image, image and viewer" that was "part of a shake-up which contaminates all purified categories" (he meant those imposed by Greenberg and Michael Fried).

Although prefigured in the 1970s and even before, 1982-84 can be seen as the moment both of the flowering of a feminised post-Modernism and of the nascent emancipation of gay consciousness itself. Some of the terms of this emancipation were captured in a panel discussion that followed the *Extended Sensibilities* exhibition in New York at the end of 1982. In that discussion Bertha Harris (author of *Confessions of Cherubino, Catching Saradove,* and *Lover*) accused the "heterosexual appetite for usefulness" of persistently reinforcing "connections with history, inheritance, antecedents, friends, neighbours, tribes, and so forth, and in so doing giving us the illusion that a future exists." The singular privilege of the homosexual sensibility was "to make things stop happening." Harris suggested that the gay artist or writer cleaves to two principal decisions: "first, that reality is interesting only when it is distorted, and second, that reality lacks interest because it is controlled by usefulness which is pertinent only to the heterosexual continuum. The positive decision our hypothetical artist makes is to attach himself or herself to the inexpedient and impertinent." Edmund White (author of *A Boy's Own Story* and *The Beautiful Room is Empty*), though denying that "gay" was an ahistorical or trans-social construct, sought to define heterosexual tastes in terms of understatement mixed with control, of preachiness combined with a tendency to conformity. Affluent, white, male gay taste he characterised in terms of ornamentation, an interest in the luxurious proliferation of detail, an oblique angle of vision, fantasy, theatricality, and "in terms of content, an interest in, and an identification with, the underdog."

The irony of such identifications in 1982 lay in the fact that its terms were just about to undergo a tragic change of resonance. The emergence of AIDS in San Francisco, Los Angeles, and New

102. Protest march through New York City on the 24 June 1990 against the inactivity of the American government in taking steps to combat the spread of AIDS.

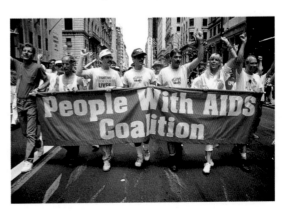

York in 1981, its official recognition in 1982 and its rapid spread thereafter, meant that several members of the American art community were forced to reconsider the relation between art and "content" in a new light. Harris's identification of "a human as well as an aesthetic need for risk" in homosexual and lesbian artists assumed particular unwanted meanings. A new mood of activism suddenly prevailed (FIG. 102). The New York gay art community, eloquently championed by the critic Douglas Crimp, called for education programmes, non-discriminatory advertising, medical and social support agencies, and a recognition of the ways in which gay men and women had become ritually displaced as an audience for art. Not only was the interface between politics and art now rapidly changing, but the identification and description of gender within art-political discussion was evolving quickly too.

A further consequence of the AIDS crisis in America – it has not devastated the European art community in anything like the same degree – was a desire, for the most part unstated, to put the prescriptions of left-wing and Conceptualist theory, identified as male, academic, white, and heterosexual, to one side. The experiences and images of the body, as opposed to the materials and

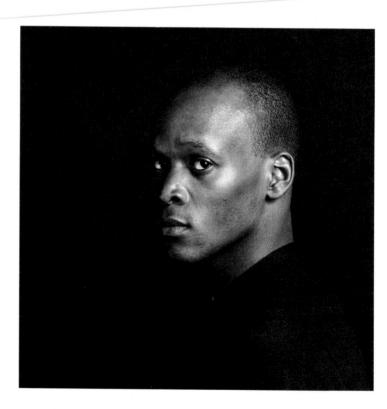

103. ROBERT MAPPLETHORPE
Don Cann, 1981. Black and white photograph.

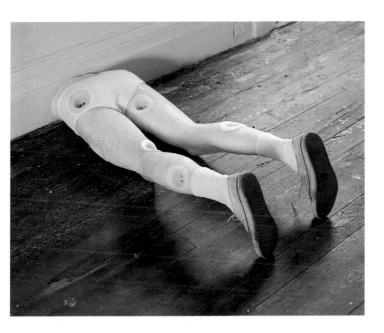

104. ROBERT GOBER
Untitled, 1991-93. Wood, wax, human hair, fabric, fabric painting, shoes, 11 x 17 x 44$\frac{1}{2}$" (28 x 43 x 113 cm). Museum für Moderne Kunst, Frankfurt.

devices of representation, became, in such circumstances, perhaps the dominant general concern among younger artists at the time.

The spectrum of work identified with the gay community and its desire for non-stereotypical visibility now ranged from Robert Mapplethorpe's celebratory photo-works of the male anatomy or the portrait head (FIG. 103) – work described by Edmund White as having "ended the invisibility of blacks" – to Robert Gober's more recent pieces simulating body-parts in beeswax and placed in unexpected positions within the gallery space (FIG. 104). Frequently decorated with candles or impregnated with plastic "drains," the pieces resonate with a sense of the body's vulnerable, prostrate, and potentially hospitalised condition. "There was the butt with music, the butt with drains and the butt with candles," Gober said recently, "and they seemed to present a trinity of possibilities from pleasure to disaster to resuscitation."

Before his death from AIDS in 1992, the artist and writer David Wojnarowicz became identified with a defiant dismantling of dominant images of gays as libertines or corpses and with vociferous opposition to government inactivity in face of the epidemic. In *Untitled* (1992), he directly identifies the bandaged outstretched hands of a beggar with those of a crippled and hence marginalised AIDS-infected artist in need of care (see FIG. 100, page 143). The covering text, from the chapter "Spiral" in Wojnarowicz's book *Memories That Smell Like Gasoline*, ends:

"I am shouting my invisible words. I am getting so weary. I am growing tired. I am waving to you from here. I am crawling and looking for the aperture of complete and final emptiness. I am vibrating in isolation among you. I am screaming but it comes out like pieces of clear ice. I am signalling that the volume of all this is too high. I am waving. I am waving my hands. I am disappearing. I am disappearing but not fast enough." Like Gober's, Wojnarowicz's art is unashamed about narrative, imagery and the signified, and is prepared to mobilise sign-systems explicitly in order to comment directly on prominent issues of the day.

West-Coast post-Modernism

The referent itself, as opposed to the politics of the signifier, had long been a conspicuous focus of interest among fringe cultures such as those of Chicago or the American West Coast. Gay artists in San Francisco and Los Angeles in particular have effortlessly accommodated themselves to the narrative drift – and in their own inimitable way. A show such as *Helter Skelter: LA Art in the 1990s*, held in Los Angeles early in 1992, set out to celebrate what its organisers called "the darker side of contemporary life," the visions of "alienation, obsession, dispossession or perversity typical of the City". Associated too with a depraved *fin-de-siècle*, Los Angeles art was now represented as in thrall to apocalyptical scenarios of necrophiliac sex, fantasy violence,

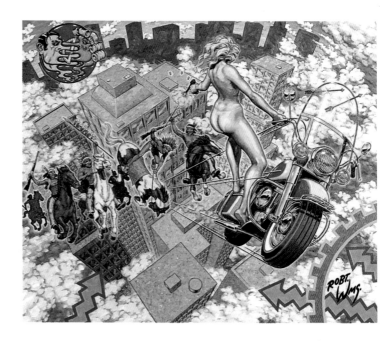

105. ROBERT WILLIAMS *Mathematics Takes a Holiday. Scholastic Designation: The Physics of Relative Motion Brings the Victim to the Bullet as the Ratio of Abstraction is Always Altered in Favour of Those Who Find It to their Advantage to Judge the Moon as a Hole in the Sky. Remedial Title: Piss-Pot Pete's Daughter Soils Apache Loincloths on a Jabberwocky Trajectory,* 1991. Oil on canvas, 3'4" x 3'10" (1 x 1.2 m). Collection Robert and Tamara Bane, Los Angeles.

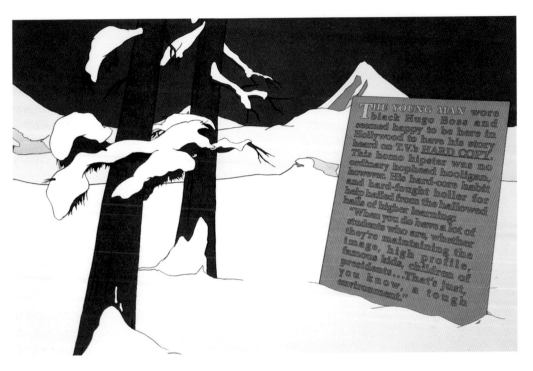

THE YOUNG MAN wore
black Hugo Boss and
seemed happy to be here in
Hollywood to have his story
heard on T.V.'s HARD COPY.
This homo hipster was no
ordinary hophead hooligan,
however. His hard-core habit
and hard-fought holler for
help hailed from the hallowed
halls of higher learning.
"When you do have a lot of
students who are, whether
they're maintaining the
image, high profile,
famous kids, children of
presidents...That's just,
you know, a tough
environment."

drug-induced alienation, or plain fear. The writings of Benjamin Weissman and Dennis Cooper are symptomatic. The paintings of an artist like Robert Williams (FIG. 105), who worked on hot-rod customising and Zap Comix in the late 1960s before coming to art, can be distinguished from their comic-book sources mainly by their commitment to visual and narrative overload, functioning as a formal counterpart to that disorientation and exoticism that West Coast artists have liked to call their own. Other varieties of apocalypticism from the Los Angeles region can be found in the art of the Philippine-born Manuel Ocampo, the performance and video art of Paul McCarthy, and in the cynical collage meditations on the institutionalised violence of corporation, church and state by Llyn Foulkes.

A very different narrative tendency, one that has stemmed in part from a West Coast gay sensibility and in part from the California Institute of the Arts, where many of the artists trained, has been an interest in teenage aesthetics: the work of Larry Johnson, Raymond Pettibon, Jim Shaw, and some aspects of the work of Mike Kelley. To look at Larry Johnson's recent work is to be made aware of various ironic levels of engagement with Hollywood animation language (specifically the Disney tradition), and of the use of verbal texts in an engaging but deeply inauthentic register (FIG. 106). The verbal rhyming, the graphic

106. LARRY JOHNSON
Untitled Negative (H),
1991. Ektacolor print, 5'1"
x 7' (1.5 x 2.1 m).

Like Warhol, but with greater menace, Johnson is interested not in emotion but in "the precepts that accompany emotion: the confession, the self-explanation, the release, the testimonial, the testimony, the things that have come to signify what is meaningful," rather than the supposedly meaningful in itself.

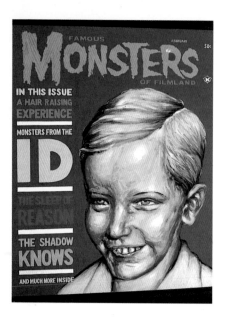

107. JIM SHAW
Billy's Self-Portrait, panel
from *My Mirage* narrative,
1987-91. Gouache on board,
17 x 14" (43 x 35.5 cm).

style, and the visual scenarios of Johnson's scenes all index a sub-teenage world of fantasy adventure, glib jokes, and mindless absorption in advertising messages. Johnson's works in this genre come in sequences, each one apparently more "inconsequential" than the last. Johnson is in favour of art that can be "got" in "about the same time as it takes to read a daily horoscope or beauty tip."

Or take Raymond Pettibon, who in repeated small panels employs a range of graphic effects from comic-book drawing to produce stereotypes of travel, heroism, detection, mystery, and other stock situations of popular action strips. Despite the familiarity of his source materials and the apparent banality of his "stories," Pettibon's scenes and narratives are, in fact, slightly skewed. Portentous, half-formed thoughts, verging at one extreme on the existential or metaphysical (re-written *bonsmots* of the likes of Ruskin and Hawthorne) and at the other on the interior monologue, litter his drawings. Jim Shaw, who completes the trio, seems to sink back into the *Saturday Evening Post* ethos of the 1960s: his *My Mirage* narrative of 1987-91 utilised what he called "as many aesthetics of the period as could be crammed in." In the panels which compose the piece, Billy the protagonist grows up a Christian, but runs the gauntlet of secular temptation only to seek innocence again in psychedelia, having read about it in *Time* and watched it on CBS (FIG. 107). But in revulsion against these new forms of depravity, Billy becomes a born-again Christian in a vain attempt for innocence. In the same work, Shaw has teenagers aimlessly speculating about the anti-heroes who absorb their free time: Donovan, Frank Zappa, Timothy Leary, and the like. Mildly flirting with involvement in drugs and other minor forms of criminality, Shaw knows (and knows that we know) that his characters are merely acting out rituals of fairly innocuous resistance to the social system to which they belong.

Given that "youth culture" has constituted one of Western civilisation's most potent inventions since the 1950s, it is somewhat surprising that its actual mores (as opposed to its advertised qualities) did not surface more fully in culture before. Though its ostensible content is puerilism and miscreancy, however, the aesthetic strategies of this art are themselves neither puerile nor miscreant. From the messy, adolescent confusions of Jim Shaw's Billy or Larry Johnson's camp nostalgia to other explorations such as the painful world of sexual discovery delineated in Larry Clark's photo-essay, *Teenage Lust* (1975), or the world of the cowboy junkie in his *Tulsa* (1971), or the transgressive biking and clubland gangs of Richard Prince's recent work – the whole pubescent panoply has established a certain *verité* in the face of disapproving grown-up certainties more regularly applied to art. For one thing, camp is no longer apolitical, even if Warhol might have claimed so. Secondly, the new puerilism signifies ever more urgently how artifice is the key term in dominant constructions of all social and sexual identities. More cynical and worldly than most of Pop art – its protagonists are well into their thirties or forties – puerilism may be credited with a thoroughly adult understanding of the ironic tone. It has discovered an unexplored arena of "primitivism," eroticism, and perversity rolled into one. Its attention to adolescence as a transitional phase between childhood and adulthood may even be seen eventually to have prepared the ground for similar incursions into the hidden subversive agendas of the middle-aged or the very old.

An interest in narrative stemming from a non-straight and post-Modernist sensibility is not, of course, confined to particular sexual identities, media, or topics of interest. Like the first-generation gay art of Johns, Rauschenberg, and Warhol, the discoveries of a new and once marginal sensibility have fanned out widely into Western culture in a process that may be seen as inherently free-ranging and unpredictable. An examination of personal and social positioning – fictionalised or real – has frequently occupied centre-stage. For example, the fascination with identity just described has migrated from the rectangular wall-picture to the more disordered formalities of the installation genre in the work of Mark Dion, Jack Pierson, Laurie Parsons, and Karen Kilimnik, as well as across a wider international field.

Installation and the déclassé

Installation – the idea descends from Dada and Surrealism and re-emerges in Fluxus, Conceptual art, and other radical movements such as German sculpture of the 1980s – involves guiding attention away from singular objects onto complexes and relations structured within the viewing space itself, where that space is now taken as a physical context rather than as a neutral background for the work.

The narrating of social and private identities has proved highly amenable to the installation form, since the installation can fictionalise a space in a way that singular objects seldom can.

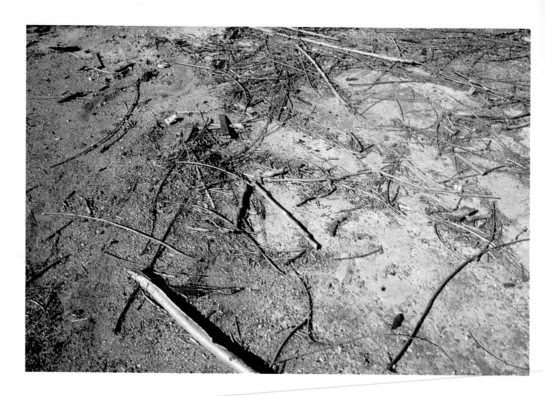

108. LAURIE PARSONS
Stuff, 1988. Branches,
rocks, debris, etc., 16" x
1200' square (40.6 cm x
365 m square). No longer
extant.

Stuff hovers ambiguously
between a project that was
never finished, and a
document. Parsons says that
"it was just a photograph of
an outdoor spread of
natural material. I did
collect the whole tableau,
but then it was
inadvertently discarded
from the space where I had
been keeping it." She adds:
"sooner or later I would
have done so anyway, I'm
pretty sure."

The preoccupation with teenagedom drifts inexorably towards a fascination with dirty and over-used goods in the group of works illustrated here. What this art does is well exemplified by Laurie Parsons' loose assemblies of random or cast-off materials which take into three dimensions many of the adolescent concerns that the picture-makers were scouting in two. Photographing random collections of debris or already familiar scenes, such as her own bedroom, "as thoughts, forays, whatever," Parsons lodges the resulting slides with her dealer, but only sometimes counts them as art (FIG. 108). For a show in New York in 1988 she exhibited her own desk, littered with the usual papers in disarray – but in the back room, not in the gallery space. As the critic Jack Bankowsky has pointed out, it's more or less the world of Richard Linklater's 1991 film, *Slacker*, the world of the "pre-semester doldrums of a middle-American university town," in which slackers – drifting student types grouped aimlessly around a series of cultish interests – "worship at their own jerry-built altars and proselytise for a private religion," for whom "anarchy percolates...but never exceeds a slow boil." In a similar spirit, a 1991 installation by Jack Pierson entitled *One Man's Opinion of Moonlight* ushered the audience into a simulated bohemian walk-up, replete with a junk drawer full of what junk drawers are typically full of – empty match-boxes, coasters, a dead battery and some pencils. But if Pierson has lived within the image-system of the aimless bohemian, drinker or uncoordinated student type, Parsons has cultivated a life-style of *faux-naïf* "honesty" that she wants to have counted as art. Telling us that she wants to make art beyond the gallery, evade the institutions of art, re-encounter the real – all vanguard attitudes of the 1960s if not before – she offers striking opportunities for negotiating a practice to one side of, but still within, the art institutions she so evidently doubts.

A similar appetite for the half-finished within the compass of an adolescent life is to be found in the recent installations of Karen Kilimnik. Her "slack art" takes the form of specific re-creations of possible events that never (presumably) quite happened. One enters a disordered space in which, apparently, something either has happened or is about to happen. Objects and surfaces are at their neglected, unswept worst, covered with trash and neglect (FIG. 109). Such installations can be read autobiographically: "I'm such a slob," says Kilimnik, "everything seems destined to wind up on the floor as though I was too lazy to pick up whatever it is." Better, they can be read as the artist's response to glamour-stars and their super-charged lifestyles – in this case Madonna – from the point of view of someone who has just missed the show. Yet to describe Kilimnik's installations this way is to position oneself as spectator of the static theatre presented. It is to accept the objects and remnants displayed at face value, in terms of the story they suggest or the real-life scenario they simulate. It is to acknowledge that theatricality – the *bête*

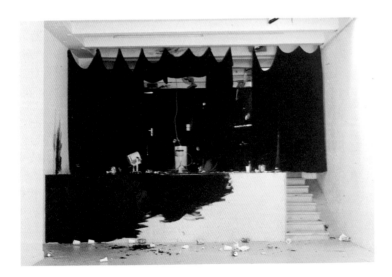

109. KAREN KILIMNIK *Madonna and Backdraft in Nice*, 1991. Fog machine, black velvet, fish line, flashlight, fireman's helmet, 2 hats, cellophane, photographs, electric fan, and cassette tape. Dimensions variable. Installation at the Villa Arson, Nice.

noire of formalist Modernists in the 1960s – has developed to the point at which narrative is constructed explicitly as illusion, as in the theatre, but with all the iconographical richness that a static tableau allows.

Slack art in its generality works against idealisation. Given its preoccupation with the unfinished and the second-hand, it can also be construed as a reworking of the mechanisms of viewer expectation. For slack art works on the basis of a twin strategy of fascination and disappointment: fascination at the prospect of observing someone else's deserted projects or their personal junk (that most intimate of residues), but simultaneously disappointment at the realisation that as artistic spectacle it is degraded or incomplete.

Most slack art can be seen as a rejection of the appropriation aesthetics of Koons, Bickerton, and Steinbach which launched a meditation on the commercially and glossily new. Even the physically more threatening tableaux of another American, Cady Noland, fall under this latter description. When Noland re-arranges the props and devices of sporting events, police investigations, and nationalist emblems such as the American flag, she evokes a realm of personalised violence that seems somehow redolent of the mid-West or Southern states (FIG. 110). Yet the effectiveness of her pieces lies in her taking the hard paraphernalia of containment – aluminum, galvanised steel, and iron – and bringing them abruptly into (and against) the spatial vehicle of the gallery with a startling confidence that gains from their very unsuitability as "art."

110. CADY NOLAND
The Big Shift, 1989. Mixed media including pole, grille, rings, flags, bug sprayer, bungee cord, handcuffs, 5'6" x 14' x 6" (1.6 m x 4.2 m x 15 cm). Collection Jeffrey Deitch.

In such pieces Noland loosely incorporates "redneck" objects such as handcuffs and flags with a deceptive informality suggestive of what a *New York Times* critic called "the struggles and emotional vacancy of the American heartland, especially its Southern half."

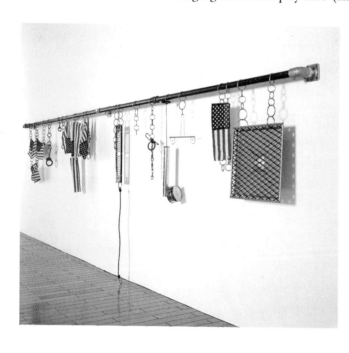

In one regard an aesthetics of disappointment can be traced to Robert Smithson's *Artforum* writings of the 1960s. In an essay entitled "Entropy and the New Monuments" Smithson voiced a pioneering admiration for "disrupted and pulverized" sites far away from the neatly curated spaces of the city centre. "Near the super highways surrounding the city," Smithson wrote, "we find the discount centres and cut-rate stores with their sterile façades...the lugubrious complexity of their interiors has brought to art a new consciousness of the vapid and the dull." Such a consciousness was successfully evoked for Smithson in the "monumentally inactive" contemporary works of Robert Morris and Sol LeWitt; but it resonates equally in the new art of the slacker.

In both, arguably, the situation of the spectator is frequently problematised in ways that have little to do with the work's overt content. In Mike Kelley's installations, for example, one is sometimes at a loss to know whether the "vapid and dull" is interesting at all: that, indeed, is their interest.

Kelley also belongs to a generation of middle-aged artists who mobilise an adolescent sensibility to mock middle-class rituals of religious piety, family, and official history as symptoms of adult rationality. A work of 1988 entitled *Pay For Your Pleasure* has a series of crudely painted banners depicting forty-two writers, artists, and philosophers (of the order of Baudelaire, Goethe, Degas, and Sartre) which bear quotations to the effect that genius is outside the law. To emphasise the link between creativity and criminality, Kelley then arranged these banners along a corridor that led to a final amateur work by a local criminal-turned-artist: for the Chicago showing, a self-portrait by the Illinois mass child-murderer, John Wayne Gacey, dressed as Pogo the Clown; for Los Angeles, the freeway killer, William Bonin; for Berlin's *Metropolis*, the murderer Wolfgang Zocha. A collection-box near the door solicited donations for victims' rights groups.

111. MIKE KELLEY *Craft Morphology, Flow Chart*, 1991. Thirteen groups of tables with 113 soft toys and black and white photographs. Installation at the Carnegie Museum of Art, Pittsburgh, 1991-92.

Another of Kelley's recent tactics has been to display soiled soft toys from the playpen in various guises: stitched into a wall-hung tapestry, mounted against each other in situations of mock-violence or playful ambiguity, or simply positioned on a table top (FIG. 111). "I try to present the wear and tear of the prototype and not romanticise it," says Kelley, "because there's nothing I hate more than romantic, nostalgic art... My work is perched between nostalgic assemblage artists on

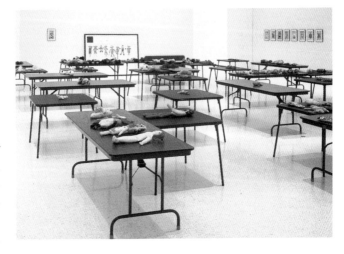

the one side and this classical commodity art on the other side. It's not about idealisation." It is possible to read Kelley's various tableaux in terms of what they ostensibly refer to: childhood toys as evocations of nursery memories, blankets as reminiscent of the playpen. But his work is increasingly understood as an allegory of adult projections embodied in toy manufacture and use. Kelley makes the point that the doll as the perfect image of the child becomes feared and rejected – hence repressed – when dirty. It begins to speak of abuse and neglect, even becoming demonised as an unwanted presence. The myth of childhood innocence lies at the origin of the process: in modern, developed culture, says Kelley, "the doll pictures the person as a commodity more than most. By virtue of that, it's also the most loaded in regard to the politics of wear and tear."

On another level Kelley's trangressions are attacks on the taste and assumptions of avant-garde art itself: the Duchampian ready-made is deployed with deliberate lack of grace. Significantly, too, Kelley rails against the high-mindedness of classic Modernism, especially its unresolvable dichotomy between abstraction (Mondrian) and expressiveness (Matisse), which Kelley transcends by appeal to low-art cartooning, grotesquerie, and various paradigms of the feminine. Minimal art – one of Kelley's central targets – is described by him as "reductive, essentially heroic primal forms [which] lend themselves easily to the role of the authority figure. Thus it is only right that we should want to defame them." Minimal art, he says, is "something that needs to be pissed on."

Installation has also proved a notable feature of some East European art of the period. Ilya Kabakov had been a leading Moscow Conceptualist in the 1970s and at that time composed wry "albums" recording the life-progress of characters whose private identities were markedly at odds with their designated social ones. Kabakov was also one of the founders of Collective Actions, who from the mid-1970s performed Minimalist or "empty" performances in remote locations in reaction against the poorly cultivated life of the cities.

Kabakov's first journey outside the Soviet Union took him to Czechoslovakia in 1981, the year of his celebrated essay "On Emptiness," and the beginning of his *Ten Characters* series that would last for most of the decade. There followed a group of installations such as *The Man Who Flew Into Space from His Apartment* (1988), which reconstructed the domestic remnants of a man who confronts an identity crisis by catapulting himself into space through the roof of his cramped quarters in a communal dwelling house. Such works share with Western slack art the authentic detail of the human trace, from which the human presence has departed and from which a nostalgic reverie of loss and

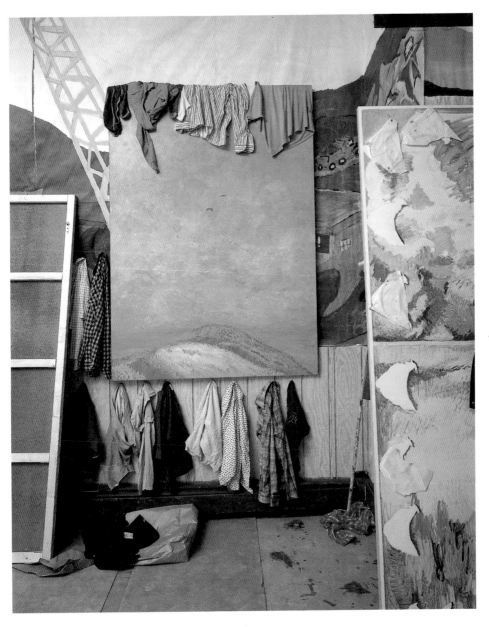

transience can arise. Kabakov is eloquent on the possibilities of the installation genre. "By its very nature," he says, "it may unite – *on equal terms*, without recognition of supremacy – anything at all, and most of all phenomena and concepts that are extraordinarily far from one another. Here, politics may be combined with the kitchen, objects of everyday use with scientific objects, garbage with sentimental effusions." In a multi-part work of 1990, Kabakov constructed an explicit story out of the props and

112. Ilya Kabakov
*He Lost His Mind,
Undressed, Ran Away
Naked*, 1990.

113. AIMEE MORGANA
The *Ecstasy* series, 1986-87.
Installation view at the
Postmasters Gallery, New
York.

A viewer peeps into the box
entitled *Perversity*,
containing scented silk
flowers, amethysts, and
other exotica coloured
purple, while listening to a
David Bowie song on a set
of headphones. Echoing
Huysmans's novel *Against
Nature*, as well as
Duchamp's *Precision
Optics*, Morgana's boxes
exploit the self-awareness of
the viewer as voyeur as well
as providing a panoply of
rich sensory effects.

devices of art. The viewer walked into a crowded, labyrinthine space inhabited by large-format paintings of "happy" Communist life such as a construction site and a camp for pioneers. They were placed, however, in "terrible disorder in two rows," Kabakov explained (FIG. 112). "On some of them for some reason clothes are hanging – underclothes, socks, shirts: the paintings are partly realistic, and partly depict all kinds of plans and schedules." Texts lay nearby on a table, telling how an inhabitant of a crowded apartment "becomes tormented by the fact that he doesn't fulfil his obligations to do things at a certain time, to meet deadlines. He begins to go crazy, hanging up his clothes on these schedules and regulations, right down to his underwear. He hangs out everything that he has, then runs from his 'Red Corner' naked." Kabakov has said that the technique of installation "consists in ensuring that the viewer can never for a single moment grasp whether he is confronted by an image or a thing... in my case the game is played in such a way that the viewer cannot work out whether he is confronted by ethnography or a semiotic system...An installation is a technique of producing a critique, of constant, permanent, criticism!"

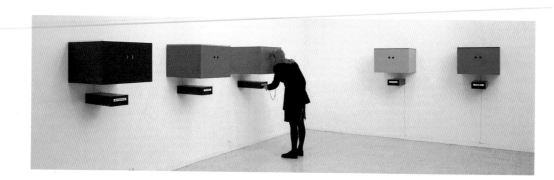

Narrating the Body

Narrative structures implicit in the installation genre have proved effective in other ways as well. What seems characteristic of Kabakov, as of Kelley, is a claustrophobic maximalisation of material, as part of a general reaction against the austerities of Minimal art. On one level this reaction constitutes a protest against the authority and logic invested by male artists and critics in reductive geometrical form. On another, it constitutes an attempt to turn Minimalism's cold formulae into bearers of "human" content, specifically the marks of the body, its social history and its biological travails.

In the *Ecstasy* series (FIG. 113), for example, Aimee Morgana (née Rankin) set up a Judd-like series of wall-boxes with peep-holes that reveal highly charged sensuous or erotic scenes on the themes of Perversity, Possession, Sadness, Sex, Fear, Suffocation, Attraction, Bliss, and Fury. Protesting against male "theory," but equally seeking a position related to that theory, Morgana has recently said that "the system of logic which models our think-ing process is showing signs of wear and tear." "Sometimes dis-course fucks me nicely and I don't begrudge myself the plea-sure," she continued. "Sometimes I like to use it to fuck it back – discourse as a sort of strap-on prosthetic dick." To vary the metaphor only slightly, her stated preference has been for "an exuberant orgy of mental gymnastics that would encourage a fluid interchange of meaning...the pleasurable rubbing of one idea against another to see what sparks fly."

When Morgana speaks of the "revolutionary power of women's laughter," one begins to understand the motivations which animate her own and other modifications to the male Minimalist cube. Debby Davis has made cubes that are anything but pure: they are cast from the forms of compressed, dead ani-mals. Extending Jackie Winsor's original "feminine" Minimalism (see FIG. 12, page 23), Liz Larner has exploited cubic and rectangular forms as containers of phials of dis-ease or as lead-and-steel boxes cov-ered with corrosive chemicals used in the manufacture of bombs. The art historian Anna Chave has written recently of male Minimalism that it embodies a rhetoric of power that in some of its more unwholesome man-ifestations aligns it with the social psychology of fascism. Spurning the strictures of "left" critics and Mod-ernist theory alike, these protests ask to reintroduce iconography, the social self, and the body, back into the conventions of inno-vative sculpture and painting.

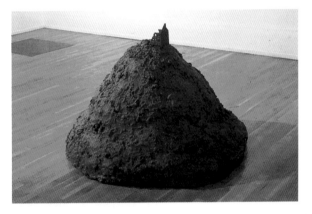

114. JOHN MILLER
Untitled, 1988. Styrofoam, wood, papier mâché, modelling paste, acrylic, 34¹/₄ x 48 x 42" (86 x 121 x 106 cm).

The sculpture depicts houses, tenements, and other buildings smeared with brown substance, atop what looks like a fetid excremental pile. Its brute disregard of traditional languages of Modernist sculpture stands for Miller's equally stern disregard for "art" in its more conventional manifestations.

An equally urgent narrativizing agenda has been followed, again internationally, in relation to the concept of the "abject body." Made articulate on a theoretical level by the publication in English of Julia Kristeva's *The Powers of Horror: An Essay on Abjection* (1982), and of Georges Bataille's *Visions of Excess: Selected Writings 1927-1939* (1985), the term connotes anything which contaminates or defiles, anything which is surplus, ejected or base, anything which evokes psychological trauma or threatens the stability of the body-image. Mike Kelley, for instance, has spoken of the prevalent "intense fear of death and anything that shows the body as a machine that has waste products or that wears down." John Miller's coprophile sculptures have attempted to organise contradictions between the ubiquitous hygiene of the gallery and evidence of the "extreme" body of a kind seldom seen since the self-immolating performances of Hermann Nitsch, Stuart Brisley, or Gina Pane in the 1960s and early 1970s, or the even earlier coprophile installations by Sam Goodman and Boris Lurie of the No! group in America in the years 1959-64 (FIG. 114).

The presence of bodily fluids – shit, piss, vomit, milk, sperm, and blood – in the recent work of the New York artist Kiki Smith has brought into focus, through narrative or iconographic vocabulary, the baleful hierarchy of the "civilised" body which

115. Sue Williams
Your Bland Essence, 1992. Acrylic and enamel on canvas, 5' x 5'8" (1.5 x 1.7 m). Regen Projects, Los Angeles.

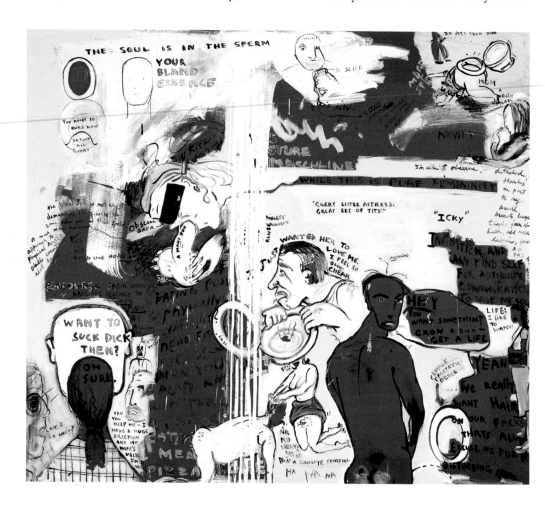

elevates the rational and functional while it represses the instinctual and emotive. Smith emphasises that our bodies are constantly "stolen from us...we have this split where we say the intellect is more important than the physical: we have this hatred of the physical." She speaks of "reclaiming one's own vehicle of being here," of "integrating the spirit and soul and physical and intellect in a kind of healing and nurturing way, even if it should mean attending to those things that the body won't easily contain." Emphasising that "women's experience is much more acutely through the body," Smith then reads that experience as a powerful social metaphor. "You're constantly changing, with a fluidity that's not to be lost," says Smith. "You're a flexible thing, not this inert definition."

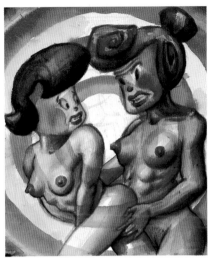

116. NICOLE EISENMAN *Betsy Gets It*, 1992. Ink on paper, 14 x 11" (35.5 x 27.9 cm).

Eisenman's mocking satires of sexual stereotypes are, like her large wall murals, impermanent. They are quickly executed images that are often "performed" shortly before a show.

In a related register, women artists have been bucking what they perceive as the over-cerebral tendencies of Conceptual art to articulate feelings of rage and frustration, particularly as (and on behalf of) victims of rape, sexual stereotyping, and homophobia. Sue Williams's painting style is that of badly drawn pictures and messages scrawled in desperation in public toilets. Her use of this *faux-naïf* graphic style is to propagate a range of current feminist concerns: the attitudes prevalent among men towards the women they profess to love, the confusions of the porn/anti-porn debate, the censorship of sexually explicit art by the National Endowment for the Arts (NEA), and other topical causes of disquiet (FIG. 115). No longer comic or ironic, but embodying the bitter voice of a rape victim in trauma, Williams's painting is a no-nonsense protest art that uses the public arena of the gallery as its billboard. It is also determinedly "ugly," as painting goes. The issue is not whether its ugliness disqualifies it as art – on the contrary, a commitment to certain kinds of ugliness has often been a precondition of art – but whether the venom of its attack is enough to prevent Williams's art from sliding back into well-mannered style. The case of the French-born lesbian artist, Nicole Eisenman, is parallel, though distinct. Her wall paintings and smaller works on paper are clearly anti-men and derisive of the art which men validate. A large mural, *The Minotaur Hunt* (1992), shows a Picassoesque minotaur, standing for aggressive male sexuality, being pleasurably hunted, forced into submission, and put to death. Eisenman's smaller drawings enlarge on illicit acts of lesbian sex (FIG. 116) or enact a merciless satire at the expense of the male member.

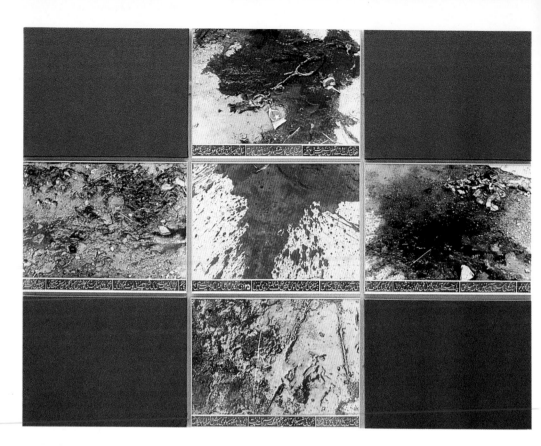

117. RASHEED ARAEEN
Green Painting I, 1984-85.
Mixed media, 9 panels,
overall 5′8″ x 7′5″ (1.7 x
2.2 m). Collection Arts
Council of Great Britain.

The Discourse of Race

A no less significant assault has come from artists concerned
with race and the politics of geography, but again from outside
the Western Duchampian tradition. That there can be no stylistic uniformity in the work of contemporary artists from India,
aboriginal Australia, or Africa must be obvious. What they
share, however, is a perception and a theorisation of how those
entering the white, urbanised NATO-centred orbit as modern
artists have renegotiated terms of recognition and legitimation
that are acceptable, not to whites, but to themselves.

The Pakistani-born Rasheed Araeen, both as an artist and as
editor of the influential journal *Third Text*, founded in 1987, has
long wrestled with his perceived marginalisation within the
British and Western art world by the employment of strategies
that are intended to destabilise the viewer's space. In *Green
Painting I* (FIG. 117), Araeen disposed four green panels (the
colour of the Pakistani flag) around photos of blood spattered
on the streets (images from a Muslim animal-slaying festival that
may also be read as references to organised political violence),

adorned with a series of Urdu newspaper headlines on Benazir Bhutto's house arrest and Richard Nixon's visit to Pakistan. The work deploys the established grid-conventions of Western Modernist abstraction, at the same time placing its ostensible content beyond the recognition-threshhold of most West European viewers. In thus courting recognition by *both* sets of observers of the *wrong* readings, Araeen points to the lip-serving and hypocritical incorporation by the West of the politics of the other, so-called "third," world. The competent spectator of such a work arguably has no single or simple identity behind which to hide. The structure and significations of the painting work to defeat it.

As Araeen has repeatedly warned in his writings, the problem lies largely not with the colonised, but with the colonisers: – the white North European and American establishment. Aesthetically, the problem dates from at least the eighteenth century and surfaced powerfully in early Modern art with the efforts of Gauguin, Picasso, and others to enact forms of "primitivism" as routes to a deeper, supposedly more authentic, consciousness. The fact that that search provides only stereotypes of the white mind's desire to escape itself – in fantasies of the "oriental," the "native," the "natural," and so forth – has now become a significant source of tension within the dominant culture everywhere.

The great curatorial attempt of the late 1980s to establish a global vision in which artists of any nation could be celebrated as contemporary was the blockbuster exhibition *Magiciens de la Terre*, mounted by Jean-Hubert Martin and Mark Francis at the Centre Georges Pompidou in Paris in 1989. Martin's declared aim to "show artists from the whole world, and to leave the ghetto of contemporary Western art where we have been shut up over these last decades," though resulting in a colourful and much-reviewed spectacle, courted the familiar danger of wielding modern-art notions forged in the West in order to recover exotic notions of "magic" perceived to be lacking at home. By placing works by artists such as Nuche Kaji Bajracharya from Nepal, Dossou Amidou from Benin, southern Nigeria (FIG. 118), Sunday Jack Akpan from Nigeria, the Inuit artist Paulosee Kuniliusee, and the Australian Northern Territory artist, Jimmy Wululu, next to already legitimated figures such as John Baldessari, Hans Haacke, and Nam June Paik, *Magiciens* invited awkward questions about the pursuit of quasi-colonialist motives in contemporary dress. As Benjamin Buchloh argued in an interview with Martin, the project ran

118. DOSSOU AMIDOU (b. 1965) *Masque*. Painted wood, 18½ x 12 x 15¾" (47 x 30 x 40 cm).

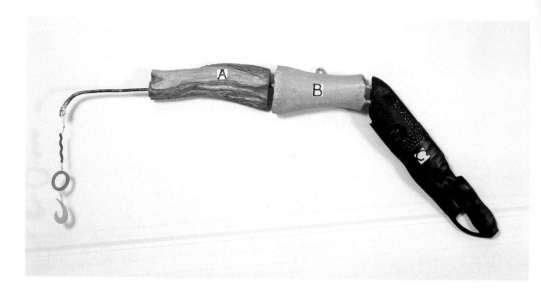

119. JIMMIE DURHAM
Wood, 1990. Acrylic paint
on wood and plastic, 18 x
54 x 3" (46 x 137 x 7 cm).
Collection Galerie
Micheline Szwajcer,
Antwerp.

Durham's laconic works
express not a Cherokee
identity, but the identity
offered to the Cherokee by
the white settler. "One of
the most terrible aspects of
our situation today is that
none of us feel that we are
authentic. We do not feel
that we are real Indians...
For the most part we feel
guilty, and try to measure
up to the white man's
definition of ourselves."

the risk of "cultural and political imperialism to request that
these [remote] cultures deliver their cultural products for our
inspection and consumption"; that it fell prey to the "cult of a
presumed authenticity which would like to force other cultural
practices to remain within the domain of what we consider the
'primitive' and the original 'other'."

The plight of artists from those nations with histories of sys-
tematic displacement by whites, such as the First Nations artists
of North America, has been especially severe. The Cherokee
artists Edgar Heap-of-Birds and Jimmie Durham have been
absorbed into the Western system, but only through a recognition of those symbols of identity in terms of which they first
became visible as artists: in Durham's case, skulls, feathers, fragments of wood and sticks, and self-effacing jokes about the body
(FIG. 119). Durham's significance, however, lies in his ability to
double-guess the hapless Western curator, who still instinctively
colonises his subject as the native "other." "Authenticity is a
racist concept," says Durham, "which functions to keep us
enclosed in 'our world' (in our place) for the comfort of a dominant society" – a society transfixed by notions of self-presence,
ownership, and the supposedly autonomous individual. Yet
"none of the words you call us by are words we call ourselves."

Attempts to salvage not a racial identity but a way of speaking about the dominant discourses that shape how identity is discussed have begun to animate marginalised artists in Canada
such as the Cree artist Jane Ash Poitras, or the Mohawk artist
Shelley Niro. Niro's work parallels that of Sherrie Levine and

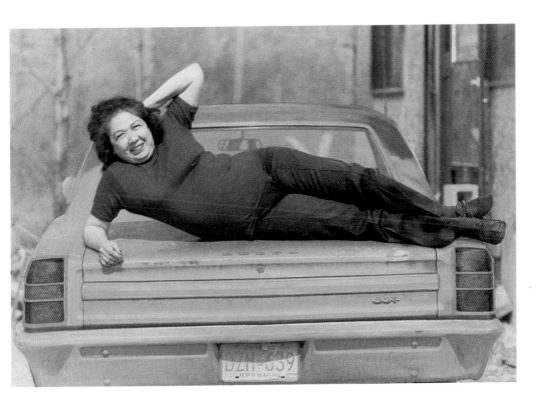

120. SHELLEY NIRO
The Rebel, 1987. Hand-tinted black and white photograph, 6½ x 9½″ (16.5 x 24 cm). Collection of the artist.

Cindy Sherman, not only formally and strategically, in using the photo-document to refuse the expectations of male culture, but also to unlock the fixed perceptions through which whites regard groups whose traditions they have replaced with their own. In *The Rebel*, Niro photographed her mother reclining sensuously on the mud-splattered trunk of the family car (FIG. 120). Parodying the advertisers' stereotype image of the model draped on the hood, Niro's small, hand-coloured print begins to contest the dominant culture's cherished concepts of beauty, ownership, and status. Such works effortlessly join the discourse of Western art by adopting its languages and codes – even its avant-gardist ones – to subversive ends. Here, the marginal uses its marginality precisely to occupy, and by occupying to redefine, the centre.

Of course, the attempt to bring matter from the sexual, racial, and especially psychological margins into the centre of a given culture brings with it an increased likelihood of stark and often fierce opposition from within. Particularly in matters of religion and sexual morality, and in countries (such as the United States) with extreme contrasts in the social mix, the results have been and will continue to be explosive.

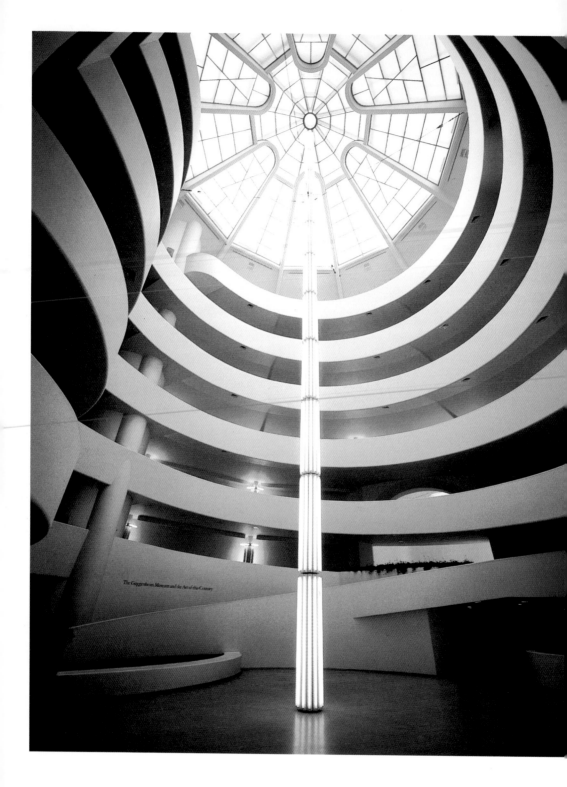

The Guggenheim Museum and the Art of this Century

SIX

Coda: Future Prospects

121. DAN FLAVIN
Untitled (to Tracy, to celebrate the love of a lifetime), 1992. Fluorescent light, dimesions variable. Installed at the Solomon R. Guggenheim Museum, New York.

The central question of this book has been the rise, precarious survival, and development of the traditions of Minimal and Conceptual art from the 1970s through to the 1990s, measured against the pressure of other cultural tendencies that would seek to dilute or deplete them. In some ways the most powerful conflict has been between the Conceptualist position and work rich in declared significance that belongs within a referential or narrative mode: work that wishes to speak directly of issues of gender, race, and identity. Such work, that elevates legible content over form and strategy, became the most general category of advanced art in the decade to 1995. Though the distinction is seldom absolute, narrative art, ranging from maximal installation art through gay and lesbian to "slack" and ethnic art, has gravitated towards just those attitudes and resources that were excluded from the pantheon of hegemonic, male, Modernist art and the criticism which supported it.

Conceptualists will argue that an art of iconography and open signification tends to complicity with the museum and gallery system; that, because of its indifference to issues of form and strategy, narrative art will prove unable to continue the critical enterprise invented in the nineteenth century of an "art of modern life" – initially Impressionism – whose purpose was to deny overtly accessible meaning and to abruptly state the contradiction present between formal ambition and the cultural expectations of its supporting class. A genuine avant-garde, it will be argued, needs a measure of unpopularity in order to consolidate its philosophical and economic independence from the culture from which it in turn borrows its formal effects. In even the best narrative art, that independence looks sorely stretched.

The more accomplished art of the Conceptualist tradition, by contrast, has tended to the theoretically difficult, the over-ambitious and the sometimes obscure. Its audience has remained small and its defenders few. And yet important claims have attended it. Annette Michelson, writing in 1969 about Robert Morris, claimed that his works "command recognition of the singular resolution with which a sculptor has assumed the philo-sophical task which, in a culture not committed on the whole to speculative thought, devolves with particular stringency upon its artists." Thomas Crow has recently argued that this statement "is among the most accurate justifications for the exacting requirements that the best work in Minimal and Conceptual art imposes upon its audience. One could expand upon it to say that in a culture where philosophy has been largely withdrawn into technical exchanges between academic professionals, artistic practice in the Duchampian tradition has come to provide the most important venue where demanding philosophical issues could be aired before a substantial lay public."

Of course, such claims are generally to be understood as having application back inside, and not somewhere beyond, the endlessly revised and contested continuum of Modernism. Even the most conservative form of the Modernist doctrine – Green-bergian or Friedian formalism – had identified the larger cultural evolution as a process of continual self-purification of art's various specialised media. And the challenge to orthodox Modernism mounted by Minimal and Conceptual art began by insisting that visual art be practised always as visual art alone. Overt imagery has remained largely proscribed in these movements in favour of devices and techniques acting upon the image itself: negation, displacement, interruption, nihilism and incompetence (Clark's list, more or less). Taken together, such claims provide one kind of answer to the conundrum of how Modernist art can sustain a revolutionary commitment in an historical period which has had little room for revolutions, let alone for the dis-senting sub-cultures necessary to them.

The difficulty, as recent art in the narrative vein has shown, is that Conceptualism's formal gestures are themselves increasingly seen in emblematic, iconographic terms. Thus Dan Flavin, though belonging to the generation of non-painting iconoclasts of the later 1960s, recently placed his own soaring pink neon structure in the centre of the Guggenheim Museum in a gesture that was instantly perceived as a flesh-coloured phallic totem, a celebration of gay sexual pride at the heart of contemporary culture itself (FIG. 121).

It is a reading which captures the newest dilemma of contemporary art in its most general form: on the one hand, the desire to embrace images and values which speak to a wide public in a sensuously rich, formally expert way; on the other, the need to intensify the Conceptual manner still further by resort to as yet unformulated techniques of evasion, mystification, and displacement of the normative expectations of the culture. The Duchampian tradition may be depleted, despairing, and often arcane. It may have breaks and holes in it (FIG. 122). Yet it arguably still represents the most vital engine of avant-garde Modernism we have, moreover one which will ensure that the best advanced art will never be effortlessly or easily "understood."

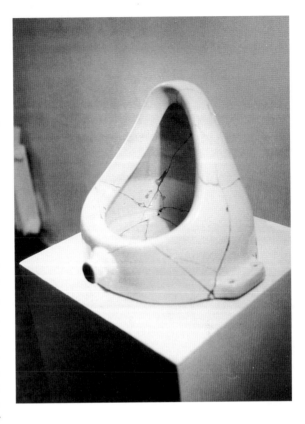

122. AVDEI TER OGANYAN
Some Questions of Contemporary Art Restoration, 1993.

In this epitaph to Conceptual art's vicissitudes, an object similar to Marcel Duchamp's *Urinal* of 1917 was smashed and then repaired with glue. Like other projects within the contemporary Russian avant-garde, Ter Oganyan's performances present caustic reflections on the Modernist past, though with apparent indifference to the vagaries of art-world attention.

Equally, the culture of NATO and the West, though divided by such tensions, is now also under pressure to extend itself far beyond essentially local conflicts within the advanced consumer world – conflicts that it has tried to articulate through objects, their status as forms and commodities, their relation to the body and the museum, and increasingly through a relation to the eco-system. Certainly, this culture will have to accommodate new geographical and political pressures that simply cannot be predicted – pressures that, if the future resembles the past, will tend to widen the philosophical claims and resources of the art object in unforeseen and unforeseeable ways. Within this widened system, it is to be hoped that Conceptual practice which favours reflection and sustains a critical viewpoint will continue to contest the centre stage with forms of art which point away from reflection towards entertainment, rapid stimulation, and assimilation by lesser journalism and the agencies of publicity. But almost anything is possible.

Politics	Scientific and sports events

1970

1972	Nixon elected president for second term (USA)	**1972**	Apollo 16 lands on moon
1973	USA withdraws troops from Vietnam		Pocket calculator invented
	War between Israel and Arab states	**1973**	First colour photocopier marketed (Japa
1974	Nixon resigns following Watergate hearings		

1975

1975	General Franco dies (Spain)	**1975**	First joint space mission between US an
	North Vietnamese capture Saigon, ending war		USSR
	Khmer Rouge seize power in Kampuchea		F–16 fighter developed (USA)
1976	Jimmy Carter elected president (USA)	**1976**	Olympic Games held in Montreal
	Death of Mao Zedong (China)		US space-probe Viking I lands on Mars
1977	Democratic elections take place in Spain	**1977**	Apple II microcomputer marketed (USA
	Steve Biko dies in police cell (South Africa)	**1978**	First test-tube baby born (UK)
1978	Pope John Paul II succeeds Pope Paul VI	**1979**	Personal stereo introduced
1979	Ayatollah Khomeini takes power in Iran		Compact disc developed
	US Embassy hostages taken (Iran)		
	Margaret Thatcher becomes prime minister (UK)		

1980

		1980	Ozone-layer depletions cause concern
1980	Ronald Reagan elected president (USA)		Olympic Games held in Moscow
1981	François Mitterrand elected president (France)	**1981**	Facsimile machines enter widespread u.
1982	Solidarity trade union outlawed in Poland		Microcomputer developed
	Helmut Kohl elected chancellor (West Germany)	**1982**	Cruise missiles adopted by US Air Force
1983	Thatcher wins second term as prime minister (UK)	**1983**	First US woman travels in space
	Anti-nuclear protests in UK, France, West		AIDS virus isolated (France)
	Germany, and USA	**1984**	Top quark molecule discovered (Geneva
1984	Reagan wins second term (USA)		Olympic Games held in Los Angeles
	Ethiopian Civil War intensifies		

1985

1985	Mikhail Gorbachev elected president (USSR)	**1986**	Challenger spacecraft explodes
	Gorbachev and Reagan agree to reduce arms		Chernobyl nuclear reactor explodes (Uk
	African famine continues	**1987**	Compact video disc introduced
1986	Ferdinand Marcos ousted (Phillipines)		Montreal Protocol on CFC emissions
1987	Irangate inquiry criticises Reagan (USA)	**1988**	Olympic Games held in Seoul (South Ko
	Conservatives win third term (UK)		Transatlantic fibre optic cable laid
	Stock markets crash on Black Monday	**1989**	San Francisco earthquake
1988	George Bush elected president (USA)		Cordless telephones become widely ava
	Mitterrand re-elected president (France)		10,000,000 fax machines in use worldw
1989	Protesters killed in Tiananmen Square (China)		Stealth bomber makes maiden flight
	Death of Ayatollah Khomeini (Iran)		
	Democratic elections take place in USSR		
	Berlin wall opened, Germany unified		

1990+

1990	Nelson Mandela released (South Africa)	**1990**	Global warming threat recognised
	Iraq invades Kuwait, US troops sent to Persian Gulf	**1991**	BCCI banking scandal uncovered
	John Major elected prime minister (UK)		Tomahawk missile used in Gulf War
	Kohl elected chancellor of Germany		10,000,000 cases of HIV estimated worl
	Democratic elections take place in Poland	**1992**	Olympic Games held in Barcelona (Spai
	Boris Yeltsin elected president of Russia		COBE satellite explores cosmic backgrou
1991	Gulf offensive launched by NATO against Iraq		(USA)
	Formal dissolution of USSR takes place		Digitalised video launched
	Civil war begins in Yugoslavia	**1993**	"Information super-highway" concept
1992	Conservatives win fourth term (UK)		promoted (USA)
	Bill Clinton elected president (USA)		Internet system links 5,000,000 users
1993	Vaclav Havel elected president of Czech Republic	**1994**	FIFA World Cup (USA)
1994	White rule in South Africa formally ended		

Visual arts	Other cultural events
1972 *Documenta 5* exhibition (Kassel) **1973** Death of Picasso **1974** Beuys, *Coyote* performance (New York)	**1972** John Berger: *Ways of Seeing* Bernardo Bertolucci directs *Last Tango in Paris* **1973** E.F. Shumacher: *Small is Beautiful* **1974** Alexander Solzhenitsyn exiled from USSR
1975 *The Fox* journal published (New York) **1976** *The Human Clay* exhibition London) *October* magazine launched (New York) Death of Max Ernst Carl Andre *Bricks* controversy (UK) **1977** *Documenta 6* (Kassel) *Pictures* exhibition (New York) Pompidou Centre opens (Paris) *Heresies* magazine published (New York) **1978** Death of Giorgio de Chirico Death of Harold Rosenberg	**1975** Nobel Peace Prize: Andrei Sakharov Saul Bellow: *Humboldt's Gift* Solzhenitsyn: *The Gulag Archipelago* **1976** *Taxi Driver* directed by Martin Scorsese Michel Foucault: *Discipline and Punish* **1977** *Star Wars* directed by George Lucas **1978** Graham Greene: *The Human Factor* **1979** *Apocalypse Now* directed by Francis Ford Coppola *Berlin Alexanderplatz* directed by Rainer Werner Fassbinder
1980 *Picasso's Picassos* exhibition (New York) Baselitz and Kiefer sensations at Venice Biennale **1981** *A New Spirit in Painting* exhibition (London) Roland Barthes's *Camera Lucida* published *Westkunst* exhibition (Cologne) **1982** *Zeitgeist* exhibition (Berlin) *Documenta 7* (Kassel) **1983** Baudrillard's *Simulations* published **1984** *Primitivism in 20th-Century Art* exhibition (New York)	**1980** Deaths of Roland Barthes, Jean-Paul Sartre John Lennon shot (USA) William Golding: *Rites of Passage* **1981** Salman Rushdie: *Midnight's Children* **1982** *E.T.* directed by Steven Spielberg *Blade Runner* directed by Ridley Scott **1983** Umberto Eco: *The Name of the Rose* *Gandhi* directed by Richard Attenborough **1984** Michael Jackson: *Thriller* (LP) Milan Kundera: *The Unbearable Lightness of Being*
1985 Saatchi Gallery opened (London) Death of Marc Chagall **1986** *Damaged Goods* exhibition (New York) Ludwig Museum opened (Cologne) Los Angeles MOCA opened Death of Joseph Beuys **1987** *Documenta 8* (Kassel) Death of Andy Warhol **1988** *American/German Art of the Late 80s* exhibition (Düsseldorf and Boston) **1989** *Magiciens de la Terre* exhibition (Paris) Serra's *Tilted Arc* destroyed	**1985** Live Aid raises money globally for famine relief Deaths of Heinrich Böll, Italo Calvino *Amadeus* directed by Milos Forman **1986** *Caravaggio* directed by Derek Jarman **1987** Nobel Prize for Literature: Joseph Brodsky Tom Wolfe: *Bonfire of the Vanities* **1988** Salman Rushdie: *Satanic Verses* *Satanic Verses* causes worldwide controversy *Fatal Attraction* directed by Adrian Lyne **1989** Khomeini orders *fatwah* against Salman Rushdie Death of Samuel Beckett
1990 *Between Spring and Summer* exhibition (Washington) **1991** *Metropolis* exhibition (Berlin) MOCA Frankfurt opened **1992** *Helter Skelter: LA Art in the 90s* exhibition (Los Angeles) SoHo Guggenheim opened (New York) **1993** *Abject Art* exhibition (New York) *Documenta 9* (Kassel) **1994** *Bad Girls/ Bad Girls West* exhibitions (New York and Los Angeles)	**1990** *Teenage Mutant Ninja Turtles* directed by Steve Barron **1991** *Silence of the Lambs* directed by Jonathan Demme *Terminator 2* directed by James Cameron Nobel Prize for Literature: Nadine Gordimer **1992** Euro Disney opened in Paris AIDS quilt exhibited, Washington, D.C. Madonna's *Sex* sells 100,000 at launch **1993** *Schindler's List* directed by Steven Spielberg **1994** Death of the influential art critic Clement Greenberg

Bibliography

The literature of advanced art in the 1970s, 1980s, and 1990s is widespread and necessarily uneven in quality. Dispersed through journals, small-circulation exhibition catalogues and reviews, the best accessible writing of the period is to be found in anthologies of essays and interviews with artists, though catalogues should be consulted for a wider array of images. The following short list of sources is generally available.

ANTHOLOGIES OF ARTISTS' STATEMENTS AND INTERVIEWS

FERGUSON, RUSSELL, WILLIAM OLANDER, MARCIA TUCKER, and KAREN FISS (eds), *Discourses: Conversations in Postmodernist Art and Culture* (New York: New Museum of Contemporary Art, 1990)

HALLEY, PETER, *Collected Essays, 1981-87* (Zurich: Bruno Bishofberger Gallery; and New York: Sonnabend Gallery, 1988)

MEYER, URSULA, *Conceptual Art* (New York: Dutton, 1972)

SIEGEL, JEANNE (ed.), *Artwords: Discourses in the 60s and 70s* (New York: Da Capo, 1985)

— *Art Talk: the Early 80s* (New York: Da Capo, 1988)

WALLIS, BRIAN (ed.), *Blasted Allegories: An Anthology of Writings by Contemporary Artists* (New York: New Museum of Contemporary Art; Cambridge, Mass., and London: MIT Press, 1989)

ANTHOLOGIES OF CRITICAL ESSAYS

BANN, STEPHEN, and WILLIAM ALLEN (eds), *Interpreting Contemporary Art* (London: Reaktion, 1991)

BATTCOCK, GREGORY (ed.), *Minimal Art: a Critical Anthology* (New York: Dutton, 1968)

— *Idea Art: a Critical Anthology* (New York: Dutton, 1973)

BURGIN, VICTOR (ed.), *Thinking Photography* (Basingstoke: Macmillan, 1982

DUNCAN, CAROL, *The Aesthetics of Power: Essays in Critical Art History* (Cambridge: Cambridge University Press, 1993)

FOSTER, HAL (ed.), *Discussions in Contemporary Culture* (Seattle: Bay Press, 1987)

— *The Anti-Aesthetic: Essays on Postmodern Culture* (Seattle: Bay Press, 1983)

HARRISON, CHARLES, *Essays on Art and Language* (Oxford: Blackwell, 1991)

HARRISON, CHARLES, and PAUL WOOD (eds), *Art in Theory 1900-1990: an Anthology of Changing Ideas* (Oxford: Blackwell, 1992)

LIPPARD, LUCY, *From the Centre: Feminist Essays on Women's Art* (New York: Dutton, 1976)

NOCHLIN, LINDA, *Women, Art and Power and Other Essays* (London: Thames and Hudson, 1989)

SQUIRES, CAROL (ed.), *The Critical Image: Essays on Contemporary Photography* (Seattle: Bay Press, 1990)

WALLIS, BRIAN (ed.), *Art After Modernism: Rethinking Representation* (New York: New Museum of Contemporary Art, 1984)

EXHIBITION CATALOGUES

Abject Art: Repulsion and Desire in American Art (New York: Whitney Museum of American Art, 1993)

Bad Girls (New York: New Museum of Contemporary Art, 1994)

Bad Girls West (Los Angeles: UCLA Wright Art Gallery, 1994)

The Bi-national: American and German Art of the Late 80s (Boston: ICA, and Düsseldorf: Städtische Kunsthalle; Cologne: Dumont, 1988)

Bi-nationale: German Art of the late 80s (Düsseldorf: Städtische Kunsthalle; Boston: ICA; Cologne: Dumont, 1988)

Damaged Goods: Desire and the Economy of the Object (New York: New Museum of Contemporary Art, 1986)

Documenta (Kassel: 1972, 1977, 1982, 1987, 1993)

Endgame: Reference and Simulation in Recent Painting and Sculpture (Boston: ICA, 1986)

GUDIS, CATHERINE (ed.), *Helter Skelter: LA Art in the 90s* (Los Angeles: Museum of Contemporary Art, 1992)

JOACHIMEDES, CHRISTOS, NORMAN ROSENTHAL, and NICHOLAS SEROTA (eds), *A New Spirit in Painting* (London: Royal Academy of Arts, 1981)

JOACHIMEDES, CHRISTOS, and NORMAN ROSENTHAL (eds), *Metropolis* (Berlin: Martin-Gropius-Bau, 1991)

JOACHIMEDES, CHRISTOS, and NORMAN ROSENTHAL (eds), *Zeitgeist* (Berlin: Martin-Gropius-Bau, 1982)

Magiciens de la Terre (Paris: Centre Georges Pompidou, 1989)

ROSS, DAVID (ed.), *Between Spring and Summer: Soviet Conceptual Art in the Era of Late Communism* (Washington, D.C.: Tacoma Museum of Art; Boston: ICA, 1990-91)

SUSSMAN, ELIZABETH (ed.), *On the Passage of a Few People Through a Rather Brief Moment in Time: the Situationist International 1957-1972* (Paris: Centre Georges Pompidou; London: ICA; Boston: ICA, 1989-90)

THEORETICAL MONOGRAPHS

BARTHES, ROLAND, *Camera Lucida* (New York: Hill and Wang, 1981)

BAUDRILLARD, JEAN, *Simulations* (New York: Semiotext(e), 1983)

BURGIN, VICTOR, *The End of Art Theory: Criticism and Postmodernity* (Basingstoke: Macmillan, 1986)

CRIMP, DOUGLAS, *On the Museum's Ruins* (Cambridge, Mass., and London: MIT Press, 1993)

DEBORD, GUY, *Society of the Spectacle* (Detroit: Black and Red, 1970)

FOUCAULT, MICHEL, *Discipline and Punish: the Birth of the Prison* (London: Penguin Books, 1977)

FRASCINA, F., J. HARRIS, C. HARRISON, and P. WOOD, *Modernism in Dispute: Art Since the Forties* (New Haven and London: Yale University Press, 1993)

HOME, STEWART, *An Assault on Culture: Utopian Currents from Lettrisme to Class War* (Stirling: AK Press, 1991)

SONTAG, SUSAN, *On Photography* (London: Penguin Books, 1978)

JOURNALS AND MAGAZINES

Artforum, Art in America, Art Journal, Artscribe, Avalanche, Flash Art, Frieze, October, Parkett, Studio International, Tema Celeste, Third Text

Picture Credits

Collections are given in the captions alongside the pictures. Sources for illustrations not supplied by museums or collections, additional information, and copyright credits are given below. Numbers to the left refer to figure numbers unless otherwise indicated.

Title pages: as 69

1   © The Solomon R. Guggenheim Foundation, New York; photo: Robert E. Mates and Paul Katz. © ADAGP, Paris and DACS, London 1995
2   Courtesy Galerie Marie-Puck Broodthaers, Brussels
3   Dallas Museum of Art, General Acquisitions Fund, and a matching grant from the National Endowment for the Arts. © ARS, NY and DACS, London 1995
4   Courtesy the artist. © DACS 1995
5   Courtesy the artists
6   Courtesy the artist; photo: Jerzy Gladykowski
7   Judy Chicago, 1973; photo: © Donald Woodman
8   Range/Bettmann/UPI
9   © Lynda Benglis/DACS, London/VAGA, New York 1995, and Annie Liebowitz
10 Courtesy the artist, New York
11 Courtesy the artist, Brussels
12 Courtesy Paula Cooper Gallery, New York; photo: Efraim Lev-Er
13 Courtesy the artist, New York
14 Courtesy the artist, New York
15 Courtesy the artist, New York
16 Courtesy the artist, New York
17 Courtesy the artist, California
18 Courtesy the artist; photo: Janet Anderson
19 Courtesy Galerie Stadler, Paris
20 Courtesy Ronald Feldman Fine Arts, New York; photo: Caroline Tisdall. © DACS 1995
21 Courtesy the Holly Solomon Gallery. © The Estate of Gordon Matta-Clark
23 Courtesy Ronald Feldman Fine Arts, New York
24 Victor and Margarita Tupitsyn Archive, New York City
25 Courtesy Heiner Bastian, Berlin (Cy Twombly, *Catalogue Raisonné of the Paintings*)
26 Courtesy Leo Castelli Gallery, New York. © ARS, NY and DACS, London 1995
27 Courtesy the artist, New York; photo: Eddie Owen
page 43 detail of 32, courtesy the artist; photographer Friedrich Rosenstiel, Cologne
28 Courtesy the artist, Cologne
29 Courtesy the artist; photo: David

Reynolds, New York City
30 The Bridgeman Art Library, London
31 Courtesy Gallery Bruno Bishofberger, Zurich. © Sandro Chia/DACS, London/VAGA, New York 1995
32 Courtesy the artist; photographer Friedrich Rosenstiel, Cologne
33 Courtesy Sotheby's, London
34 Courtesy the artist, Cologne
35 Courtesy Lisson Gallery, London
38 Courtesy Waddington Galleries, London. © David Salle/DACS, London/VAGA, New York 1995
39 Courtesy Anthony Reynolds Gallery, London
40 Courtesy Leo Castelli Gallery, New York
41 Courtesy the artist, New York
43 Courtesy the artist and Edward Totah Gallery, London. © DACS 1995
45 Courtesy Gagosian Gallery, New York
46 Courtesy Sidney Janis Gallery, New York. Valerie Jaudon/DACS, London/VAGA, New York 1995
47 Courtesy Max Protetch Gallery, New York; photo: Steven Sloman
page 73 detail of 65, courtesy Postmasters Gallery, New York; photo: Tom Powel
48 Courtesy Anthony d'Offay Gallery, London
50 Courtesy Metro Pictures, New York
51 Courtesy the artist, New York
52 Courtesy John Weber Gallery, New York
53 Courtesy Thomas Ammann, Zurich
54 Courtesy the artist, Paris
55 Courtesy the artist, Germany
56 Courtesy Lisson Gallery, London
58 Courtesy Lisson Gallery, London; photo: Gareth Winters
59 Courtesy the artist New York; photo: Ken Schles
61 Rex Features Ltd, London
62 Courtesy the artist, New York
63 Courtesy the artist, New York
64 Courtesy the artist, Illinois
65 Courtesy Postmasters Gallery, New York; photo: Tom Powel
66 Courtesy John Weber Gallery, New York
67 Courtesy the artist, New York; photo: Steven Sloman
68 Courtesy Mary Boone Gallery, New York
69 Courtesy the artist, New York
71 Victor and Margarita Tupitsyn Archive, New York City
page 73 detail of 95, courtesy Hal Bromm Gallery, New York; photo: Lee Stalsworth
73 Courtesy the artist and Margarete Roeder Gallery, New York
74 Courtesy the artist, Paris. © ADAGP, Paris and DACS, London 1995

75 Courtesy Galerie Buchmann, Basel
76 Courtesy the artist, London
77 Courtesy Galerie Philomene Magers, Cologne
78 Courtesy Lisson Gallery, London
79 Courtesy Gimpel Fils, London
80 Courtesy Anthony d'Offay Gallery, London
81 Courtesy the artist, Geneva; photo: Tom Warren, New York
82 Photo Florian Kleinefenn, Paris
83 Courtesy the artist, Berlin
84 Courtesy the artist, Dusseldorf
85 Courtesy DIA Center for the Arts, New York; photo: Nic Tenwiggenhorn
86 Courtesy Galerie Maz Hetzler, Berlin
87 Courtesy the artist; photo: Ulrich Görlich. © DACS 1995
88 Courtesy Museum für Moderne Kunst, Frankfurt am Main; photo: Rudolf Nagel
89 Courtesy the artist and Barbara Gladstone Gallery; photo: Bill Orcutt
90 Courtesy the artist, Dusseldorf. © DACS 1995
91 Courtesy Johnen & Schöttle, Cologne. © DACS 1995
92 Courtesy the artist, Dusseldorf
93 Courtesy Galerie Ghislaine Hussenot, Paris. © ADAGP, Paris and DACS, London 1995
94 Courtesy Marian Goodman Gallery, New York
95 Courtesy Hal Bromm Gallery, New York; photo: Lee Stalsworth
96 Courtesy Pace Gallery, New York City; photo: Kim Steele. © ARS, NY and DACS, London 1995
97 Work commissioned by Artangel and Becks. Courtesy of Artangel, London; photo: Sue Ormerod
98 Courtesy Galerie Crousel, Paris
99 © Barbara Gladstone Gallery, New York; photo: David Regen
page 143 detail of 110, courtesy Paula Cooper Gallery, New York
100 Courtesy P.P.O.W, New York; photo: Adam Reich
101 Courtesy Daniel Weinberg Gallery, San Francisco
102 Rex Features Ltd, London
103 © 1981 The Estate of Robert Mapplethorpe
104 Courtesy Paula Cooper Gallery, New York; photo: Andrew Moore
105 Courtesy Robert Bane Editions, Los Angeles
106 Courtesy 303 Gallery, New York
107 Courtesy Rosamund Felsen Gallery, Santa Monica, California
108 Courtesy the artist, New Jersey
109 Courtesy 303 Gallery, New York
110 Installation view Touko Museum,

Index

176   *Index*